D1352491

Total
Business 2

HEINLE
CENGAGE Learning™

Total Business 2 Teacher's Book
John Hughes

Publisher: Jason Mann

Head of Inventory: Jane Glendening

Head of Content & Media Production: Alissa Chappell

Production Controller: Tom Relf

Typesetter: Starfish Design, Editorial and Project Management Ltd. UK

Cover design: White Space

© 2009 Heinle, Cengage Learning

ALL RIGHTS RESERVED. No part of this work covered by the copyright herein may be reproduced, transmitted, stored or used in any form or by any means graphic, electronic, or mechanical, including but not limited to photocopying, recording, scanning, digitizing, taping, Web distribution, information networks, or information storage and retrieval systems, except as permitted under Section 107 or 108 of the 1976 United States Copyright Act, or applicable copyright law of another jurisdiction, without the prior written permission of the publisher.

For permission to use material from this text or product, submit all requests online at **cengage.com/permissions**.

Further permissions questions can be emailed to **permissionrequest@cengage.com**.

ISBN: 978-0-462-09867-8

Heinle, Cengage Learning EMEA
Cheriton House, North Way, Andover, Hampshire, SP10 5BE, United Kingdom

Cengage Learning is a leading provider of customised learning solutions with office locations around the globe, including Singapore, the United Kingdom, Australia, Mexico, Brazil and Japan. Locate our local office at: **international.cengage.com/region**

Cengage Learning products are represented in Canada by Nelson Education Ltd.

Visit Heinle online at **elt.heinle.com**
Visit our corporate website at **cengage.com**

Printed in the United Kingdom
3 4 5 6 7 8 9 10 – 13 12 11

Total Business 2

Teacher's Book

John Hughes

Summertown
Publishing

HEINLE
CENGAGE Learning™

Australia • Brazil • Japan • Korea • Mexico • Singapore • Spain • United Kingdom • United States

Contents

Total Business

Total Business is a three-level business English course for pre-work students and business people wishing to improve their English and their employment prospects. It is also suitable for in-company training.

The core lessons offer:

- modern, business-related topics to engage students and involve them in the practice of everyday business
- an integrated grammar syllabus offering extensive functional practice
- varied activities and learner strategies to motivate and support students in their studies.

Student's Book

The Student's Books for all levels contain twelve modules divided into the core lessons of *Business topic, Business skills* and *Learning strategies*. This modular division of material makes it flexible to the needs and requirements of each class.

BUSINESS TOPIC LESSONS focus on vocabulary and grammar. They cover a wide range of business topics: see pages 8 and 9 for a breakdown of topic coverage.

BUSINESS SKILLS LESSONS cover high frequency business skills, laying the foundations for effective communication.

LEARNING STRATEGIES LESSONS work on both the receptive and productive skills (listening and reading, speaking and writing) by placing learning tasks within the context of business.

Back of book material

Each Student's Book contains additional material at the back of the book, including:

- Pairwork and groupwork materials
- Useful expressions
- Listening scripts
- Grammar reference (*Total Business 2*)
- Business idioms (*Total Business 3*).

The Student's Books contain the audio CDs.

Workbook

The Workbooks feature stimulating input texts and motivating activities which consolidate and extend the topics and skills presented in the Student's Books. They also provide further business practice.

Each Workbook includes the answer key.

Audio CDs

There are two CDs for *Total Business* 1 and 2, and one for *Total Business* 3. They contain all the listening material for the module lessons. Activities include: dialogues, interviews, reports, case studies and telecommunication texts.

Teacher's Books

The comprehensive Teacher's Books contain:

- reduced Student's Book spreads for easy reference as you teach
- step-by-step teaching notes and answers
- listening scripts
- extra activities
- suggestions for alternative activities / how to modify the book activity for pre-work students
- twenty-four brand new photocopiable activities and teaching notes
- suggestions in the lesson notes for when to use the photocopiable activities.

To accompany Total Business…

Summertown Readers

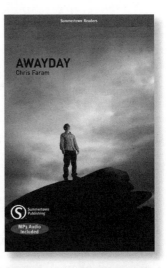

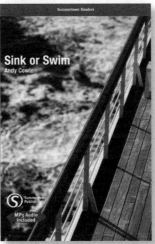

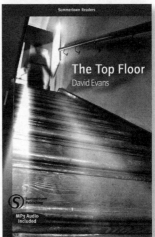

Topic areas covered in the *Total Business* course

You can see in the table below how the topic coverage in *Total Business* covers a wide range of business topics. If you are using the course selectively, focusing either on skills or vocabulary, you may wish to take this mapping into account, to ensure adequate coverage of all the topics. The business topic lessons are labelled 1.1, 2.1, 3.1, etc. The business skills lessons are labelled 1.2, 2.2, 3.2, etc. The flexibility of this organisation allows each topic to be approached from the most suitable angle.

Topic area	*Total Business* 1
Personal identification	1.1 World of work 1.2 Personal and professional details 3.1 Company biography 12.2 Job applications
The office, general business environment and routine	2.2 Making arrangements 5.1 Career choices 9.2 Meetings
Entertainment of clients, free time, relationships with colleagues and clients	10.2 Organising a conference
Travel and meetings	6.1 Business travel 6.2 Travel arrangements
Using the telephone	4.2 Business communications
Health and safety	11.1 Health and safety 11.2 Reporting accidents
Buying and selling	4.1 International business 7.2 Orders and contracts
Company structures, systems, processes	2.1 Work in progress 8.1 Manufacturing processes 8.2 Problems and solutions 12.1 The job market
Products and services	7.1 Products and services
Results and achievements	3.2 Company performance 5.2 Achievements and plans
Business issues	9.1 The future 10.1 Career development

Total Business 2	Total Business 3
1.1 Ways of working	1.1 Working life
5.2 Participating in a meeting 6.2 Emailing	3.1 Communication at work 3.2 Email exchange 5.2 Discussing options 7.2 Report writing 8.2 Formal meetings 10.2 The language of proposals 11.2 Effective writing
5.1 The workplace	12.1 Crossing cultures 12.2 Social English
1.2 Making contacts	10.1 Travel and entertainment
3.2 Leaving and taking messages 9.2 Getting through	6.2 Telephoning
Secondary focus in other lessons	1.2 Asking and answering questions
7.1 Sales 7.2 Selling 11.1 Ethical economics	4.1 The art of selling 6.1 Purchasing power
2.1 Company benefits 2.2 Presenting your company 6.1 Recruitment 10.2 Solving problems	9.1 Innovation
12.2 Handling questions	9.2 Negotiating
11.2 Discussing trends	2.1 Growing the company 2.2 Presenting facts 4.2 Presenting figures
3.1 Starting a business 4.1 Advertising 4.2 Delegating 8.1 Training 8.2 Showing you're listening 9.1 Branding 10.1 Management 12.1 Business law	5.1 Money and finance 7.1 Managing people 8.1 Being responsible 11.1 The economy

MODULE	BUSINESS TOPIC	BUSINESS SKILLS	LEARNING STRATEGIES
1	**1.1 Ways of working** *page 6* **Vocabulary:** Different ways of working **Reading:** How to job-share **Listening:** Working from home **Grammar:** Present tenses **Speaking:** A mini-presentation	**1.2 Making contacts** *page 10* **Vocabulary:** Job responsibilities **Reading:** Life's all about making connections **Listening:** Starting a conversation **Speaking:** Developing a conversation **Writing:** Business correspondence	**1.3 Speaking: Talking about yourself** *page 14*
2	**2.1 Company benefits** *page 16* **Vocabulary:** Benefits and incentives **Reading:** Is working for Xerox too good to be true? **Vocabulary:** Expressions with *take* **Speaking:** Asking questions about jobs **Grammar:** The past **Writing:** A letter of application	**2.2 Presenting your company** *page 20* **Vocabulary:** Company terms **Listening:** Presentations **Pronunciation:** Pausing, intonation and stress **Speaking:** Giving a presentation **Writing:** A memo	**2.3 Reading: Checking for errors** **Writing: Internal communications** *page 24*
3	**3.1 Starting a business** *page 26* **Vocabulary:** Types of business **Reading:** We wanna hold your hand **Listening:** Advice on franchises **Listening:** Planning a seminar **Grammar:** *will* and the future **Speaking:** Discussing a schedule	**3.2 Leaving and taking messages** *page 30* **Listening:** Leaving messages **Speaking:** Leaving a voicemail message **Writing:** Taking notes and messages	**3.3 Listening: Short messages** *page 34*
4	**4.1 Advertising** *page 36* **Vocabulary:** Types of advertising **Listening:** Advertising on the web **Speaking:** A short presentation **Reading:** Advertising standards **Grammar:** Modals	**4.2 Delegating** *page 40* **Reading:** How to delegate **Listening:** A bad delegator **Pronunciation:** Sentence stress **Speaking:** Delegating **Writing:** A report	**4.3 Reading: Vocabulary and collocations** *page 44*
5	**5.1 The workplace** *page 46* **Reading:** Art at work **Listening:** An interview with an art consultant **Grammar:** Reporting **Listening:** Some opinions on art **Speaking:** A meeting about artwork	**5.2 Participating in a meeting** *page 50* **Reading:** Meetings are great **Vocabulary:** Verb collocations **Speaking:** Expressions for meetings **Listening:** Report on a meeting **Writing:** Minutes of a meeting	**5.3 Speaking: Short presentations** *page 54*
6	**6.1 Recruitment** *page 56* **Reading:** Employment news **Vocabulary:** Hiring and firing **Listening:** Employment case studies **Speaking:** Employment issues **Grammar:** Passives	**6.2 Emailing** *page 60* **Reading:** Clicking the habit **Vocabulary:** Emailing terms **Reading:** Internal communication and emails **Writing:** An email	**6.3 Reading: Linking ideas** *page 64*

Overview

1.1 Business topic: Ways of working

VOCABULARY   Different ways of working

READING   How to job-share

LISTENING   Working from home

GRAMMAR   Present tenses

SPEAKING   A mini-presentation

1.2 Business skills: Making contacts

VOCABULARY   Job responsibilities

READING   Life's all about making connections

READING   Starting a conversation

SPEAKING   Developing a conversation

WRITING   Business correspondence

1.3 Learning strategies: Talking about yourself

Answering personal questions

Expressing opinions and preferences

Speculating

Asking someone to repeat something

PHOTOCOPIABLE

© 2009 Heinle, Cengage Learning

Useful language from Module 1

Wordlist

attend	flexitime	networking	shift work
company	freelance	part-time	socialising
consultancy	group	produce	specialise in
control	in charge of	report to	success
deal with	involved in	responsible for	teleworking
department	job-sharing	run	temping

Expressions

Do you two know each other already?

Have you always lived in ...?

How do you do?

How do you know him?

I deal with ...

I specialise in ...

I usually report to ...

I work for ...

I'd like to introduce you to ...

I'm in charge of ...

I'm involved in ...

I'm responsible for ...

Is that something you might be interested in ...?

Is this your first time at ...?

May I join you?

Nice to meet you ...

Pleased to meet you too.

So have you enjoyed ...?

We were both at [name of company] together.

We've spoken on the phone a few times.

Would you like a ...?

Yes, it was very interesting.

You're a colleague of ..., aren't you?

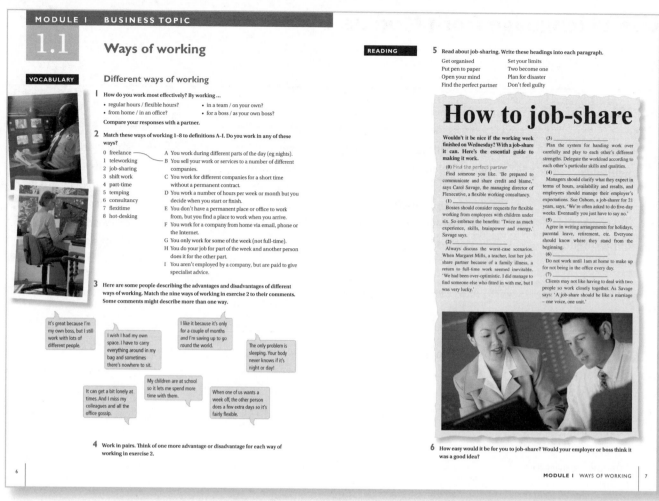

Student's Book pages 6 and 7

Different ways of working

VOCABULARY

1 Put students into pairs or small groups to discuss how they work most effectively.

Alternative

If you teach pre-work learners, write this list of questions on the board to help them discuss the points more easily:

How do you study English most effectively?
By working ...
- *at the same time every day/at different times of the day?*
- *early in the morning/late at night?*
- *on your own/with others?*
- *at home/at your place of study (school or college)?*

2 Students match the terms to the definitions. If you teach students who are in work, or perhaps also work part-time, ask if any of them are familiar with these ways of working, eg ask them:
Would it be possible to telework in your job?
How would you feel about job-sharing?
Have you ever suggested to your boss the idea of flexitime?

Answers
1 F 2 H 3 A 4 G 5 C 6 I 7 D 8 E

Pronunciation
Read the following words aloud and ask students to underline the word stress or stressed word: *freelance, teleworking, consultancy, flexitime*. Afterwards, drill the students and make sure they can pronounce the words properly. Note also that two-part words like *job-sharing, shift work, part-time, hot-desking* carry virtually equal stress in both words.

Extension
Ask the class which ways of working they would like to try.

3 Students match the comments to the different ways of working.

Possible answers
Freelance, temping, consultancy:
It's great because I'm my own boss but I still get to work with lots of different people.

Teleworking:
It can get a bit lonely at times. And I miss my colleagues and all the office gossip.

14

Job-sharing:
When one of us wants a week off, the other person does a few extra days so it's fairly flexible.

Shift work:
The only problem is sleeping. Your body never knows if it's night or day!

Part-time, teleworking:
My children are at school so it lets me spend more time with them.

Temping:
I like it because it's only for a couple of months and I'm saving my money to go round the world.

Hot-desking:
I wish I had my own space. I have to carry everything around in my bag and sometimes there's nowhere to sit.

4 Put students into groups to discuss more advantages and disadvantages. If time is short, give each group one way of working. Collate their ideas on the board in a table as shown below.

Possible answers

	Possible advantages	Possible disadvantages
freelance	you choose the job	no job security
teleworking	organise your work time	you need to be good at self-organisation
job-sharing	more free time	need to coordinate with other person
shift work	gives you your days free	tiring
part-time	more free time	less money
temping	lots of variety	hard to progress your career
consultancy	well paid	no job security
flexitime	good for work-life balance	not good for people who like routine
hot-desking	saves the company money	disruptive to employees

How to job-share

READING

5 Ask students to read the whole text before they put the headings with the correct paragraphs. Tell them that they won't need to understand every word to complete this reading task.

Answers
1 Open your mind
2 Plan for disaster
3 Get organised
4 Set your limits
5 Put pen to paper
6 Don't feel guilty
7 Two become one

6 Students can discuss these two questions as a class.

Extension 1
Put students into pairs. Student A is the employee and Student B is the employer. Tell them to imagine Student A wants to start job-sharing with another colleague. They must try to convince their employer that it is a good idea and mention the advantages. Student B should be sceptical and mention disadvantages. Set a time limit of three minutes for each conversation. Then students change partners and swap roles.

Extension 2
Ask students to think of other possible work related questions then write everyone's ideas on the board. Finally, you can ask students to work in pairs. One student asks some of the questions. The other student tries to answer them. At this early stage of the course, focus on the positive aspects of their responses in your feedback. The main aim is for students to practise talking about different areas of business.

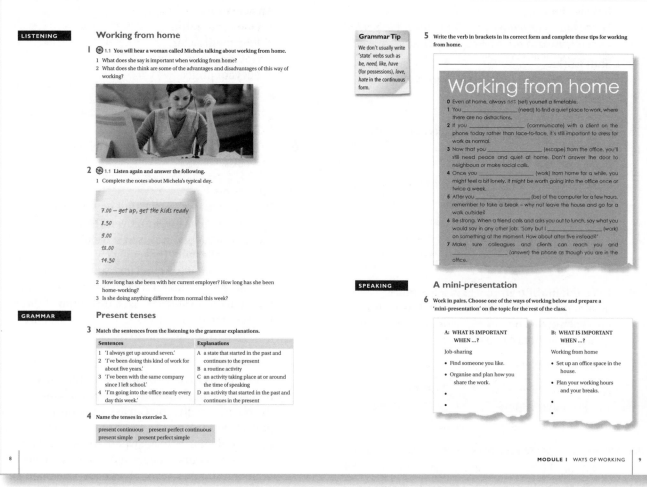

Working from home

LISTENING Track 1 (CD1)

1 🔘 1.1 You may need to play the recording twice for students to listen and take notes.

Answers
1 Have a timetable and stick to it.
2 Advantages:
– you spend more time with the children
– more flexibility
– the company saves money on office space
– no commuting.
   Disadvantages:
– sometimes you work in the evening
– you miss people and office news.

1.1 Listening script
I = Interviewer   M = Michela
I OK Michela. You work from home now. Can you tell me about a typical day?
M Sure, I always get up around seven and the first thing I do is get the kids ready for school. I take them at eight thirty and then I always start work at nine.
I Do you ever have a day where you decide to have the morning off and start work later?

M No, you can't do that. It's important with home-working to have a timetable and stick to it. If you end up watching TV or doing the cleaning then it isn't for you. So I have lunch at twelve and finish work at two thirty to get the children.
I Was that why you gave up your office job?
M Yes, I wanted to spend more time with the children. It gives me more flexibility. Sometimes I need to work in the evening but usually it isn't a problem.
I So how long have you been doing this kind of work?
M For about five years. I've been with the same company since I left school, but with the Internet and technology it's easy now to be at home.
I So your employer doesn't mind.
M No. It means the company saves money on office space and as long as I get the work done, they're happy. Sometimes I still go into work to meet clients and so on. For example, I'm going in nearly every day this week because we have visitors from another company and I can't really invite them over to my house. Besides, it's nice to go in every so often. I like to see people and catch up on the gossip and the news with my colleagues. I miss that side of going into work every day.
I Is there anything else you miss?
M Ermm. No, not really. And I'll tell you what I really don't miss and that's having to spend two hours commuting on the bus and train every day …

2 (CD) 1.1 Play the recording again. Students complete the notes.

Answers
1 7.00 – get up, get the kids ready
    8.30 – take kids to school
    9.00 – start work
    12.00 – have lunch
    14.30 – finish work
2 She's been with her current employer since she left school, but she's been home-working for five years.
3 She's going to the office every day to meet visitors.

Present tenses

GRAMMAR

3 Students match the sentences to the explanations. Tell them that the sentences come from the listening.

Answers
1 B   2 D   3 A   4 C

4 Students name the tenses in exercise 3.

Answers
1 Present simple
2 Present perfect continuous
3 Present perfect simple
4 Present continuous

Photocopiable activity 1.1
See page 156.

5 Refer students to the Grammar Tip and clarify that state verbs are usually in the simple form. As students write the verb forms in the text, refer them to page 128 in the Grammar Reference at the back of the Student's Book.

Answers
1 need
2 communicate
3 have escaped
4 have been working
5 have been
6 'm working
7 answer

A mini-presentation

SPEAKING

6 This exercise gives students the opportunity to bring together many of the ideas and vocabulary looked at in the module so far. Working in pairs, each student prepares a mini-presentation based on A or B. Refer students to the previous reading and listening from this module to help them prepare ideas. Then students give their presentation to each other. You could set one minute as a time limit. Make notes on any problems with vocabulary and give feedback.

You could ask any students giving especially good presentations to present to the class.

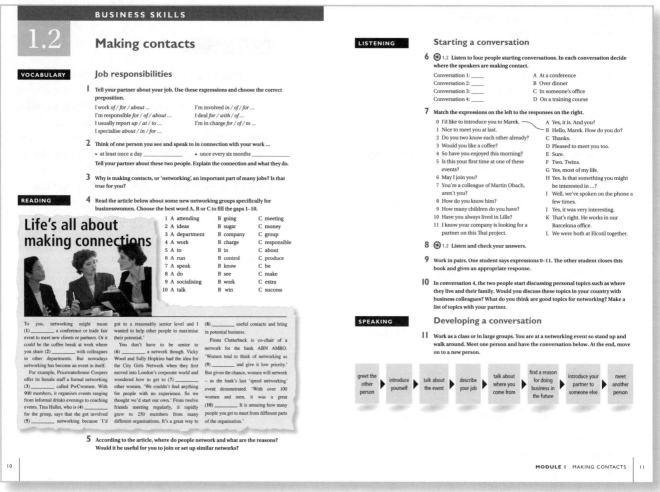

Student's Book pages 10 and 11

Job responsibilities

LISTENING

1 Ask students to underline the correct preposition before they start speaking in pairs.

Answers
work for
responsible for
report to
specialise in
involved in
deal with
in charge of

Alternative
For pre-work or unemployed students, make copies of the business cards on page 157 and give one to each student. They imagine they have the job on the card and make sentences with the expressions.

2 This exercise encourages students to use the third person form of the verbs in exercise 1.

Alternative
Pre-work learners can describe people or friends they see at their place of study.

3 Students with work experience can tell the rest of the class their response to this question. If no students formally 'network' in your class, ask students why they think networking is important.

Possible answer
'Networking' is the skill of making contacts and can help people progress in their career through knowing the 'right' people. The skill is important in areas such as sales where you need to develop relationships with potential customers.

Life's all about making connections

READING

4 Students read and choose the best answer. Ask them to compare their answers with a partner.

Answers
1 A   2 A   3 C   4 C   5 B   6 A   7 B   8 C
9 A   10 C

5 Ask students to underline the parts of the text which tell you where people network and the reasons why. Then ask students to give their answers and discuss the second question as a class.

Answer

People network at:
- conferences
- trade fair events
- coffee breaks
- formal 'networking' events

The reasons are:
- to help people maximise their potential
- to get to know other people
- for people with little experience.

Starting a conversation

LISTENING Track 2 (CD1)

6 1.2 Students listen and match the conversations to the locations.

Answers
1 C   2 A   3 D   4 B

1.2 Listening script

Conversation 1
R = Richard   W = Woman   M = Marek
R Hello?
W Hello, Richard. I'd like to introduce you to Marek.
R Oh yes. Hello, Marek. How do you do? Nice to meet you at last.
M Hello, Richard. Pleased to meet you too.
W Oh, do you two know each other already?
M Well, we've spoken on the phone a few times.
R But we've never actually met. Anyway, take a seat. Would you both like a coffee?

Conversation 2
A Would you like a coffee?
B Oh thanks.
A Milk?
B Yes, please, and a sugar … thanks.
A So have you enjoyed this morning?
B Yes, it was very interesting. The first speaker was particularly good.
A Is this your first time at one of these events?
B Yes, it is. And you?
A No. I've been coming for years. The company pays and if the location is good then I come. I remember the best year we had was in Monaco …

Conversation 3
M = Marie   W = Woman
M May I join you?
W Sure.
M You're a colleague of Martin Obach, aren't you?
W That's right. He works in our Barcelona office. How do you know him?
M We were both at Elcotil together. He left about a year before me.
W Oh, are you Mandy?
M Marie.
W Marie. That's right. Sorry, I knew it began with an M. Yes, Martin said you were doing this course and that I should say hello …

Conversation 4
A Well, this is nice.
B Well, it's quite simple but the food is very traditional and it's popular with the locals. On Sundays I often bring the family here.
A That's nice. How many children do you have?
B Two. Twins. A boy and a girl. They've just started school.
A Wow. Twins.
B And you?
A No, not yet. And have you always lived in Lille?
B Yes, most of my life. I worked in Paris for a while and in your country, of course. But all my relatives are here. What about your family?
A Oh, they're spread out. I see my parents from time to time but my sister lives in Norway with her husband so we don't get together much. Anyway, I know your company is looking for a partner on this Thai project.
B Yes. Is that something you might be interested in …

7/8 1.2 Students match the expressions to the responses and then check by listening. If they find the first stage difficult, they can do the matching task while they listen to the recording.

Answers
1 D   2 I   3 C   4 J   5 A   6 E   7 K   8 L
9 F   10 G   11 H

9 Students practise the expressions and responses in a controlled way. Note that the student with the book closed doesn't have to give exactly the same response as those in the book. Write any good examples of responses generated by students on the board afterwards to share with the rest of the class.

10 Typically students will suggest topics like *weather, travel, countries, work* and *language*. However, note that with some cultures, topics such as *politics, religion or family* may not be appropriate. If you have a class with students from many different cultures or experience of travel, open this up for discussion and draw on students' experiences of dealing with different cultures.

Developing a conversation

SPEAKING

11 Before you begin, give students time to study the flowchart. Elicit from them the type of expressions they might use at each stage of the flowchart. If possible, clear space in the classroom for students to walk around and simulate networking with each other. If there isn't space, students could work in pairs and follow the flowchart.

Photocopiable activity 1.2
See page 157.

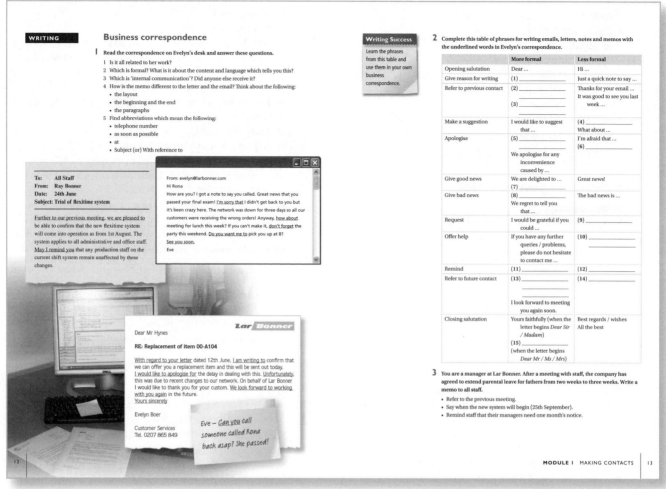

Student's Book pages 12 and 13

Business correspondence

WRITING

This first writing section provides a general overview of different correspondence.

1 Give students a time limit of 10 minutes to answer the questions.

Answers
1 The email and post-it note are not related to her work.
2 The memo and the letter are formal because they are giving information and replying to a customer with a complaint. The language uses quite long and fixed expressions.
3 The memo is 'internal communication' because it was sent within the company. Everyone in the company received a copy of it.
4 The memo uses the *To/From/Date/Subject* headings. It doesn't require an opening salutation line (*Dear ...*) or closing salutation (*Best ... Yours ...*). Memos often have only one paragraph.
5 Tel. / asap / @ / RE

2 Refer students to the Writing Success tip. Ask them to complete the table using words from the correspondence in exercise 1. The table will give students a very useful reference for further writing during their course.

Answers
1 I am writing to ...
2/3 Further to our previous meeting / With regard to your letter dated ...
4 how about
5 I would like to apologise for
6 I'm sorry that ...
7 we are pleased to
8 Unfortunately
9 Can you
10 Do you want me to
11 May I remind you ...
12 Don't forget
13 we look forward to working with you ...
14 See you soon
15 Yours sincerely

3 If students do the task in class, you could put them into pairs to write it together.

Encourage students to keep their memos succinct and to the point. Students will find it helpful to use the memo on page 12 as a model.

Possible answer

To: All Staff

From: [Name of student]

Date: 25th July

Subject: Parental Leave

Further to our previous meeting, I am pleased to confirm that parental leave for fathers has been extended to three weeks. The new system will come into operation as from 25th September. May I remind you that your managers will require one month's notice?

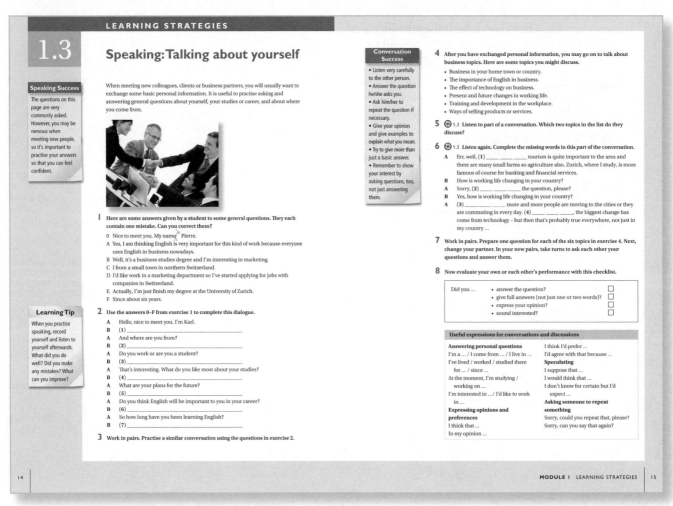

Student's Book pages 14 and 15

Read the introductory paragraph with the students. Refer students to the Speaking Success tip.

Track 3 (CD1)

1 This exercise looks at some typical mistakes that students make when talking about themsleves.

Answers
A Yes, I **think** English …
B … I'm interest**ed** in marketing.
C **I'm** from …
D I'd like **to** work …
E Actually, I'm just finish**ing** my degree …
F **For** about six years.

2 Students complete the conversation with corrected answers 0–F.

Answers
1 0   2 C   3 E   4 B   5 D   6 A   7 F

3 To set this up, the student playing the part of B can close their book and answer the A's questions in exercise 2 in their own words. Refer students to the Learning Tip which suggests that students record and self-evaluate their performance. If possible, record them in the classroom and let them listen and note any common errors.

4 Refer students to the Conversation Success tip. Note that these questions don't rely on specialist knowledge and pre-work students should be able to respond as well as in-work students. Let students read the topics and briefly discuss with the class how difficult they would find these to give a short comment on. If any students look concerned about the topics, point out that the Student's Book covers all of these (and more) both in terms of content and language.

5 1.3 Play the extract.

Answers
B asks about:
– business in your home town or country
– present and future changes in working life.

1.3 Listening script
B And where do you live exactly?
A I'm from a small town in northern Switzerland, but at the moment I'm studying for a business degree so I live in Zurich.

B What types of business are most successful in your town?

A Er, well, I suppose that tourism is quite important to the area and there are many small farms so agriculture also. Zurich, where I study, is more famous of course for banking and financial services.

B How is working life changing in your country?

A Sorry, can you repeat the question, please?

B Yes, how is working life changing in your country?

A I think that more and more people are moving to the cities or they are commuting in every day. In my opinion, the biggest change has come from technology – but then that's probably true everywhere, not just in my country ...

6 1.3 Students listen again and complete the gaps. Encourage students to keep a note of these phrases as they are useful for general discussion.

Answers
1 I suppose that
2 Can you repeat
3 I think that
4 In my opinion

7 In pairs, students prepare questions on the topics in exercise 4. Students take their questions and work with another partner. Each student takes turns to ask and answer the questions.

Possible questions
1 What kind of business is very important in your home town?
2 Do you think English will continue to be important for business in the future?
3 Which technology has had the biggest effect on business in recent years?
4 In what ways do you think working life will change in the next ten years?
5 If you had a choice of work training, what would it be? Why?
6 How effective is selling over the phone?

8 Students can assess their speaking skills in exercise 7 using the checklist.

Extension
Now that students have practised both personal information questions (in exercise 3) and further business-related questions (in exercise 7), they can find new partners and practise asking and answering these questions again. They will find it helpful to refer to the Useful expressions summary at the bottom of page 15 and, again, they can use the checklist in exercise 8 to evaluate their performances.

Overview

2.1 Business topic: Company benefits

VOCABULARY	Benefits and incentives
READING	Is working for Xerox too good to be true?
VOCABULARY	Expressions with *take*
SPEAKING	Asking questions about jobs
GRAMMAR	The past
WRITING	A letter of application

2.2 Business skills: Presenting your company

VOCABULARY	Company terms
LISTENING	Presentations
PRONUNCIATION	Pausing, intonation and stress
SPEAKING	Giving a presentation
WRITING	A memo

2.3 Learning strategies: Checking for errors / Internal communications

Types of incorrect words

Writing an internal communication

PHOTOCOPIABLE

© 2009 Heinle, Cengage Learning

Useful language from Module 2

Wordlist

branch	headquarters	promotion	take part in
call centre	holding company	recognition	take seriously
cash bonus	manufacturing	research and	take with a pinch
corporation	parental leave	development	of salt
distribution centre	pension	reward	trademark
division	perks	subsidiary	turnover
flexible	plant	take care	warehouse
found (a company)	position	take on	

Expressions

Presenting

Good morning and thanks for coming.

Today I'd like to tell you about …

If you have any questions, I'll be happy to answer them at the end.

In my brief presentation we'll begin by looking at …

First of all there's …/ and finally there's …

Then I'll give an overview of …

OK, let's move on to look at …

One thing I'd like to point out is …

Take a look at this chart, which shows …

Here you can see …

Finally, I'd like to talk about …

So that brings me to the end of my presentation.

Thanks for listening.

Are there any questions?

MODULE 2   BUSINESS TOPIC

2.1   Company benefits

VOCABULARY

Benefits and incentives

1 What is most important to you when choosing a job? Rank the following in order of importance from 1 to 10.

_____ an impressive job title
_____ a good salary
_____ flexible working hours
_____ opportunities for promotion
_____ days off and long holidays

_____ training and staff development
_____ a pension
_____ opportunities to travel
_____ parental leave
_____ a company car

Work in pairs. Compare your lists and give reasons for your answers.

2 2.1 Listen to five short recordings. Which of the benefits and incentives in exercise 1 is each person referring to?

Speaker 1: _____
Speaker 2: _____
Speaker 3: _____
Speaker 4: _____
Speaker 5: _____

READING

3 Read the article about Xerox on page 17. What benefits and incentives does the article mention for employees at Xerox?

Exam Success

This task is similar to Part Three of the BEC Vantage Reading Test. It's helpful to read the whole text before trying to answer any of the questions.

4 Choose the best answer, A, B or C for questions 1–5 about the Xerox article.

1 The journalist of this article thinks that
   A staff at Xerox are not telling the truth about the company.
   B Xerox offers great benefits to staff.
   C people haven't worked at Xerox long enough to know if it's a good company.

2 Where does the company tend to find its new managers?
   A From existing staff.
   B On training courses.
   C Only from graduates.

3 Why doesn't Kim Moloney have her own desk?
   A Because she isn't important enough.
   B Because there isn't space at head office.
   C Because she often travels and is away on business.

4 As well as recognising its staff though promotion, Xerox
   A gives cash bonuses.
   B provides a number of perks.
   C gives unpaid leave to take trips of a lifetime.

5 One common feature of Xerox staff is that they tend
   A to work hard.
   B to get promoted.
   C not to change employer.

Is working for Xerox too good to be true?

What a lovely place Xerox is to work! Kim Moloney, a client services executive, can't say enough nice things about her employer. 'It's a very special environment,' she says. 'People describe Xerox as a family and I was amazed at the number of people who have worked here for so long.'

It's tempting to take Moloney's comments with a pinch of salt, especially considering that when you've been working somewhere for only two years, as she has at Xerox, everyone seems old and established. But there's truth behind her enthusiasm.

Take Carole Palmer, the group resources director. She joined Xerox in 1978 as a temp and has been in her present role for seven years. 'Xerox has been good to me over the years,' she says. 'It has supported me through qualifications … and last year I took part in the vice-president incumbent programme.'

Human resources is taken seriously at Xerox, Palmer says, and the company has a policy of promoting from within (which would explain Moloney's amazement at her colleagues' longevity). The company takes on only fifteen to twenty graduates each year and Moloney was part of an intake who joined having already acquired a couple of years' work experience.

She started as a project manager for Xerox Global Services before moving into sales. Now her responsibility is to 'grow and maintain customer relationships.'

Moloney is based at the head office in Uxbridge. 'It's great in terms of working environment,' she says. 'We've just got a new provider in the canteen and … we have brainstorming rooms and breakout areas.'

Much of Moloney's role is visiting clients, so she doesn't have a permanent desk at head office. 'I'm a hot-desker, which is good because you get to sit with different people in the hot-desk areas. And you're given a place to store your things.'

Head office staff numbers between 1,200 and 1,500 people, Palmer says. The company has four other main offices in the UK. The nature of the organisation, which encompasses sales and marketing, global services (the biggest division), developing markets, research and development and manufacturing, means that the opportunities at the company vary from service engineers to sales roles and consultants.

Perks include a final-salary pension scheme and various discount schemes. The reward and recognition scheme is a little different, and rather nice: 'Each manager has a budget every year to recognise and reward staff,' Palmer says. 'It can be in the form of a meal for two, or a bottle of wine. It can be up to £1,000. There's the recognition, and then there's putting money behind it.'

Moloney, however, likes the non-cash rewards. 'Xerox takes care of all its staff but it also recognises the people who put in the added effort,' she says. 'It offers once-in-a-lifetime incentive trips, and recently I organised a sailing trip for my team.'

The idea of working abroad with the company appeals to her, and she says that her career goal is to be part of the senior management team. Here's another employee, it would seem, who is in it for the long haul.

VOCABULARY

Expressions with *take*

5 There are six expressions in the article with the word *take*. Find them and match them to these meanings.

1 not completely believe something is true or likely _____
2 looks after _____
3 for example _____
4 participated in _____
5 employs _____
6 regarded as important _____

MODULE 2 COMPANY BENEFITS

Student's Book pages 16 and 17

Benefits and incentives

VOCABULARY Track 4 (CD1)

1 Ask students to work alone as they rank the ten items and then compare and discuss in pairs. Make sure they give reasons.

Extension

Put students in pairs and tell them to practise a presentation entitled what is important when choosing a job? Students can use some of the ideas listed in exercise 1.

2 2.1 Students listen out for five of the benefits and incentives in exercise 1.

Answers

1 a company car
2 flexible working hours
3 parental leave
4 an impressive job title
5 a pension

2.1 Listening script

Speaker 1 It's great because usually it means my wife can use the one at home and we even take mine away at weekends. I work for quite a relaxed company and they don't seem to mind how I use it for leisure.

Speaker 2 I thought it wouldn't change the way I worked after the first six months, but as they got older it actually became more complicated with getting them to school or if they wanted to do activities in the afternoon. But my boss has been really good about it and some days I can do a half day if I want and then I might work later on other days – or I take work home, which I don't like doing, but it's the only way …

Speaker 3 It's actually the law now so they had to let me have it. It was only two weeks but at least I had time to help my wife out. Mind you, after all the late nights and crying I was really happy to get back to work for a while and have a rest!

Speaker 4 I've just been promoted from Assistant IT Technician to Chief Operational Network Administrator. It means I get a bit of a pay rise and new business cards with my name on. I'm not sure if I get my own office though.

Speaker 5 The problem for me is that I won't have enough to live on when I'm 60 and I can't afford a private plan. So I'll probably try and keep working for a few more years, and anyway, I heard the government is planning to raise the age of retirement …

Is working for Xerox too good to be true?

3 Set students a time limit of about three minutes to answer the question. The aim is to find any benefits and incentives, but tell students not to read in too much detail at this stage.

Answers
opportunities for promotion, training and staff development, a pension
*Note that the article also mentions a 'reward and recognition scheme' which is another form of incentive.

4 Now students read the article in much more detail to answer questions 1–5. Refer them to the Reading Success tip on reading the complete text before answering any questions.

Answers
1 B   2 A   3 C   4 B   5 C

Expressions with *take*

VOCABULARY

5 As a quick lead-in, ask students to brainstorm collocations and expressions they can think of with *take*, eg *take a day off, take a taxi, take a break, take off*, etc.

Answers
1 take (Moloney's comments) with a pinch of salt
2 takes care of
3 Take (Carole Palmer)
4 took part in
5 takes on
6 takes seriously

Extension
Ask students to write six new sentences using *take* from the exercise. They can relate the sentences to their own work or life, eg *I'd take the news of a pay rise with a pinch of salt.*

SPEAKING

Asking questions about jobs

1 Work in pairs. Use the prompts to ask questions 1 to 6 about working for Xerox. Look back at the article on the previous page to help.

0 Q: why / like / the company? Why do you like the company?
 A: It's like a family.
1 Q: long / working / the company? _____
 A: Two years.
2 Q: when / join? _____
 A: In 1978.
3 Q: was / first job? _____
 A: A project manager.
4 Q: what / responsible? _____
 A: Growing and maintaining customer relationships.
5 Q: where / based? _____
 A: At Uxbridge.
6 Q: would / like / in the future? _____
 A: Work abroad and be part of the senior management team.

2 If you or your partner works for a company, ask each other the questions in exercise 1.

GRAMMAR

The past

3 Read this profile of a company employee. Underline the three verb forms and write each underlined verb next to the correct tense definition.

Steve Bennett started as a project manager in global services and since then has moved into sales. He has only been working at the company for two years.

Past simple: refers to a specific point in the past. _____
Present perfect: refers to a present situation with a link to a point in the past. _____
Present perfect continuous: refers to a present action that started in the past and is still continuing. _____

4 Complete the information about Xerox and one of its employees by underlining the correct verb form.

The company (0) *existed / has existed* since 1906 but in fact Xerox (1) *begun / has begun* as The Haloid Company. It then (2) *trademarked / has trademarked* the word Xerox in 1948 and eventually (3) *became / has been becoming* the Xerox Corporation in 1961.

Carole Palmer (4) *was / has been* with the company since 1978 and she (5) *worked / has been working* as the group resources director for the last seven years. 'Xerox (6) *has been / has been being* good to me over the years,' she says. 'It has supported me through qualifications … and last year I (7) *took part / 've taken part* in the vice-president incumbent programme.'

5 Read this application for a job. Write the verb in brackets in the past simple, present perfect or present perfect continuous.

Dear Sir or Madam,
I (0) saw (see) your advert for the post of Client Services Executive in yesterday's newspaper and I would like to apply for the position.

As you can see from my attached CV, I (1) _____ (work) for my current company for over two years. I (2) _____ (join) MacKintyre and Co in 2007 and since then, I (3) _____ (have) many opportunities to develop my skills. However, I (4) _____ (consider) a career change with a new challenge for a number of months and this seems like the perfect moment to make that move.

I see from recent press reports that your company (5) _____ (expand) its operations in China and therefore I would like to draw your attention to my degree in Oriental Studies and Mandarin which I (6) _____ (complete) in 2006. Combined with my current MBA, which I (7) _____ (study) for part-time at the local university, I feel that I would be an asset to your company.

Please also note that my current manager (8) _____ (agree) to write a reference and can be contacted on 0207 857 6785.
I look forward to hearing from you.

Yours faithfully
Daniel Lewis

WRITING

A letter of application

6 Read this advert for a job. You would like to apply for it and have written some notes about your experience. Use the handwritten notes to write a letter of application (120–140 words) similar to the one in exercise 5 above.

Personal Assistant to Overseas Sales Manager
We are currently seeking someone to work in a busy and expanding department. You will have experience in secretarial duties. Good knowledge of English and at least one other language is preferred. You will need to travel abroad with the Sales Manager and organise schedules. Opportunities for promotion.

completed course at college
worked 2 years as receptionist and secretary
lived in Rome summer 2006 – fluent Italian
been working for travel agency for last 6 months

18

MODULE 2 COMPANY BENEFITS 19

Student's Book pages 18 and 19

Asking questions about jobs

SPEAKING

1 Tell students to imagine they were the journalist writing the article on Xerox on the previous page. They need to create the questions they asked during the interviews with Kim Moloney and Carole Palmer. The article offers clues as to the tense needed for each question. This exercise should be a review for students at this level and provides some basic questions for asking about a job.

Answers
1 How long have you been working for the company?
2 When did you join (the company)?
3 What was your first job?
4 What are you responsible for?
5 Where are you based?
6 What would you like to do in the future?

2 Students practise asking and answering the questions. If possible, try to pair students who haven't yet met in the class. Make sure the answers use the correct tense and give feedback.

The past

GRAMMAR

3 Students match the three verb forms to the correct tense definitions.

Answers
Past simple: *started*
Present perfect: *has moved*
Present perfect continuous: *has been working*

Refer students to the Grammar reference on page 128. Suggest they also re-read the information on the present perfect and present perfect continuous in Module 1. Remind students that we tend not to use continuous forms with stative verbs. Also point out that verbs like *work* and *live* can often be used in the present perfect and present perfect continuous form with little change in meaning. The main change in emphasis is that the continuous form emphasises that the action is ongoing.

You could also draw these timelines on the board to help clarify the meaning:

Past simple

Past   Now

Present perfect

Past   Now

Present perfect continuous

Past   Now

4 Students underline the correct verb form. When checking answers, ask students to try and explain their choice.

Answers
1 began
2 trademarked
3 became
4 has been
5 has been working
6 has been
7 took part

Photocopiable activity 2.1
See page 158.

5 Students complete the letter of application with the verbs in different tenses.

Answers
1 have been working
2 joined
3 have had
4 have been considering
5 has expanded / has been expanding (we are unsure if the expansion has ended)
6 completed
7 have been studying
8 has agreed

A letter of application

WRITING

6 Begin by asking students if they have ever applied for a job. Elicit the process, eg *Where did you find out about the job? Did you have to write a letter or fill in a form?*

Ask students to underline key information and remind them to include the handwritten notes and stay within the word limit.

If you are short of time this could be set as homework. If it is done in class, students could work in pairs and draft the letter together.

Possible answer

Dear Sir or Madam

I saw your advert for the post of Personal Assistant to Overseas Sales Manager in yesterday's newspaper and I would like to apply for the position.

As you can see from my attached CV, I have been working for a travel agency for the last six months, which I have really enjoyed. Before that I worked as a receptionist and secretary for two years.

I have a good knowledge of English as I completed a course at college and I am also fluent in Italian having lived in Rome for the summer in 2008.

Please note that my current manager has agreed to write me a reference. I look forward to hearing from you.

Yours faithfully

[student's name]

BUSINESS SKILLS

2.2 Presenting your company

VOCABULARY

Company terms

1 Work in pairs. Play this game.

You each have five words. Prepare three definitions of each word but only one definition is correct. For example, if the word is 'turnover', your three definitions might be:

A a company's total profits   B a company's total costs   C a company's total spending

Your partner should guess that answer A is correct. Here are your five words each:
Student A: distribution centre, warehouse, holding company, call centre, plant
Student B: headquarters, subsidiary, branch, corporation, division

If you are unsure of your word, then check the definitions on these pages:
Student A: File 2.1 on page 126   **Student B:** File 2.2 on page 131

LISTENING

Presentations

2 2.2 Listen to three extracts from a presentation about Xerox. Which of the words in exercise 1 does the speaker mention when he talks about the Xerox Corporation?

3 Can you say all the following figures from the key facts about the Xerox Corporation?

Fact Sheet XEROX®

Key facts	
16,000,000,000	_____
978,000,000	_____
160	_____
55,000	_____
½	_____
4	_____
6	_____
5,000,000,000	_____
2,000,000,000	_____
1906	_____
112,000,000,000	_____

4 2.2 Listen to the presentation again and write what each figure refers to.

5 The presenter follows this traditional three-part structure for a presentation.

A	B	C	D	E	F
Introducing the presentation	Explaining the structure of the presentation	Presenting the first part	Presenting the second part	Presenting the final part	Ending the presentation

2.2 Listen and match stages A–F to the expressions below. Write the letter after the expression.

1 Today I'd like to tell you about …	A
2 So that brings me to the end of my presentation.	__
3 Are there any questions?	__
4 OK, let's move on to look at …	__
5 Good morning and thanks for coming.	__
6 Here you can see …	__
7 Finally I'd like to talk about …	__
8 If you have any questions, I'll be happy to answer them at the end.	__
9 Then I'll give an overview of …	__
10 One thing I'd like to point out is …	__
11 Take a look at this chart, which shows …	__
12 With a turnover of … the company develops / manufactures / markets …	__
13 In my brief presentation we'll begin by looking at …	__
14 First of all there's … / and finally there's …	__
15 Thanks for listening.	__

PRONUNCIATION

6 To help an audience understand your presentation, it's helpful to put short pauses between your phrases. Notice how, in the first part of the presentation, the speaker pauses where there is a / symbol.

Good morning / and thanks for coming. / Today / I'd like to tell you about / the world's / largest / document / management / company. / With a turnover of nearly sixteen billion dollars the Xerox Corporation develops and markets innovative technologies with products and solutions that customers depend upon to get the best results for their business. In my brief presentation we'll begin by looking at some of the key figures behind the company's success and how the company is structured. Then I'll give an overview of Xerox around the world and finally I'd like to talk about some of the trends affecting our market and its future growth. If you have any questions, I'll be happy to answer them at the end.

2.3 Listen to this part again and mark in the rest of the pauses with a line (/). Now practise saying the presentation with these pauses.

7 2.4 Listen to the presenter say each part of the presentation and repeat it. Notice the intonation and sentence stress.

Presenter	Good morning	Presenter	and thanks for coming.
You	Good morning	You	and thanks for coming.

20   MODULE 2 PRESENTING YOUR COMPANY   21

Student's Book pages 20 and 21

Company terms

VOCABULARY

1 This activity checks that students know some key vocabulary before starting. The definitions are in the information files on pages 126 and 131, or students can check in their dictionaries.

During the task, make sure students know how to pronounce all the words. It may be helpful to drill the word stress in these words: *distribution, warehouse, headquarters, subsidiary, corporation, division*

Presentations

LISTENING Track 5 (CD1)

2 2.2 For this first listening, students only need to listen out for the words in exercise 1.

Answers
headquarters   corporation   divisions

2.2 Listening script

Extract 1 Good morning and thanks for coming. Today I'd like to tell you about the world's largest document management company. With a turnover of nearly sixteen billion dollars the Xerox Corporation develops and markets innovative technologies with products and solutions that customers depend upon to get the best results for their business. In my brief presentation we'll begin by looking at some of the key figures behind the company's success and how the company is structured. Then I'll give an overview of Xerox around the world and finally I'd like to talk about some of the trends affecting our market and its future growth. If you have any questions, I'll be happy to answer them at the end. So, here you can see, the turnover for last year was nearly sixteen billion dollars, with a final income of 978 million dollars. We operated from our headquarters in Rochester New York State in 160 countries with 55,000 employees, with over half of those in the USA. This next chart shows you how the corporation is split into four divisions. First of all there's Xerox Global Services …
Extract 2 And finally there's Xerox Innovation with five centres in the United States, Canada and Europe. Note that six percent of revenue was dedicated to research and development last year as the key part of our mission statement is, and I quote, 'to help people find better ways to do great work.' OK, let's move on to look at Xerox around the world in a little more detail. Take a look at this chart, which shows revenue by region. So about half our revenue is from the US market. Then Europe with over five billion

dollars and the rest of the world with over two. One thing I'd like to point out is ...

Extract 3 Finally, how is the market for the document industry looking? Well it would be unrecognisable to the people who founded the original company in 1906 and even compared to the second half of the twentieth century. More and more offices are moving from black and white printing to colour, and from paper documents to electronic documents. These are clearly the future opportunities and areas of growth in what is a total market worth an estimated 112 billion dollars ...

So that brings me to the end of my presentation. Thanks for listening. I hope it's been of interest. Are there any questions?

3 Students can work in pairs and try to say the numbers. In order to check their answers, you could play the recording again so students can listen for pronunciation.

Answers
sixteen billion
nine hundred and seventy-eight million
one hundred and sixty
fifty-five thousand
half
four
six
five billion
two billion
nineteen oh six
one hundred and twelve billion

4 2.2 Students listen again and write notes.

Answers
16,000,000,000 turnover
978,000,000,000 final income
160 countries
55,000 employees
half of 55,000 in the USA
4 divisions
6 % of revenue dedicated to research & development
5,000,000,000 dollars revenue in Europe
(over) 2,000,000,000 dollars rest of world revenue
1906 company founded
112,000,000,000 total market

Photocopiable activity 2.2
See page 159.

5 2.2 Give students time to study the flowchart and read the expressions. Then, play the recording at least once for students to match the expressions. Afterwards, students could check their answers by reading the listening script.

Answers
1 A 2 F 3 F 4 D 5 A 6 C 7 B 8 B
9 B 10 D 11 D 12 A 13 B 14 C 15 F

PRONUNCIATION Tracks 6, 7 (CD1)

6 2.3 Students might find the idea that we pause so often in a presentation quite strange, but it is a standard technique with experienced presenters, especially when talking to larger audiences. Play the recording and students mark the pauses. With more confident groups, let them try to predict where the pauses will go before listening. It might help to point out that we tend to pause whenever there is a full stop or comma, after signal phrases (*Today*/*Firstly*/*Next*), to separate key information (eg the name of a company), or to emphasise information (as in the presentation about Xerox – *the world's/largest/document/management/company*). Students can check their answers in the listening script on page 135 where the pauses are indicated already.

2.3 / 2.4 Listening script

Presenter   Good morning / and thanks for coming. / Today / I'd like to tell you about / the world's / largest / document / management / company. / With a turnover of nearly sixteen billion dollars / the Xerox Corporation develops / and markets / innovative technologies / with products and solutions / that customers depend upon to get the best results / for their business. / In my brief presentation / we'll begin by looking at / some of the key figures / behind the company's success / and how the company is structured. / Then / I'll give an overview of Xerox around the world / and finally / I'd like to talk about some of the trends / affecting our market / and its future growth. / If you have any questions, / I'll be happy to answer them at the end. /

7 2.4 This is designed as a drill and helps to focus students on intonation and stress, as well as pausing. It's a useful strategy that they can learn to apply to their own presentations. Drill it as a class, or students could also practise on their own at home.

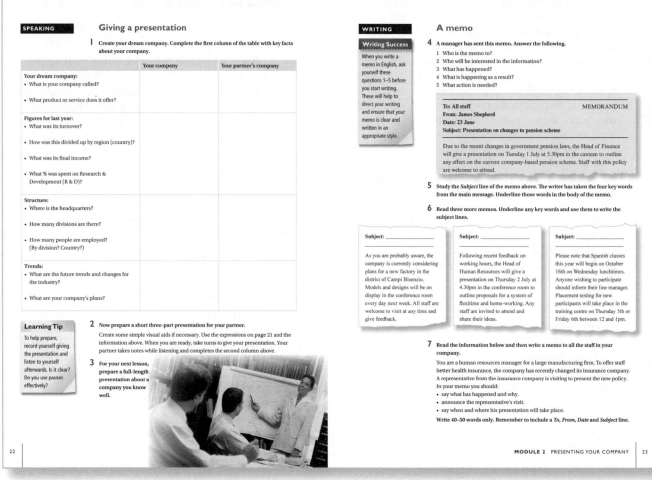

Student's Book pages 22 and 23

Giving a presentation

SPEAKING

1 Ask students what kind of company they would like to run if they had the chance. Tell them this is their 'dream' company and they are going to create it. Working alone, they make up facts and figures to fill in the first column of the table. The aim of the task is to give controlled practice of the expressions for presenting. Their ideas can be as far-fetched as they like.

2 Refer students back to the expressions in exercise 5 on page 21. Students work in pairs and give their presentations. They may find it helpful to repeat their presentations at least twice so they could also change partners. The person listening takes notes and could also offer feedback and suggestions on possible improvements.

Extension

After students have given their presentations to partners, you could ask them to do the same again to the class. Also, students could follow the advice in the Learning Tip and record their presentation or transcribe it, marking pauses as they did in exercise 6 on page 21.

3 Students prepare a full-length presentation about a company for their next lesson. This could be their own company or one they know well. Alternatively, students could research a company using information on its website and use this as the basis for a presentation.

A memo

WRITING

Ask students if they receive memos at work. What are they about? Who writes them? With pre-work learners, ask them if they can define what a memo is.

4 Refer students to the Writing Success tip before they read the instructions.

Answers
1 All staff.
2 Any staff with a company-based pension scheme.
3 There have been changes in the government pension laws.
4 This will affect the current company-based pension scheme.
5 A presentation will be given by the Head of Finance on the changes and any effects.

5 The next two exercises help students to write effective subject lines. Make sure students realise the importance of a subject line, which is to summarise the key content of the memo and help the reader to identify the purpose easily.

Answer
presentation, changes, pension, scheme

Extension
Before students do exercise 6, ask them to apply questions 2–5 from exercise 4 to each of the memos in exercise 6. Note that all the memos are to 'All staff'.

6 Students should begin by underlining any key words. They could compare these with a partner. Then they will need to choose the best three or four words to keep the subject lines brief.

Possible answers
Memo 1: Display of new factory plans
Memo 2: Presentation on flexitime and home-working
Memo 3: Spanish classes

7 This could be done in class (perhaps with students in pairs) or set for homework.

Possible answer

To: All Staff

From: [name of student]

Date: 1ˢᵗ October

Subject: Presentation of new insurance policy

To offer staff a better health insurance scheme, we are now working with a new insurance company. Please note therefore that a representative from this company will present the new staff policy on 9th October at 2pm in the conference room. All staff are welcome to attend.

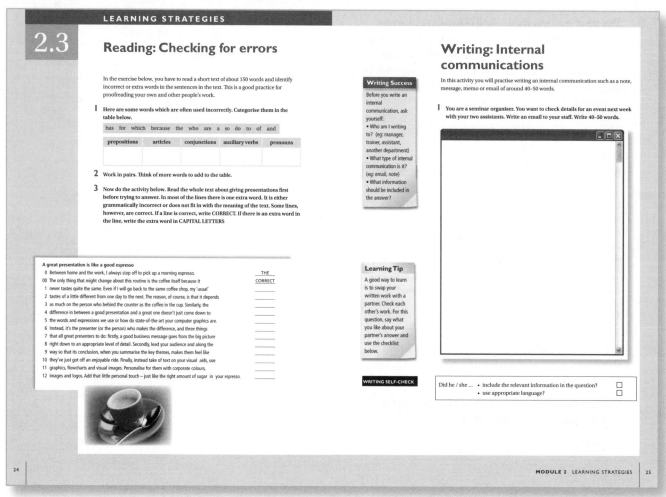

Student's Book pages 24 and 25

I Students complete the table with words that are often used incorrectly.

Answers

prepositions	articles	conjunctions	auxiliary verbs	pronouns
for	the	because	has	which
to	a	so	are	who
of		and	do	

2 After students work in pairs, ask everyone to feed back to the class so ideas can be shared. It's also a good idea for students to use good dictionaries so they can check the word types beforehand.

Possible answers

prepositions	articles	conjunctions	auxiliary verbs	pronouns
in	an	when	have	it
at	(no article)	while	does	him
by				that

3 Ask students to read the rubric carefully. They should always read the whole text first before trying to answer. You might want them to work in pairs and discuss possibilities. Draw their attention to the fact that many of the words will be those looked at in exercises 1 and 2, although other types of words may still be incorrect (see 10 in this text).

Answers

1 WILL
2 OF
3 WHO
4 IN
5 DO
6 CORRECT
7 TO
8 AND
9 CORRECT
10 TAKE
11 FOR
12 CORRECT

Writing: Internal communications

I Refer students to the Writing Success tip. Students will be fairly familiar with this type of task now as they were introduced to the format on page 12 of Module 1 (exercise 3) and page 23 of Module 2 (exercise 7). For this reason, you can ask students to work alone. Allow 10–15 minutes.

Possible answer

> From: [student's name]
>
> Subject: Confirmation of seminar details
>
> Date: XXXX
>
> To: Assistant seminar organisers
>
> Please note that I have booked Rooms 101 and 102 for the seminar next week. I'd be grateful if you would now confirm this booking and the final schedule for the event with security. Also note that Mr Singh will be one hour late on the Monday morning.

WRITING SELF-CHECK

Refer students to the advice in the Learning Tip. They should swap their work with a partner. It's helpful if students become used to commenting on and being supportive of each other's work.

Overview

3.1   Business topic: Starting a business

VOCABULARY	**Types of business**
READING	**We wanna hold your hand**
LISTENING	**Advice on franchises**
LISTENING	**Planning a seminar**
GRAMMAR	***will* and the future**
SPEAKING	**Discussing a schedule**

3.2   Business skills: Leaving and taking messages

LISTENING	**Leaving messages**
SPEAKING	**Leaving a voicemail message**
WRITING	**Taking notes and messages**

3.3   Learning strategies: Short messages

Predicting missing information

Listening for specific words

PHOTOCOPIABLE

© 2009 Heinle, Cengage Learning

Useful language from Module 3

Wordlist

branch out	franchise	luggage	sole trader
charge	franchisor/	online database	subscription
concept	franchisee	partnership	trademark
entrepreneur	grant (a licence)	profit margin	trade name
entrepreneurial	growth	run (a company/	venture
spirit	invest	business)	
fee	launch	set up	

Expressions

Call me on ...

Can I help you?

Can I take a message?

Could I ask who's calling?

Could you call me back?

Could you give me your mobile number?

Hello, this is a message for ...

I'd be very grateful if you'd return my call ...

I'll be in the office tomorrow.

I'll call you back in about an hour.

I'll have to check with another presenter.

It's P for Paris ...

It's with regard to ...

It's ...

Let me read that back to you.

So that's M as in Madrid ...

So that's two in the afternoon.

Sorry, let me check.

The reason I'm calling is that ...

This is ...

You can email me at r dot ...

You can get me any time between ...

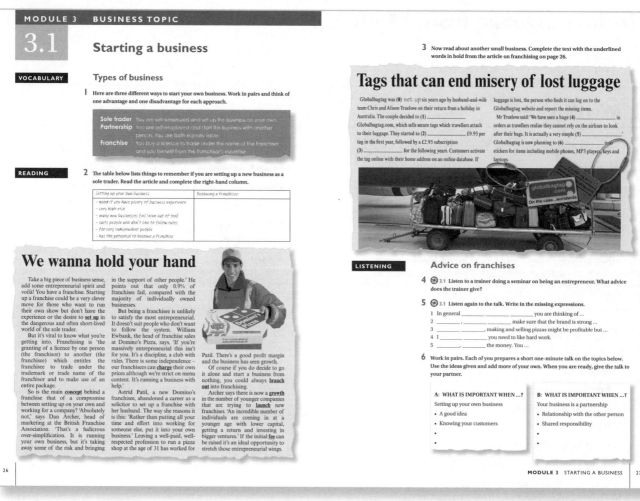

Student's Book pages 26 and 27

Types of business

VOCABULARY

1 Find out what the equivalent terms are in their country and language. As well as asking students to think of one advantage and disadvantage for each approach, ask them to give an example of a business they know which matches each of the three definitions. If your students are inexperienced, you could write the six answers on the board randomly and ask students to match them to the business type.

Possible answers

	Advantage	Disadvantage
Sole trader	You take all the profit.	If you go bankrupt, you lose everything.
Partnership	You share the pressure.	You might disagree on strategy.
Franchise	The business model is given to you so there is less risk.	Part of your profits goes to the franchisor.

We wanna hold your hand

READING

2 Students read and underline key information to help them fill in the right-hand column.

Possible answers

Becoming a franchisee:
- good if you don't have much business experience
- less risky than being a sole trader
- you have a business relationship with someone else
- only 0.9% of franchises fail
- doesn't suit people who don't like to follow other systems/people
- offers some independence and you don't work for someone else

Extension

Put students into two groups. Each group writes five comprehension questions for each other about the text, eg *What are you granted in a franchise? (A licence.)* Then they swap their questions and try to answer them.

3 Elicit the meaning of the underlined words in bold in exercise 2. Students should read the whole text first before trying to complete the text about Globalbagtag.

Answers
1 launch
2 charge
3 fee
4 growth
5 concept
6 branch out

Extension

If you have an entrepreneurial class of students, put them into groups. Begin by brainstorming typical problems that travellers have on holiday or on long journeys. Then tell the groups to choose one problem and think of a commercial way to help with this problem, eg many travellers have to wait a long time at airports. Perhaps your students can discover a way to make this process less problematic. Give groups 10 minutes to come up with an idea and then ask them to present it to the class. Note that the ideas can be as crazy as they like. The aim is for them to make use of some of the vocabulary from this section, eg *Our group intends to set up a company which helps business travellers. Our main concept is to …*

Advice on franchises

LISTENING Track 8 (CD1)

4 🔘 3.1 The trainer develops some of the ideas from the reading on the previous page. Students make notes on the advice given.

Answers
- You must be someone who likes to follow rules and have support from others.
- Choose a strong brand and something you are interested in.
- You need start-up capital.

3.1 Listening script

T = Trainer   **M** = Man

T So. That's the end of my talk. Are there any questions? Yes?
M Thanks for your talk. It was very interesting. I've been thinking of starting my own business and I wondered what you thought of franchises.
T That's a good question. In general, it's important when you are thinking of becoming a franchisee to be someone who likes to follow rules and have support from others. Entrepreneurs tend to be people who don't like following tried and tested routes, so if you don't like doing what other people want, then franchising isn't for you.

Secondly, I'd say make sure that the brand is strong and that it's something you are interested in. For example, making and selling pizzas might be profitable but do you want to be doing it for the next five years? I also think you need to like hard work. People shouldn't think that running a franchise is less work than being a sole trader.

Finally, there's the money. You still need start-up capital. This can be as low as five thousand pounds and as high as two hundred and thirty thousand pounds for a well-known brand like Domino's Pizza …

5 🔘 3.1 Students listen again for useful expressions.

Answers
1 it's important when
2 Secondly, I'd say
3 For example
4 also think
5 Finally, there's

6 Students will now be familiar with this task from Module 1. Students should find the discussion and reading from earlier in this module helpful in preparing ideas for their talk. If you think some students will find it difficult to come up with ideas, put all the Student As together and all the Bs. They can discuss their ideas for the talks. Then pair As and Bs for the one-minute talks.

Extension

Give feedback on the talks. Students could then change roles and give the other talk to a new partner.

Photocopiable activity 3.1
See page 160.

LISTENING

Planning a seminar

1 🔊 3.2 **Listen to a message on a voicemail about a seminar. Complete the information on this message pad.**

> Business Circle Conferencing
> Name: Mr Ray (1)
> Name of event: (2)
> He can't come to the buffet on (3) .... because his train
> doesn't arrive until after (4) .... Please send the schedule
> to his email which is (5)

2 🔊 3.3 **Vanessa and Kirsten are in charge of organising the seminar at Business Circle Conferencing. Vanessa calls Kirsten to confirm the final arrangements. Add the missing information to Vanessa's notes.**

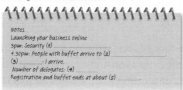

> Notes
> Launching your business online
> 3pm: Security (1)
> 4.30pm: People with buffet arrive to (2)
> (3) .... : I arrive.
> Number of delegates: (4)
> Registration and buffet ends at about (5)

GRAMMAR

will and the future

3 **Read these sentences from the first message. Match the sentences to an explanation of the use of the verb, A–E.**

1 We will send it to you immediately.
2 I'm coming to the event next week called 'Launching your business online'.
3 My train doesn't arrive until nine fifteen.
4 I probably won't get to the training centre until Monday morning.
5 I'm going to take a taxi straight to the hotel.

A *Going to* + verb to emphasise a planned decision or intention.
B *Will* for making a (likely / unlikely) prediction.
C Present continuous for describing future planned arrangements.
D Present simple for regular timetabled events.
E *Will* for promising action.

4 🔊 3.3 **Listen to the second conversation again. Write in the missing words in these sentences.**

1 The buffet _____ _____ _____ up until four thirty.
2 I don't think anyone _____ _____ _____ before five.
3 I assume that we _____ _____ _____ by nine.
4 I hope they _____ _____ _____ by then!

5 **Answer these questions about the sentences in exercise 4.**

1 Which sentences are in the future continuous and refer to future events which are fixed and can be confirmed?
2 Which sentences are in the future perfect and say that something will end by a certain time?

6 **Underline the appropriate verb form in each sentence.**

0 I'm just phoning to confirm that I *will be* / *am* in my office by ten.
1 Don't worry. I promise that I *'ll call* / *'m calling* you back straight away.
2 Inflation probably *won't rise* / *won't have risen* above three percent this year.
3 We *'ll run* / *'re running* seminars every day next week so I can't take any time off, I'm afraid.
4 After that, I *'ll have* / *'m going to have* a rest in my room before this afternoon's session starts.
5 The hotel has a scheduled shuttle bus to the training centre. I think it *is going to leave* / *leaves* every half hour, but let me check for you.
6 Security *open* / *will be opening* the building at eight tomorrow instead of nine.
7 We begin at nine. So by the time he arrives at nine thirty, the first session *will have started* / *will be starting*.
8 He says he's *going to leave* / *'ll have left* at three to catch a flight even though he knows it doesn't finish until four.
9 I'm sure you *'re receiving* / *'ll be receiving* something in the post in the next couple of days, but I can check with my colleague if you like.

SPEAKING

Discussing a schedule

7 **You and your partner are in charge of a training event. Here is the schedule to email out to all participants.**

> **New in Business: a Seminar for Young Entrepreneurs**
> Monday 15th February
> 9.00–9.30 Registration and coffee
> 9.30–11.00 Introductions and talk: 'A good idea does not necessarily make money'
> Speaker: Fiona Brewster
> 11.30–1.00 Workshop and mini-presentations by each participant
> 1.00–2.00 Lunch
> 2.00–3.00 Talk: 'Online businesses — the myth and the truth'
> Speaker: Laszlo Reiner
> 3.30–5.00 Workshop: Title to be confirmed

However, before you confirm these details, read some correspondence and make any changes and notes on the schedule. Finally, meet with your partner to discuss and confirm the final version.

Student A: Turn to File 3.1 on page 126.
Student B: Turn to File 3.2 on page 131.

28

MODULE 3 STARTING A BUSINESS   29

Student's Book pages 28 and 29

Planning a seminar

LISTENING Tracks 9, 10 (CD1)

1 🔊 **3.2** Students listen and fill in the information.

Answers
1 Naunton
2 Launching your business online
3 Sunday evening
4 nine fifteen/9.15
5 r.naunton@worldsyouroyster.com

3.2 Listening script

Recorded message Thank you for calling Business Circle Conferencing. Please state your name and address. Then give the name of the event you'd like information on and we will send it to you immediately. Please speak after the tone.
Ray Hello. This is Mr Ray Naunton. That's N-A-U-N-T-O-N. I'm coming to the event next week called 'Launching your business online' and so you've already got my details. Anyway the reason I'm calling is that I won't be able to arrive in time for registration and the buffet on the Sunday evening. My train doesn't arrive until nine fifteen, so I'm going to take a taxi straight to the hotel. So I probably won't get to the training centre until Monday morning. I hope that's OK. Anyway it's just to confirm that I will be there for the course. Oh, and could someone send me the schedule for the two days? You can email it to me at r dot naunton at worldsyouroyster dot com. Worldsyouroyster is all one word. That's w-o-r-l-d-s-y-o-u-r-o-y-s-t-e-r. And all in lower case. Thank you

2 🔊 **3.3** Students listen to a call about the event in exercise 1.

Answers
1 are opening the room at 3   2 set up   3 4pm
4 twelve   5 seven

3.3 Listening script

K = Kirsten   **V** = Vanessa

K Hello, Kirsten speaking.
V Hi, Kirsten. It's Vanessa. I'm just calling to check details for the group on Sunday evening.
K Sure. Security are opening the room at three. Is that early enough?
V Yes, the buffet won't be setting up until four thirty so that's plenty of time. I'll get there at four and I don't think anyone will be arriving before five. According to my records, we have twelve. Is that right?
K Yes. Everyone has confirmed. Oh that reminds me. We've had a message from Mr Naunton to say he won't be here until after nine so he's checking straight into the hotel. There's no point in inviting him to come after then, is there? I mean, I assume that we'll have finished by nine.

V By seven, I hope. Well, I hope they'll have gone by then! If they want to get to know each other any longer, they can use the hotel bar.

K Fine. I think that's everything, then. Do you need me to be there?

V No. There's no point in both of us interrupting our weekend. It doesn't need two of us.

K Great. See you on Monday. Bye.

V Bye.

will and the future

GRAMMAR Track 10 (CD1)

3 Students match sentences to different verb forms used to refer to the future.

Answers
1 E 2 C 3 D 4 B 5 A

4 3.3 Students listen again and write verb forms in the future perfect and future perfect continuous.

Answers
1 won't be setting   2 will be arriving
3 'll have finished   4 'll have gone

5 Clarify the two forms on the board like this:

Future continuous: *will* + *be* + *...ing*
Future perfect: *will* + *have* + past participle (or *will* + present perfect)

You might want to refer students to the grammar reference on page 128 for more help before starting the next exercise.

Answers
1 Sentences 1 and 2 are future continuous.
2 Sentences 3 and 4 are future perfect.

6 Students check their understanding by choosing the correct verb forms.

Answers
1 'll call   2 won't rise   3 're running
4 'm going to have   5 leaves   6 will be opening
7 will have started   8 's going to leave
9 'll be receiving

Discussing a schedule

SPEAKING

7 There are two stages to this pairwork activity. First of all, students need to turn to their files on pages 126 and 131 and read the correspondence. Using the information, they make changes to the schedule on page 29. Before students proceed to the speaking stage, check that they have made the necessary changes to the schedule. To help ensure this, students could work in an A group and a B group.

Possible changes (in bold):

Student A:

9.15–9.30 Registration and coffee (**Should we put everything back by fifteen minutes?**)

9.30–11.00 Introductions and workshop: 'You **might want it but does your customer?'**

Speaker: R Thorne

3.30–5.00 Talk: 'A good idea does not necessarily make money'

Speaker: Fiona Brewster.

Student B:

11.30–1.00 Talk: 'A good idea does not necessarily make money'

Speaker: Fiona Brewster. (She can't do 9.30? What do we replace her with at 9.30?)

Workshop and mini-presentations by each participant. (**When do we do this?**)

1.15–2.00 Lunch (**Can we shorten lunch or put events back by fifteen minutes?**)

2.00–3.00 Workshop: Online businesses – the myth and the truth.

Speaker: Laszlo Reiner (**He wants to speak for two hours!***)*

Finally, working in pairs students report on the changes to their schedules and try to prepare a finalised schedule. At the end, each pair presents their version and gives reasons. Note that there is not one correct version.

Possible final version
Everything has been moved back by fifteen minutes because of security and the people organising lunch. R Thorne is the only speaker who wants to talk straightaway and F Brewster speaks mid-morning as requested. Because L Reiner wants two hours, this has been changed and the day will end on time with mini-presentations by each participant.

New in Business: A Seminar for Young Entrepreneurs

Monday 15th February

9.15–9.45 Registration and coffee

9.45–11.15 Introductions and workshop: 'You might want it but does your customer?'

Speaker: R Thorne

11.45–1.15 Talk: 'A good idea does not necessarily make money'

Speaker: Fiona Brewster

1.15–2.15 Lunch

2.15–4.15 Workshop: Online businesses – the myth and the truth.

Speaker: Laszlo Reiner

4.30–5.00 Mini-presentations by each participant.

Throughout this exercise, monitor for good use of different future forms and afterwards correct any errors or suggest alternative future forms.

MODULE 3.2   LEAVING AND TAKING MESSAGES

BUSINESS SKILLS

3.2 Leaving and taking messages

LISTENING

Leaving messages

1   3.4 **Listen to five voicemails for Vanessa at Business Circle Conferencing. Decide what the speaker's purpose is in each call.**

1 _____	A to ask for permission
2 _____	B to complain about a mistake
	C to confirm something is OK
3 _____	D to request information
	E to offer information
4 _____	F to cancel arrangements
	G to request help
5 _____	H to change a booking

2   3.4 **Look at stages 1–7 for leaving messages. Listen to each of the messages again and tick the stages each caller follows.**

	Call 1	Call 2	Call 3	Call 4	Call 5
1 Say who the message is for					
2 Say who you are					
3 Give the reason for calling					
4 Spell any difficult words					
5 Request a return call					
6 Leave your contact details					
7 Say when you will be available					

3 **Match the following expressions to stages 1–7 in exercise 2. Write the number of the correct stage next to each expression.**

0	Hello, this is a message for ...	1
A	It's ...	___
B	You can email me at r dot ...	___
C	The reason I'm calling is that ...	___
D	It's with regard to ...	___
E	This is ...	___
F	So that's M as in Madrid ...	___
G	You can get me any time between ...	___
H	Could you call me back?	___
I	It's P for Paris ...	___
J	Call me on 0207 ...	___
K	I'll be in the office tomorrow.	___
L	I'd be very grateful if you'd return my call ...	___

SPEAKING

Leaving a voicemail message

4 **Prepare to leave a message on a colleague's voicemail. Make notes below.**

Your contact details (telephone no / email)	
Who are you calling? What's the message about?	
What action do you want the person to take (eg call you back, meet you somewhere)?	

5 **Work in pairs. Take turns to leave your messages. Your partner notes down the key information on this form.**

Important message

message for: _____

_____ called.

Message:
_____
_____
_____

Action:
_____
_____
_____

Student's Book pages 30 and 31

Leaving messages

LISTENING Track 11 (CD1)

1   3.4 Draw students' attention to the fact that there are two extra unnecessary answers in A–H.

Answers

1 D   2 H   3 B   4 G   5 C

3.4 Listening script

Call 1 Hi, Vanessa. It's Ralph again. Sorry, I forgot to ask earlier if you can send me details of next month's seminars. I've got two people who really need some help with spreadsheets and accounting software. I remember you said that you had some computer courses planned. Anyway, send me details on those and anything else you have coming up. Thanks. Oh. You can email it to me if that's easier. It's R for Ralph. Dot. Hensher. At Henckel. That's H-E-N-C-K-E-L dot D-E. Thanks. Bye.

Call 2 Hello. My name is Maria Monblot. The reason I'm calling is that I have a booking for next week's business breakfast meeting. I'm afraid I won't be able to attend but I would like to come to next month's instead. I assume it is on the last Wednesday of the month as usual. Please confirm this. You've already got my number but just in case, it's 768 4556.

Call 3 Hello. This is Jochen Anderson. I am booked in to run the seminar on design on the 25th. I've just received the schedule for the day and it appears that I am speaking at nine thirty. That isn't what I agreed with you. We said I would be at eleven and that I would have ninety minutes not one hour. You've also described it as a talk but I'm giving a workshop. Please get back to me about this as soon as possible. I'll be in my office between two and five o'clock.

Call 4 Hi, Vanessa. It's Kirsten. Just to let you know that Jochen Anderson is trying to get hold of you. He left a message on my home number to say he isn't happy about the schedule for the 25th. I haven't got the details with me so I can't help really. I'm sorry, but can you call him back? He only needs the time changing and something about the title. I'm sure one of the other speakers won't mind changing. You know what he's like. See you tomorrow.

Call 5 Hello. This is Bryan in security. I'm returning your call about having the building open on Sunday. I'm just calling to say that's fine. I'll be here at midday anyway so it'll be OK for three o'clock. If there's anything else, you can call me any time on my mobile. It's 07786 678 8890.

2   3.4 Students listen again and tick the stages. Note that for the category 'Give the reason for calling', we would expect a caller to give a clear reason at the beginning of the call.

	Call 1	Call 2	Call 3	Call 4	Call 5
1 Say who the message is for	✓			✓	
2 Say who you are	✓	✓	✓	✓	✓
3 Give the reason for calling	✓	✓	✓	✓	✓
4 Spell any difficult words	✓				
5 Request a return call		✓	✓		
6 Leave your contact details	✓	✓			✓
7 Say when you will be available			✓		✓

3 Students match the expressions to the correct stage.

Answers
A 2 B 6 C 3 D 3 E 2 F 4 G 7 H 5 I 4
J 6 K 7 L 5

Extension
To draw attention to the sentence stress in some of these expressions, read the expressions aloud and ask students to underline the stressed words. Drill them.

Hello, this is a message for Gill.
You can email me at r dot naunton
The reason I'm calling is that...
It's with regard to...
So that's M as in Madrid.
You can get me any time between five and nine.
Could you call me back?
It's P for Paris.
I'll be in the office tomorrow.
I'd be very grateful if you'd return my call.

Leaving a voicemail message

SPEAKING

4 Students make up their own message. It can be similar to the kind of message they leave in their work or they can create any context they like.

5 Students work in pairs and leave their message. Afterwards, students can compare and check they have all the key information. Make sure that students use some of the expressions in exercise 3.

Student's Book reproduction

WRITING

Learning Tip

When we take notes of what people say, it's important to summarise it in a short message. Try to use fewer words and make it clear.

Taking notes and messages

1 Read what people say in 1–9 and write messages. Use words from the spoken message.

0 'Hello. This is Michael James speaking and this is a message for Lelia.'
  Michael James called for Lelia. (4 words)

1 'I'd be grateful if you could return this call on my home number.'
  Call him back _____ (4 words)

2 'I am calling to inform you that the next meeting is on the 23rd.'
  Please note _____ (8 words)

3 'Would you mind checking and letting me know the final dates?'
  Please confirm _____. (3 words)

4 'I just wanted to say that I'm sorry for any confusion.'
  He apologised _____ (3)

5 'The client is asking if it would be possible to put the meeting back.'
  He called about postponing _____ (2)

6 'If you have any further questions, don't hesitate to call me.'
  Feel free _____ him. (2)

7 'I was hoping we could bring the interviews forward. Is that possible for you?'
  Are you able to _____? (4)

8 'Can you let me know if you're available to join us later?'
  Let her know if you can _____. (3)

9 'I'm telephoning with regard to order number 01-X33. I'm not happy about it, I'm afraid.'
  She's complaining about _____. (3)

2 3.4 Listen to the five calls from exercise 1 on page 30 again. Take notes and write brief and clear messages.

| 1 | 2 | 3 |
| 4 | 5 | |

Now compare the messages with your partner's.

3 3.5 Vanessa receives a call from Jochen Anderson. Listen and take notes on any important:
• dates _____
• times _____
• numbers _____

Listen again. What phrases does Vanessa use for:
• checking and clarifying details? _____
• confirming action? _____
_____
• requesting further information? _____
_____

Check your answers in the listening script on page 136.

4 Work in pairs.
Student A: Look at File 3.3 on page 127.
Student B: You work for Business Circle Conferencing. Someone calls to speak to your colleague Kirsten but she has taken the day off today. Take a message using the form below.

To: _____
Caller: _____
Message: _____
_____
_____
_____
_____

5 Now make another similar call.
Student A: You work for Business Circle Conferencing. Someone calls to speak to your colleague Vanessa but she is in a meeting. Take a message using the form above.
Student B: Look at File 3.4 on page 132.

32

Student's Book pages 32 and 33

Taking notes and messages

WRITING Tracks 11, 12 (CD1)

1 Refer students to the Learning Tip. Being able to summarise and shorten what someone has said is a particularly useful skill in business, not only for phone messages but also for note-taking at meetings or presentations. This exercise provides controlled practice on how to do this.

Answers
1 on his home number
2 that the next meeting is on the 23rd
3 the final dates
4 for any confusion
5 the meeting
6 to call
7 bring the interviews forward
8 join us/them later
9 order number 01-X33

2 3.4 Students listen to the recordings again from exercise 1 on page 30. They may need to hear them twice. Ask students to take note of the key words the first time they listen, and finalise their messages on the second listening.

Possible answers
1 Please email Ralph details of next month's seminars at r.hensher@henckel.de.
2 Maria Monblot wants to attend next month's business breakfast meeting not this month's. Confirm this with her on 768 4556.
3 Please call Jochen Anderson about the schedule for the 25th between two and five o'clock. He wants to change the time and length of his workshop.
4 Please call Jochen Anderson on behalf of Vanessa about the schedule on the 25th.
5 Bryan in security confirmed the opening arrangements for Sunday. Call him on 07786 678 8890 if there's anything else.

3 3.5 Play the listening twice. The first time they listen, students need to focus on the content and use their note-taking skills. On the second listening, they need to focus on useful phrases for telephoning. Afterwards, students can check their own answers to both parts in the listening script on page 136.

Answers

1

Dates: The event is on the 25th.

Times: The schedule says Jochen is speaking at 9.30pm but he's supposed to speak at 11am. He'd actually prefer to speak at 2pm.

Numbers: His mobile is 0778 890 8895.

2

Checking and clarifying details: *Let me check. So that's … / I see. / Let me read that back to you.*
Confirming action: *I'll have to check … then call you back. / I'll call you back in an hour.*
Requesting further information: *Could you give me your … ?*

Extension

When students check their answers in the Listening script, ask them to underline any other useful phrases they could use in telephone calls, eg *Can I help you?* Also ask students to suggest other phrases they could use in addition to Vanessa's:

Checking and clarifying details: *Was that A as in Amsterdam? / Can I just check I've got that?*
Confirming action: *I can confirm that … / I just want to confirm …*
Requesting further information: *I'd like to know … / Can I have … / Would you mind telling me … ?*

3.5 Listening script

V = Vanessa   J = Jochen

V Hello, Business Circle Conferencing.

J Hello. Can I speak to Kirsten, please?

V I'm sorry, she's not here today. My name's Vanessa. Can I help you?

J This is Jochen Anderson.

V Oh, hello, Mr Anderson. Kirsten said you phoned and I tried calling you at your office.

J Well, I'm on my mobile. Anyway, it's about the schedule for the training event. It isn't what was agreed.

V Sorry, let me check. So that's the event on the 25th.

J That's right. And it says I'm speaking at nine thirty.

V And you're supposed to be speaking at eleven. Yes, well I'm sure we can change it.

J Yes, but actually I think the afternoon would be better. After lunch. Can I speak at two pm? Then I can arrive in the morning.

V I see. So that's two in the afternoon. I'll have to check with another presenter and then call you back. Could you give me your mobile number?

J Certainly. It's 0778 890 8895.

V Let me read that back to you. 0778 890 8895.

J That's right.

V I'll call you back in about an hour.

J Good. Thank you.

4/5 Students roleplay two telephone conversations. One student uses notes in the information files on pages 127 and 132 and the other takes the message. The students taking the message will need to make use of the expressions in exercise 3 and the note-taking techniques in exercise 1.

Possible answers

To: Kirsten

Caller: Andrzej Welanetz

Message: Please email details of the next telephone skills course to [email address]. He's sending five people so also include details of discounts on group bookings.

To: Vanessa

Caller: Sergiusz Parteka

Message: He's sorry but he's postponing his booking for the seminar on the 13th. Please send dates for the next seminar and explain if the course fee can be refunded.

Extension

If your students also need to write emails, you could tell them to use the notes in their information files in File 3.3 and File 3.4 to write emails instead of telephoning.

Photocopiable activity 3.2

See page 161.

3.3   Listening: Short messages

In this section you will practise listening to short recorded messages and completing some information.

In each case you are listening for short answers. The texts could be forms, notes, invoices or message pads. You will hear each conversation or message twice. You need to listen in particular for information like names, numbers, dates, instructions or deadlines.

I   Study the gaps (1–12) in the forms and notes for the three conversations below. Try to predict what kind of information is missing. Is it ...

- a name?
- a number?
- a job title?
- spelling?
- equipment?
- times, dates?
- business terms?
- other?

Listening Success

- Before beginning the listening tasks on this page, study the form or notes you have to complete.
- Use the information in the notes to try and predict what you are listening for.
- Don't panic if you don't understand everything the first time. You can hear it twice!

2   3.6, 3.7, 3.8   Now listen to the recording and answer the questions. After you have listened once, play the recording again.

Conversation One
- Look at the form below.
- You will hear a message about a magazine subscription on a telephone answering machine.

Subscriptions form   *Business MONTHLY*

NAME: Ms Cynthia (1) ....
COMPANY: (2) .... solutions.
ADDRESS: On record
SUBSCRIPTION NO: (3) ....
REQUEST: Send (4) .... edition of the magazine.

Conversation Two
- Look at the notes below.
- You will hear a man calling about changes to a project.

AVH Video PRODUCTIONS

Notes

Tom Yishan called about the (5) .... we're making on the 11th.
They want to delay the filming in the (6) .... by ten days.
I've asked to put it back by (7) ....
Tom will (8) .... that with me when he has spoken to the manager.

Conversation Three
- Look at the notes below.
- You will hear a woman telephoning another department in her company about a job applicant.

MESSAGE
Message for: Michael
From: Rachel Robins, IT
RE: Job application of Rufus Nichols
Problems:
The applicant hasn't filled in all the sections of the (9) ....
She needs the (10) .... for his college tutor to get a reference.
Please confirm with Rachel when you have (11) .... the interview and she wants to know (12) .... the interview will last.

Student's Book pages 34 and 35

Ask students to read the introduction to this section.

Tracks 13, 14, 15 (CD1)

I   Students look at the gaps in the forms and notes and think about what they need to predict. Note that you cannot always predict everything, but the technique can make a big difference to a student's performance in this type of task.

Discuss students' answers as a class so everyone is clear about what is required. Here are some possible predictions:

Conversation One: a surname, a company name, a number, a month

Conversation Two: name of something being made, dates

Conversation Three: name of a form, contact details, length of time

2   3.6, 3.7, 3.8 Give students time to read the Listening Success tip first.

Answers
1 Perkins
2 Rave
3 IL0378JUL
4 (the) June
5 training video
6 printing factory
7 two weeks
8 confirm
9 application form
10 contact details
11 scheduled
12 how long

3.6 Listening script
N = Narrator   **M** = Man   **W** = Woman

Conversation One.

M   Thank you for calling Business Monthly. Please state your name, the name of your company or organisation and your address. If you already have a subscription with us please give your subscription number and the reason for your call.

W Hello. This is Cynthia Perkins – that's P-E-R-K-I-N-S. I'm the research manager at RAVE solutions. That's R-A-V-E solutions. You've got our address on record. I'm calling about our current subscription. The number is IL0378JUL. We paid for twelve issues but we've only received eleven. Please send the June edition of the magazine. Thank you very much.

3.7 Listening script

N = Narrator **T** = Tom **M** = Mari

N Conversation Two.

T Hello, this is Tom Yishan from Bright Star publishing. Could I speak to Mari Jones-Lumley, please?

M Speaking. Hello, Tom. How are you?

T Fine, thanks. Look, Mari, it's about this training video you're making for us.

M Oh no, what's happened?

T No, don't worry. Everything's fine. It's just that you know you wanted to film in the printing factory if you could. Well, I spoke to the manager and that's OK with them except that the dates we agreed aren't convenient for them. They want to know if you can put it back by ten days.

M I'd normally say yes, Tom, but we've already postponed this twice. I can't go on telling my team to cancel. Anyway, I think we have another project then.

T I'm really sorry, Mari, but it's out of my control.

M OK. Can you check with the printing manager if two weeks later would be OK and I'll have to check with my people.

T Two weeks? So that's the 25th?

M Right.

T No problem. I'll try and call him now and get back to you to confirm.

3.8 Listening script

N = Narrator **P** = Personnel Assistant
R = Rachel

N Conversation Three.

P Hello. Personnel.

R Hello, this is Rachel in IT. It's about the application of that new graduate which Michael sent over. Can I have a word with him?

P Sorry Rachel, he won't be in till tomorrow, but you can leave him a message.

R Thanks. I'm afraid I've got a problem with the application form. Rufus has done his diploma in IT at the local college but he hasn't filled in the section on references. I really need to speak to his tutor. Can Michael get hold of the contact details for him? His telephone number or email will do.

P OK. Is that all then?

R Err, I also need to know when Michael has scheduled him for interview. I think it might be tomorrow but I'm not sure. If it is tomorrow, has somebody confirmed that with Rufus because when I spoke to him briefly yesterday he didn't seem to know anything about it.

P Oh dear. Well, I'll give Michael your message and let you know.

R Well, I'll be in a meeting for the rest of the day so leave me a message about tomorrow, and someone had better ring Rufus and tell him he has an interview. And let me know how long he thinks it will take. I'm pretty busy.

P Right. Will do.

Overview

4.1   Business topic: Advertising

VOCABULARY   **Types of advertising**

LISTENING   **Advertising on the webs**

SPEAKING   **A short presentation**

READING   **Advertising standards**

GRAMMAR   **Modals**

4.2   Business skills: Delegating

READING   **How to delegate**

LISTENING   **A bad delegator**

PRONUNCIATION   **Sentence stress**

SPEAKING   **Delegating**

WRITING   **Reports**

4.3   Learning strategies: Vocabulary and collocation

Multiple-choice gap fill

Useful language from Module 4

Wordlist

banners	internet advertising	newspaper adverts	search engine
brochures	link	objectives	spam
expectations	mailshots	promotion	TV commercials
incentives	marketing	sample	word of mouth

Expressions

Also remember that …

Before we finish don't forget …

Can I borrow your expertise in something?

Can you give this priority because they need it as soon as possible?

Feel free to call me if you have any questions.

I'd like you to be in charge of all of it.

I'll need a report on this with your findings and your recommendations.

It's a good idea to …

I've asked you because …

I've got a job here that will really interest you …

Let me know how it's going once a week, please.

My third tip is (never) to …

One thing you might want to think about is …

So, let's go through this one more time to check it's clear.

The deadline for this is next Thursday.

The first thing is to …

What are you going to do?

What might be better is to …

You can do this by …

You've done a great job on this!

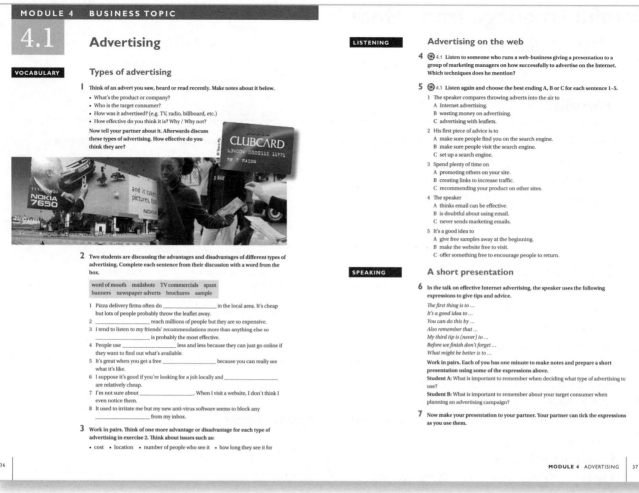

Student's Book pages 36 and 37

Types of advertising

VOCABULARY

1 Ask students to bring in a printed advert from a magazine, newspaper or off the Internet. They can use it as the basis for making notes in this first exercise. Students then discuss the billboard, person distributing leaflets, and loyalty card.

2 Before students begin, check that everyone in the class knows what the types of advertising are.

   Answers
   1 mailshots
   2 TV commercials
   3 word of mouth
   4 brochures
   5 sample
   6 newspaper adverts
   7 banners
   8 spam

3 Tell students to organise their answers in the form of a table. At the end, write their ideas on the board.

Possible answers

Types of advertising	Advantages	Disadvantages
mailshots	quick to deliver	not seen for long
TV commercials	memorable and can be fun	people remember the advert but not the product
word of mouth	you trust this form most	people can also spread bad news
brochures	give you more time to study information	expensive to produce and send out to your target market
sample	people can test before buying	expensive
newspaper adverts	read by many	read quickly or ignored
banners	you can target a market by choice of website	they disappear quickly
spam	very cheap to produce and deliver	people delete them before reading

Advertising on the web

LISTENING Track 16 (CD1)

4 🔘 4.1 Discuss with students where they find out about products and services on the Internet. Ask them where they see advertisements online, eg search engine pages, banners or pop-ups.

Answers

He mentions the following techniques:
- use search engines to put your name at the top of the listings
- get links on other sites
- through a site review
- get free advertising
- have a memorable domain name
- email campaigns (spam)
- send out a monthly newsletter
- have competitions or give something for free

4.1 Listening script

Speaker Imagine you have a new product or a new service and you want the world to know about it. One way would be to write the advertisement onto ten or a hundred or a thousand pieces of paper and drop them from the sky over your town or city. Someone on the ground might pick one up and read it. Maybe two or three people. On the other hand the wind might blow them away.

Now imagine doing the same thing but this time throwing them into the air with adverts for every other product or service in the world. You probably wouldn't do it, would you? Well, unfortunately, that's what it's like to advertise on the Internet.

Trying to make your product, service or website known to the rest of the Internet community can be very, very frustrating. Not only making it known, but getting visitors to actually visit the site can seem impossible. But there are ways to overcome the impossible when advertising on the Internet, as long as you follow three rules.

So, rule number one. The first thing is to remember that people use search engines. So whenever someone types in a keyword linked to your business, your site needs to appear in the top 50 or so listings in all of the major search engines. Any lower and no one will ever find you.

My second rule is that it's a good idea to spend some useful time and effort on getting your links on other sites. This is an excellent, though very time-consuming way to increase visitors. You can do this by sharing links with other companies, so they have a link on your site and you put one on theirs. Or perhaps through a site review which recommends your products. Also remember that the more links you have elsewhere, the more likely people are to find you through a search engine.

My third tip is never to pay for advertising on the web. I think that unless you have a very good reason, it's a waste of money. With so many ways to get free advertising, I've found very little reason to pay for things like banners to promote my site.

So those are my three starting points for anyone thinking of web advertising. Before we finish don't forget that a memorable domain name that people can easily type will help. Email campaigns can work and are an easy way to get traffic to the site, though it doesn't last long. What might be better is to have a monthly newsletter, which people sign up for. I've found this to be very effective and more positive than sending spam. Then there are contests with prizes or anything free – maybe some software or cool graphics.

Once you've got people visiting the site, keep statistics on how many people visit per day and how often people return to the site. In other words, find out who they are. How old they are. Where they come from. What they like doing in their free time. You can get this kind of information by asking them to subscribe to your newsletter for example ...

5 🔘 4.1 Give students time to study the questions first and guess any of the answers based on their first listening in exercise 4.

Answers

1 A   2 A   3 B   4 A   5 C

A short presentation

SPEAKING

6 Students need to prepare their talks so they will need about three good points.

Possible points
Student A:
When deciding what type of advertising to use:
- How much will it cost?
- Will it reach your target market?
- Is it short-term or long-term promotion?

Student B:
What is important to know about your target consumer?
- Age and gender
- Typical income
- What do they read/watch in order to select an appropriate type of advertising?

7 When students make their presentation, encourage them to use the seven expressions for giving tips in exercise 6. The partner who is listening should tick an expression every time it is used and can give a score out of seven at the end.

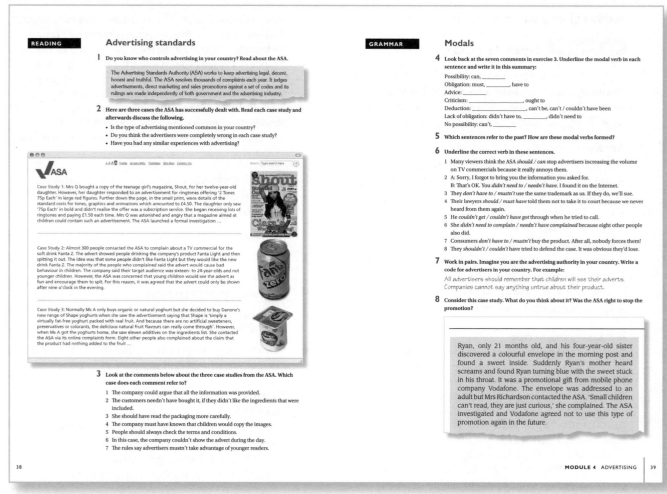

Advertising standards

READING

I Ask students if they know who controls advertising in their country. Extend this discussion if you have time and ask:
- *Do you think it's important to control adverts?*
- *Are there any adverts which you think should be stopped?*

Students then read about the ASA, a non-governmental UK organisation which tries to control advertising. Students could find out more about it at its website: www.asa.org.uk. If they don't know whether their country has a similar authority, they could research this online for the next lesson.

2 Students read each case. Discuss the three questions as a class so that you can check their understanding.

Alternative
Put students into groups of three. Each student reads one of the case studies. Students then close their books and summarise what happened in their case study to the other two students.

3 Students can work in pairs to complete this task.

Answers
1 Case study 1
2 Case study 3
3 Case study 3
4 Case study 2
5 Case study 1
6 Case study 2
7 Case study 1

Modals

GRAMMAR

4 Students begin by underlining the modal verbs in exercise 3. At this level, this exercise should be a review of modal verbs, but for some students the form of modals referring to the past may cause some difficulties.

Answers

1 could
2 needn't
3 should
4 must
5 should
6 couldn't
7 mustn't

Students then categorise these in the summary:

Answers

Possibility: *could*
Obligation: *mustn't*
Advice: *should*
Criticism: *should*
Deduction: *must (have)*
Lack of obligation: *needn't (have)**
No possibility: *couldn't*

*Note that with verbs for lack of obligation, *didn't need to* means the action didn't happen and wasn't necessary, whereas *needn't have* means it wasn't necessary but the action happened.

Extension

Students could check their answers by looking at the grammar reference on pages 128–9.

5 Discuss the questions as a class.

Answers

The modal verbs in sentences 2–4 in exercise 3 refer to the past. They are formed like this: modal verb + *have* + past participle

6 Students check their understanding and use of modals with this exercise.

Answers

1 should
2 didn't need to
3 mustn't
4 must have
5 couldn't get
6 needn't have complained
7 don't have to
8 shouldn't

7 Students work in pairs (or groups of three) to create an advertising code. You can limit the number of rules they make (eg seven) if time is short. To ensure students use modal verbs, you can also say that each rule must include at least one. Note that in this exercise the modals will refer to the present. At the end, students can compare their codes of conduct. Monitor and give on-the-spot correction or explanation for sentences with mistakes using a modal verb.

8 Students can discuss this case in small groups. It should generate use of modals referring to the past, eg *His mother should have checked the post.* Give about five minutes for the discussion. You could ask the groups to formulate three concluding sentences about the case using a modal referring to the past.

Photocopiable activity 4.1

See page 162.

BUSINESS SKILLS

4.2 Delegating

READING

1 Make a list of ten tasks you have to do this week.

attend a meeting, do English homework, clean the house …

Think about which of these tasks can be done by someone else. Who could you delegate it to? Tell your partner.

2 Read tips 1–7 below on how to delegate. Write in the missing headings A–G.

A Tailor work to the individual
B Be positive
C Give incentives
D Define the expectations and objectives
E Delegate complete tasks
F Let go
G Avoid misunderstanding

How to delegate

New managers often find it difficult to delegate the tasks they used to do. But getting others to do what you did so well is a key to good management.

1 _____ It should be challenging and make use of their specific skills – skills that you may not have.

2 _____ This is much more satisfying for the person delegated to than bits and pieces. If people feel they have ownership of a whole manageable project, they will usually rise to the challenge.

3 _____ Don't start by saying 'I know you're really busy and don't have time for this, but …' Explain why the job is important and why you have chosen them. Also explain what the rewards are – possibly financial or psychological.

4 _____ Specify what results are needed, the deadline, and how often the employee should update you.

5 _____ After you have briefed the person, ask them to explain back to you what they're going to do to ensure the instructions are clear.

6 _____ Don't check up on them. Make yourself available to answer questions but allow them space to work on their own.

7 _____ Give lots of praise, helpful feedback and constructive criticism. It boosts confidence and saves time next time.

LISTENING

A bad delegator

3 🔘 4.2 Listen to a manager talking to a member of his department. Which of tips 1–7 for delegating doesn't he follow?

4 Here are some expressions you can use to delegate. Which expressions would help with tips 1–7? Write the number of the tip next to the expression.

0 Can I borrow your expertise in something?	1
A I've asked you because … _____	___
B Let me know how it's going once a week, please.	___
C I'll need a report on this with your findings and your recommendations.	___
D So, let's go through this one more time to check it's clear.	___
E One thing you might want to think about is …	___
F You've done a great job on this!	___
G I've got a job here that will really interest you …	___
H I'd like you to be in charge of all of it.	___
I What are you going to do?	___
J Feel free to call me if you have any questions.	___
K Can you give this priority because they need it as soon as possible?	___
L The deadline for this is next Thursday.	___

PRONUNCIATION

5 🔘 4.3 We can add emphasis to these expressions by stressing one word in particular. Listen to the thirteen expressions in exercise 4 and underline the stressed word.

SPEAKING

Delegating

6 Work in pairs. Take turns to delegate the following jobs to each other. Remember to follow all the advice in exercise 2 and use some of the expressions.

- Buy some coffee from the shop across the street.
- Organise all the filing in your offices.
- Attend a trade fair for you this weekend.
- Tell another member of staff not to send personal emails in company time.
- Prepare a report on the effectiveness of the company's website.

Did you convince your partner to do everything?

Student's Book pages 40 and 41

How to delegate

READING

1 Students make a quick list of what they have to do this week (the list doesn't have to be about work). They then write the name of a person next to each task. This should also clarify the meaning of 'to delegate'.

Extension

Students work in pairs and roleplay a situation in which they try to give as many of the jobs on their list to their partner to do as possible. They should try to convince each other. Note that one strategy is to trade jobs on each other's list. Another alternative is for the students to stand and walk around the class delegating their jobs to different students in the class. At the end find out which student managed to delegate away the most jobs.

2 Encourage students to read the whole leaflet first before completing the information leaflet with the correct headings.

Answers

1 A   2 E   3 C   4 D   5 G   6 F   7 B

A bad delegator

LISTENING **Tracks 17, 18 (CD1)**

3 🔘 4.2 Students listen to a bad example of delegating, and tick the tips from exercise 2 that the manager doesn't follow.

Answers

The manager clearly doesn't follow:

1 The manager says, 'I don't want to give you anything too difficult.' so it isn't challenging.

3 He starts by saying, 'I know you're really busy but …'

5 He doesn't ask the employee to explain the instructions back to him.

6 He won't be available to answer questions.

7 He doesn't give any praise for the work the employee did on the schedules last time.

4.2 Listening script

Manager Hi, Harry. Sorry to bother you but I'm soooo busy. Could you help me? I know you're busy too but I have a meeting with the managing director tomorrow and I don't have time to do the schedules for next week. I know you did them last time I was off sick so I thought you could do them again. I don't want to give you anything too difficult, do I? So if I give you this … Sorry, I haven't had time to sort through it but you'll work it out. OK, great.

Sorry, must go. If you have any questions … err, ask Mary. I think she did the schedules last time I was on holiday so she can help too. Fine. Bye!

4 Students match the expressions to the tips in the leaflet.

Answers
A 3   B 4   C 4   D 5   E 7   F 7
G 3   H 2   I 5   J 6   K 4   L 4

Extension
Students could rewrite the listening script on page 137 so that the manager follows all the tips in exercise 2 and uses some of the expressions from exercise 4.

PRONUNCIATION

5 4.3 Ask students to predict the stressed words. They then listen and underline the stressed words.

Answers

4.3 Listening script
Can I borrow your <u>expertise</u> in something?
I've asked <u>you</u> because …
Let me know how it's going <u>once</u> a week, please.
I'll need a report on this with your findings <u>and</u> your recommendations.
So, let's go through this <u>one</u> more time to check it's clear.
One thing you <u>might</u> want to think about is …
You've done a <u>great</u> job on this!
I've got a job here that will <u>really</u> interest you …
I'd like you to be in charge of <u>all</u> of it.
What are you going to <u>do</u>?
Feel free to call me if you have <u>any</u> questions.
Can you give this priority because they need it as <u>soon</u> as possible?
The deadline for this is <u>next</u> Thursday.

Extension
4.3 Play the sentences again and students listen and repeat. Make sure they stress the underlined words.

Delegating

SPEAKING

6 Students take turns to roleplay each of the situations. During feedback give positive comments for students using expressions from exercise 4 and with the correct stressed words. You could ask any pairs doing this to present a dialogue to the rest of the class.

Photocopiable activity 4.2
See page 163.

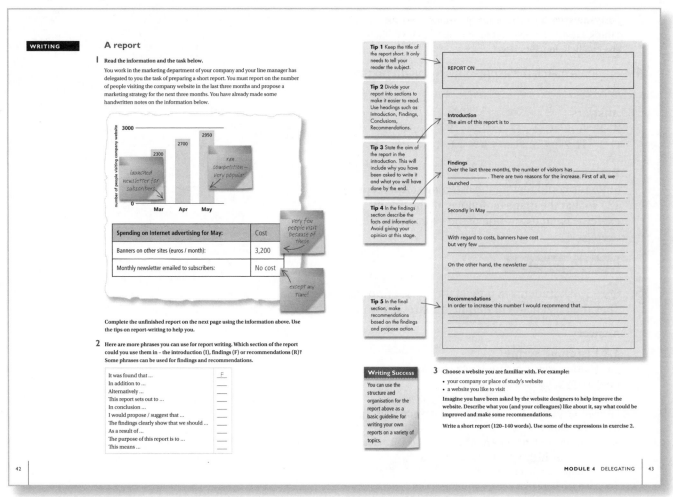

Student's Book pages 42 and 43

A report

WRITING

1 Set aside plenty of classroom time for this section so that students are clear by the end how to plan, structure and write a report.

Students need to underline key information and note the handwritten notes which will need to be included. The theme of the report refers back to the comments made by the speaker earlier in this module on what makes effective internet advertising. You could lead in by asking students to summarise what he said.

The students' task is to evaluate what makes customers visit the company website. Before students move on to writing the report, make sure everyone in the class realises that the most effective techniques seem to be a newsletter for subscribers and a competition. Using banners doesn't seem to attract many customers.

Possible answer

> **Report on visits to website and proposed marketing strategy**
>
> <u>Introduction</u>
> The aim of this report is to comment on the number of people visiting the company website in the last three months and propose a marketing strategy for the next three months.
>
> <u>Findings</u>
> Over the last three months, the number of visitors has increased by 650. There are two reasons for the increase. First of all, we launched a newsletter for subscribers. Secondly in May, we ran a competition which was very popular.
>
> With regard to costs, banners have cost 3,200 euros a month but very few people seem to visit the website as a result of these.
>
> On the other hand, the newsletter doesn't cost anything (other than my time) but has helped to increase the number of visitors.
>
> <u>Recommendations</u>
> In order to increase the number of visitors, I would recommend that we continue with the newsletter and run more competitions and quizzes. I also propose that we stop using banners and put more resources into setting up links with other sites to increase the traffic.

2 Ask students to categorise the useful phrases for report writing.

Answers

Introduction   This report sets out to ...   The purpose of this report is to ...
Findings   In addition to ...   Alternatively   As a result of   This means ...
Recommendations   In conclusion   I would propose/suggest that ...   The findings clearly show that we should ...

3 Students will need to look at websites so you could set this for homework. Or, if you have access to computers in the classroom, students could work in pairs to evaluate some websites. Refer students to the Writing Success tip on writing short reports.

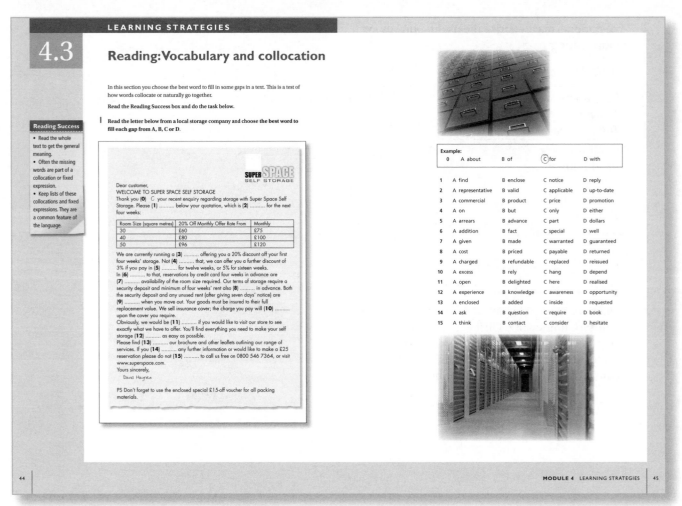

Student's Book pages 44 and 45

I Refer students to the Reading Success tip offering guidance on how to approach the task. Then ask them the following questions about the text to make sure they understand the context:
1 What kind of letter is it? (A marketing letter)
2 What type of customer might be interested? (Someone who needs storage – perhaps they are moving house.)

Answers
1 A   2 B   3 D   4 C   5 B   6 A   7 D   8 C
9 B   10 D   11 B   12 A   13 A   14 C   15 D

Extension
As a follow-up, ask students to underline any fixed expressions in the letter. This will highlight how much help these can be when completing this type of question.

Possible answers
Thank you for your recent enquiry
Please find below …
Not only that ….
In addition to that ….
payable in advance
we would be delighted if …
Please find enclosed …
do not hesitate to call us …

Overview

5.1 Business topic: The workplace

READING	**Art at work**
LISTENING	**An interview with an art consultant**
GRAMMAR	**Reporting**
LISTENING	**Some opinions on art**
SPEAKING	**A meeting about artwork**

5.2 Business skills: Participating in a meeting

READING	**Meetings are great**
VOCABULARY	**Verb collocations**
SPEAKING	**Expressions for meetings**
LISTENING	**Report on a meeting**
WRITING	**Minutes of a meeting**

5.3 Learning strategies: Short presentations

Preparing your talk

Giving your talk

Asking a follow-up question

PHOTOCOPIABLE

© 2009 Heinle, Cengage Learning

Useful language from Module 5

Wordlist

attend a meeting	hold a meeting	reach an agreement	set the agenda
commission	installation	run a meeting	take the minutes
give a presentation	move on (to the	see your point	
go along (with you)	next point)		

Expressions

Can I just come in here?

Do we all agree?

Have we reached an agreement on this?

How do you feel about that idea?

I agree.

I disagree.

I see your point, but ...

I suggest we move on to the next item on the agenda.

I think ...

I'd go along with you there.

I'd like to know more about ...

I'd like to suggest that we should ...

I'm sorry, but I just can't agree with you there.

It seems to me that ...

Let's move on.

Sorry, but I don't quite follow you.

Sorry, but ...

Sorry, I don't understand

What do you think ?

Why don't we ... ?

Would you mind telling us a little more about ... ?

Yes, but ...

MODULE 5 BUSINESS TOPIC

5.1 The workplace

READING

Art at work

1 Do you have paintings and art where you work or study? Do you like it? Does it help you?

2 Read about a company that deals with art in the workplace. Complete the information with answers A, B, C or D.

International Art Consultants

(1) _____ in 1979, International Art Consultants has been sourcing and commissioning art (2) _____ for over 25 years. We work (3) _____ clients in the corporate, hotel, healthcare and urban regeneration (4) _____ . Our clients (5) _____ from multinational companies with £1 million art budgets to organisations renting art for just £10 a week. A (6) _____ of fourteen, we are small enough to care and large enough to cope. We offer a (7) _____ combination of commercial experience, specialist art knowledge and high quality service and support. Whatever the size of the project our (8) _____ is for all our clients to be 100% satisfied with the end result. Over 75% of our work comes from (9) _____ business or referrals. We work alongside professional artists who create art of the highest artistic and technical quality, and (10) _____ our staff have different areas of specialist art knowledge and expertise. We hope that you will (11) _____ an appointment to visit us, look round the galleries, use the visual reference databases, and discuss your particular art (12) _____ with us.

1	A Founded	B Set	C Since	D Last
2	A international	B worldwide	C all	D around
3	A as	B in	C under	D with
4	A divisions	B industries	C sectors	D sections
5	A range	B report	C buy	D supply
6	A department	B building	C unit	D team
7	A original	B mix	C brand	D unique
8	A scope	B aim	C outcome	D line
9	A new	B rental	C reply	D repeat
10	A few	B all	C more	D any
11	A make	B do	C have	D attend
12	A insure	B objectives	C requirements	D paintings

LISTENING

An interview with an art consultant

3 There are five main stages for an art consultant in charge of supplying artworks. The following stages are in the wrong order. Work in pairs and number the stages 1 to 5.
- Draw up selection of possible artworks. _____
- Installation. _____
- Select or commission artworks. _____
- Art consultant makes initial visit. _____
- Present possible choices to client. _____

4 5.1 Listen to the first part of an interview with an art consultant and check your answers in exercise 3.

5 5.2 Listen to the second part of the interview. Does the consultant normally recommend traditional or modern artworks for companies? Why?

6 5.1, 5.2 Listen again to both parts of the interview. Choose the best answer (A, B or C) for questions 1–6.

1 If you are interested in having art in your workplace, the best thing to do is to
   A ask an art consultant to visit the premises.
   B look at where you want to put the paintings and decide how many you need for the size of the building.
   C decide what type of art you like.

2 The art is usually chosen
   A by the specialist.
   B by the client.
   C with both sides in agreement.

3 With a specially commissioned work of art, it's best that you let
   A the consultant tell the artist what you want.
   B the artist know what you want.
   C the artist make most of the decisions.

4 The consultant believes that choosing art for the workplace is about
   A everyone agreeing on what they like.
   B having something nice to look at.
   C letting people know what kind of company you are.

5 Why do most companies choose contemporary or modern art?
   A Because people don't like traditional art.
   B Because people don't know if it's good or bad.
   C Because it sends out a certain message about the company.

6 What does the interviewer think is a good idea?
   A To rent the art.
   B To buy the art.
   C To regularly change the art.

Student's Book pages 46 and 47

Art at work

READING

1 Discuss the questions as a class. Get students to describe some of the paintings and decoration where they work or study. Find out if they think it motivates or helps them work. Discuss what students think the purpose of art is in the workplace.

2 Students complete the text with the words in 1–12.

Answers
1 A 2 B 3 D 4 C 5 A 6 D 7 D
8 B 9 D 10 B 11 A 12 C

An interview with an art consultant

LISTENING Tracks 19, 20 (CD1)

3 Students discuss the order in which they think artworks would be supplied. Don't check answers at this stage as this will be done in exercise 4.

4 5.1 Students listen and check their answers in exercise 3.

Answers
Draw up selection of possible artworks 3
Installation 5
Select or commission artworks 4
Art consultant makes initial visit 1
Present possible choices to client 2

5.1 Listening script
I = Interviewer   **AC** = Art consultant

I I'd like to begin by asking you to imagine that I've been asked to find some art for my company's offices. Where would I start?

AC Well, the first stage in selecting art is normally for one of our art consultants to visit you on site to assess the location, the size of the area and the style of the building and so on.

I How much difference does it make where I actually put the paintings?

AC A great deal. Art needs to be placed taking into account the function of a space. Different types of art are appropriate for different areas. Once we have an idea about what kind of work it is you do and how the space is used we then begin to find artworks and present a selection of art for your business and building. We can do this on-site or you can visit our galleries. The whole thing is a two-way collaborative process.

I So you already have the painting?

AC Yes, or we can ask an artist to create works for your specific space. In this case, the client has some input but it's important to remember when choosing workplace art that art is not your brand. If you ask the artist to emphasise your company image in some way, you'll just end up with bad art. Either way, you have an art consultant who oversees and project manages the production of any commissioned artwork and makes sure it's completed and installed on time and within budget. And that also includes fitting appropriate lighting and any other maintenance and fitting.

5 5.2 Students listen for the general meaning. Elicit predictions before they listen.

Answer
Overall, the speaker seems to be suggesting that modern artworks are a better choice to show you are a modern company and 'planning for the future'. Traditional artworks say that a company is old or lacks new ideas.

5.2 Listening script
I = Interviewer   AC = Art consultant

I One thing I don't understand is how a company ever decides what to choose. I mean, art is such a personal thing. How does anyone ever agree?
AC Well, that's true. I think it's important that you don't set up committees or anything. If you have a workforce of 300 and you ask everyone, you'll get 300 different answers. No, you need to keep it small. Just one or two people. But choosing art for your offices isn't necessarily about choosing what the individual likes. The real benefits for a business are that the artwork gives a positive image to clients.
I So what's a typical type of art?
AC It's so varied but in general I suggest something strong and bold. If it's just light colours that no one can really see, it's pointless. You need art which shows your clients you have good taste and that you are successful.
I I often go into buildings and look at modern art and think, 'What is that? It isn't of anything. No people. Nothing.' Why do so many companies choose it?
AC There are a number of reasons, other than the fact that the managing director might like it. You don't want art that will offend anyone. So a painting of a man and woman with no clothes on is a bad idea. Similarly, a landscape or a painting of the countryside is the sort of thing you have in your living room at home and doesn't look very corporate. Also the art needs to say what kind of company you are. Most companies want to give clients the message that says we're modern and we're planning for the future. A classical painting says we're old and traditional. A painting by a young modern painter gives a more positive image. And remember, it doesn't have to be a painting. A sculpture in the reception area can be very effective, for example.
I Finally, all this must be very expensive. How does a company justify thousands of pounds on this kind of thing?
AC It can be expensive but of course many people rent works from us – for as little as ten pounds a week. It also means that if you change your mind after a year or so, it's easy to change the piece.
I That sounds like a good idea …

6 5.1, 5.2 Students listen to both parts of the interview again and answer questions 1–6.

Answers
1 A   2 C   3 B   4 C   5 C   6 A

GRAMMAR

Reporting

1 A company is moving offices. A consultant is asking some employees for their comments on what they would like in their new offices. Their comments are then reported. Compare the verbs in the comments with the report and complete the grammar summary that follows.

> We prefer the paintings in our old offices.

> I've always disliked the colour of the walls.

> I'll need a larger desk.

Findings	• The receptionist said she would need a larger desk.
	• 23% said they preferred the paintings in their old offices.
	• The CEO said he'd always disliked the colour of the walls.

Direct speech	Reported speech
(1) _____ (present simple)	(2) _____ (past simple)
'We are moving ...' (present continuous)	She said they were moving ... (past continuous)
(3) _____ (present perfect)	(4) _____ (past perfect)
'I worked ...' (past simple)	He said he had worked ... (past perfect)
(5) _____ (can/will)	(6) _____ (could/would)

2 Rewrite these comments to report them.
1 I am not happy with the arrangements.
   She said (that) _____.
2 We're moving next week.
   He said _____ the following week.
3 We've planned everything.
   They said they _____.
4 I left the company in 2001.
   He said that he _____.
5 I'll call back at tomorrow.
   The caller said she _____ the next day.

3 We can report speech using the word *said*. However, there are other reporting verbs which tell us what a speaker thinks. Match the reporting verbs on the left to the comments on the right.
1 concluded   A 'But we can buy new computers with that.'
2 apologised* B 'Hi. I'm just phoning to say I'll be a few minutes late.'
3 called*   C 'I'm really sorry that I've missed the deadline.'
4 agreed   D 'Can I take a day off next week?'
5 argued   E 'You're absolutely right that management is spending too much time on paperwork.'
6 asked*   F 'So to sum up, the company can offer a two percent pay rise.'

In pairs, practise reporting the comments on the right with the verbs. For example:
He asked if he could take a day off next week.

*Note that we often use *for + -ing* after *apologised*; *to say* after *called*; and *if* after *asked*.

48

LISTENING

Some opinions on art

4 5.3 A company is choosing an artwork for its reception area. Listen to five employees commenting on the five artworks below. Decide which artwork each speaker is commenting on. Number the artwork.

5 5.3 Listen again. Match the views A–H with speakers 1–5.

Speaker 1 ___ ___ ___   A ... thought that the picture should be bolder.
                         B ... commented that it didn't look like anything he knew.
Speaker 2 ___   C ... explained what it was.
                         D ... asked what it was.
Speaker 3 ___   E ... apologised for not knowing anything about art.
                         F ... said it didn't look like art.
Speaker 4 ___ ___   G ... argued that the picture should be modern and contemporary.
Speaker 5 ___   H ... suggested where to put it.

SPEAKING

A meeting about artwork

6 Work in groups of three to complete the following task.
Your company wants to buy artworks for these parts of the building:
1 The reception area   2 The coffee area   3 The conference room
Hold three short meetings. In each meeting discuss and choose one of the artworks at the top of the page for one part of the building. A different member of the group should take notes for each meeting. At the end of the meeting, this person reports back to the group what was said and what was decided. Remember to use reporting verbs.

MODULE 5 THE WORKPLACE   49

Student's Book pages 48 and 49

Reporting

GRAMMAR

1 Students underline the verb forms in the three quotes, and then underline the reported quotes in the 'Findings'. This will help them complete the grammar summary. Ask students to notice how the verb form moves back a tense. This is a general rule and students can read more on reported speech in the grammar reference on page 129.

Answers
1 We prefer
2 they preferred
3 I've always disliked
4 he'd always disliked
5 I'll need
6 she would need

2 Student rewrite the comments in reported speech.

Answers
1 She said that she wasn't happy with the arrangements.*
2 He said they were moving the following week.
3 They said they'd planned everything.
4 He said that he'd left the company in 2001.
5 The caller said she would call back the next day.

*Note that if the fact of the sentence is still true we sometimes do NOT change the verb, eg in 1, if the woman still isn't happy at the time of speaking, the speaker could say: 'She said that she isn't happy with the arrangements.'

3 Students begin by match the reporting verbs to the comments.

Answers
1 F   2 C   3 B   4 E   5 A   6 D

Having done this, students make full reporting sentences with these verbs. These may vary a little.

Possible answers
1 He concluded that the company could offer a 2% pay rise.
2 She apologised for missing the deadline./ She apologised that she had missed the deadline.
3 He called to say he would be a few minutes late.
4 They agreed that management was spending too much time on paperwork.
5 He argued that they could buy new computers with that.
6 He asked if he could take a day off next/the following week.

Photocopiable activity 5.1
See page 164.

Some opinions on art

LISTENING Track 21 (CD1)

4 5.3 As a lead-in, ask students to briefly say what type of artwork they prefer out of the five shown. Students then listen and number the artworks.

Answers
Speaker 1 The picture on the bottom left.
Speaker 2 The picture on the bottom right.
Speaker 3 The first picture.
Speaker 4 The third picture.
Speaker 5 The second picture.

5.3 Listening script
Speaker 1 But what is it? Is that a head? Or is it an animal? I can't see how that is art. I mean, it doesn't look like anything real.
Speaker 2 I agree with you that this is nice. It reminds me of being in a café in somewhere like Paris but if you put it here no one will see it. It isn't bold enough for this area. No, we need something else.
Speaker 3 This is beautiful but perhaps it would look better in someone's office. It's the sort of painting to help you relax.
Speaker 4 Well, I'm not really the right person to ask. I never go to art galleries but this looks like what you see in cathedrals. It doesn't tell you what our company is about. When people come into reception, they'll think it's a Roman temple, not a hi-tech business. Let's have something up-to-date.
Speaker 5 This is quite good for reception because it shows a man thinking, which is quite a good image for our company. It says to the visitor that this is a company with ideas. That we're constantly considering the future …

5 5.3 The sentences in A–H all use reported speech to report what speakers said in the listening. Students match the views to the speakers.

Answers
1 B, D, F
2 A
3 H
4 E, G
5 C

A meeting about artwork

SPEAKING

6 Put students into groups of three. They hold three short meetings to choose an artwork for three different locations. In each meeting, make sure that one person is taking the notes on what was said and by whom. It may be helpful to set a time limit of three minutes for each meeting. Each person then summarises the notes they took and what was decided. They should use reporting verbs during this task.

Extension
As a writing activity and for consolidation of the grammar in this module, ask each student to write up the notes from the meeting using reported speech.

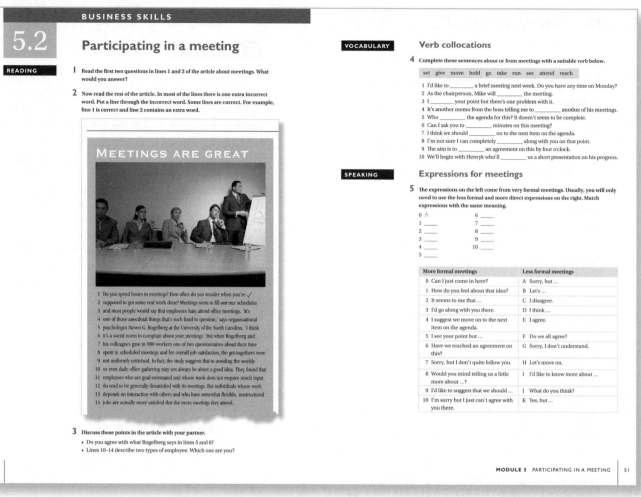

Student's Book pages 50 and 51

Meetings are great

READING

1 If your students are inexperienced or pre-work, go straight to exercise 2. Otherwise, discuss the first two questions and find out if your students think they spend hours in meetings and wonder when they are supposed to do some 'real' work.

Extension
Ask students to describe what they have meetings about, and what makes a meeting effective or what makes meetings go wrong.

2 Students correct the article.

Answers
3 attend
4 such
5 the
6 correct
7 in
8 for
9 to
10 about
11 correct
12 its
13 correct
14 that

3 Discuss these two points as a class. In lines 5 and 6, Rogelberg says it's the norm to complain about meetings so find out if students agree that this is true for where they work. In lines 10–14, the two types of employees described are those who are goal-orientated and those whose job depends on interaction with others. Students can comment on what type of employee they are and whether meetings are important for their job.

Alternative
With students who are pre-work, ask them each to say if they think they are a goal-orientated person who doesn't need much guidance or input, or someone who would prefer a job with social interaction and flexibility.

Verb collocations

VOCABULARY

4 Before completing 1–10, check that students understand these terms from formal meetings:
- *chairperson*: the person who is in charge of the meeting
- *minutes*: a written report of a meeting
- *agenda*: the list of point or 'items' to be discussed

Answers
1 hold
2 run
3 see (also *take your point* is possible but see 6)
4 attend
5 set
6 take
7 move
8 go
9 reach
10 give

Expressions for meetings

SPEAKING

5 As a lead-in to this exercise, ask in-work students to comment whether the meetings at their company tend to be formal or informal (or both). Students then match the expressions with the same meaning but different levels of formality.

Answers
1 J   2 D   3 E   4 H   5 K   6 F
7 G   8 I   9 B   10 C

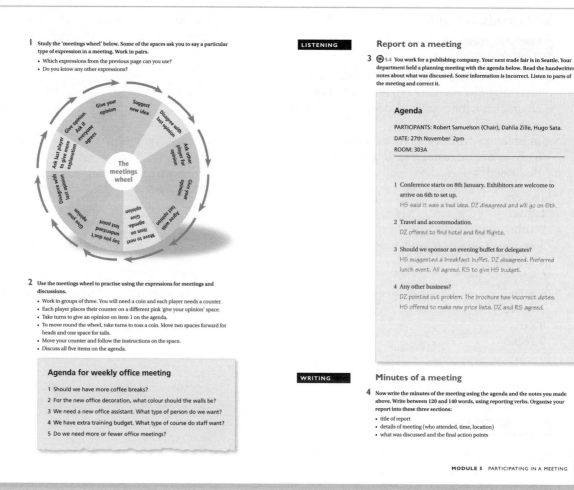

1 Study the 'meetings wheel' below. Some of the spaces ask you to say a particular type of expression in a meeting. Work in pairs.
- Which expressions from the previous page can you use?
- Do you know any other expressions?

2 Use the meetings wheel to practise using the expressions for meetings and discussions.
- Work in groups of three. You will need a coin and each player needs a counter.
- Each player places their counter on a different pink 'give your opinion' space.
- Take turns to give an opinion on item 1 on the agenda.
- To move round the wheel, take turns to toss a coin. Move two spaces forward for heads and one space for tails.
- Move your counter and follow the instructions on the space.
- Discuss all five items on the agenda.

Agenda for weekly office meeting

1 Should we have more coffee breaks?
2 For the new office decoration, what colour should the walls be?
3 We need a new office assistant. What type of person do we want?
4 We have extra training budget. What type of course do staff want?
5 Do we need more or fewer office meetings?

LISTENING

Report on a meeting

3 5.4 You work for a publishing company. Your next trade fair is in Seattle. Your department held a planning meeting with the agenda below. Read the handwritten notes about what was discussed. Some information is incorrect. Listen to parts of the meeting and correct it.

> **Agenda**
>
> PARTICIPANTS: Robert Samuelson (Chair), Dahlia Zille, Hugo Sata.
>
> DATE: 27th November 2pm
>
> ROOM: 303A
>
> 1 Conference starts on 8th January. Exhibitors are welcome to arrive on 6th to set up.
> HS said it was a bad idea. DZ disagreed and will go on 6th.
>
> 2 Travel and accommodation.
> DZ offered to find hotel and find flights.
>
> 3 Should we sponsor an evening buffet for delegates?
> HS suggested a breakfast buffet. DZ disagreed. Preferred lunch event. All agreed. RS to give HS budget.
>
> 4 Any other business?
> DZ pointed out problem. The brochure has incorrect dates. HS offered to make new price lists. DZ and RS agreed.

WRITING

Minutes of a meeting

4 Now write the minutes of the meeting using the agenda and the notes you made above. Write between 120 and 140 words, using reporting verbs. Organise your report into these three sections:
- title of report
- details of meeting (who attended, time, location)
- what was discussed and the final action points

52   **MODULE 5** PARTICIPATING IN A MEETING   53

Student's Book pages 52 and 53

---

1 This page provides students with speaking practice using the expressions from page 51. Working in pairs, students study the directions in the 'meetings wheel', eg if they see 'Give your opinion' they would choose the expressions *It seems to me that ... / I think ...* . Also ask students to think of more expressions they could use. When they think of new expressions, ask them to note how formal the expression is.

Possible expressions
Give your opinion:
It seems to me that ...
I think ...
In my opinion ...

Suggest new idea:
I'd like to suggest that we ... / Let's ... / Why don't we ... ?

Disagree with last opinion:
I'm sorry, but I just can't agree with you there. / I disagree. / No, because ...

Ask for opinion:
How do you feel about that idea? / What do you think? / How do you feel about that?

Agree with last opinion:
I'd go along with you there. / I agree. / Sure.

Move to next item on the agenda:
I suggest we move on to the next item ... / Let's move on ... / Moving on to point two ...

You don't understand the last point:
Sorry, but I don't quite follow you. / Sorry, I don't understand. / Can you explain what you mean exactly?

Ask for more explanation:
Would you mind telling us a little more about ... ? / I'd like to know more about ... / Tell us a little more about ...

Ask if everyone agrees:
Have we reached agreement on this? / Do we all agree? / Is that OK with everyone?

2 Put students into groups of three (or four if necessary) and ask them to read the instructions. Note that a 'counter' can be any small object belonging to a student (a key, a paper clip, etc.).

Students follow the agenda as they travel round the wheel. Monitor and give feedback on correct and incorrect use of expressions.

Photocopiable activity 5.2
See page 165.

Report on a meeting

LISTENING Track 22 (CD1)

3 5.4 The context for the meeting is a publishing company which plans to attend a conference and trade fair exhibition. Students need to study the agenda and the notes taken before listening to the meeting. Ask one student to say:
- how many people were at the meeting (three)
- what the purpose was (planning for a conference).

Students then listen and make changes to any incorrect information:

Answers
Point 1: DZ agreed (not disagreed) and will go on the 7th (not the 6th).
Point 2: DZ didn't offer but has already found a hotel.
Point 3: HS suggests a lunchtime reception (not breakfast buffet). DZ agrees.
Point 4: The brochure has incorrect prices (not dates). RS will make new price lists (not HS).

5.4 Listening script
RS = Robert Samuelson   **HS** = Hugo Sata
DZ = Dahlia Zille

RS OK. Point one is about the conference. It starts on the 8th but I think someone should go out early on the 6th. What do you think, Hugo?
HS Sorry, but I did that last year and sat around for a day. There was really nothing to do. I think if we go early it shouldn't be until the 7th. It really isn't worth it.
RS OK, that's fine. Do you agree, Dahlia?
DZ Sure. Do you want me to go?
RS Is that OK with you, Hugo?
HS Absolutely.
RS OK, point two. I'm assuming you're dealing with that, Dahlia.
DZ Yes, I've already found a good hotel near the fair and I'll book the flights.
RS Great. Now what about this idea to sponsor a reception for delegates? In the past, other publishers have sponsored drinks and buffets in the evening. I'd like some views on this. Hugo?
HS Well, they certainly attract people looking for a free dinner! I wonder if the evening's a good idea though.
RS Sorry, Hugo, I don't understand.
HS Well, maybe if we just offer drinks at the stand at lunchtime, we'll get more people actually looking at books and talking to us.
DZ That's a good idea, Hugo.
RS Yes, nice idea. Can you organise that, Hugo?
HS What's my budget?
RS Erm. Let me check with accounts after the meeting and I'll tell you.
DZ Sorry, Robert, but before we finish there's a problem with the prices in the brochures.
RS Really?
DZ Yes, the brochures have been updated with our list for next year but the prices are the same. We can get them reprinted but not in time for Seattle.
RS Oh no. You're joking!

DZ Sorry ...
RS Any ideas?
HS Let's just include the price list as separate from the brochure. We can say these are new for next year.
DZ But won't it show that prices have gone up? People will be able to compare next year's with this year's.
HS True. What do you think, Robert?
RS Well, we could include some offers on the new price list and show some prices haven't gone up.
DZ That might work.
HS I don't think we have a choice, Robert!
RS OK. I'll prepare that. Right, Hugo, Dahlia? Anything else?

Minutes of a meeting

WRITING

4 Students write up the minutes of the meeting using the agenda and corrected notes from exercise 3. Also refer them back to the language of reports presented on pages 42–43. If students write this in class, they could do a draft in pairs.

Possible answer

Minutes of the meeting to discuss plans for Seattle conference

Participants: Robert Samuelson (Chair), Dahlia Zille, Hugo Sata.
Date: 27th November

RS opened the meeting and suggested that someone should arrive two days early to set up. HS disagreed and suggested that one day was enough time. DZ agreed to arrive on the 7th.

DZ confirmed that she had already booked a hotel and would book the flights.

RS wanted to discuss the issue of sponsoring an event for delegates. HS suggested that a lunchtime event might attract more visitors to the exhibition stand. Everyone agreed and RS said he would give HS a budget.

DZ raised the issue of the incorrect price lists. It was agreed that RS would make new price lists and include some offers.

5.3 Speaking: Short presentations

In this section you will practise giving a 'mini-presentation' on a business theme.

1 Look at the topics on the next page and choose one of them. Which topic have you chosen? Tell your partner why. Once you've chosen your topic, you need to mention the points on the card and add some of your own ideas.

2 5.5 Now listen to Pierre. He chooses topic A. Which expressions does he use below?

Giving a mini-presentation	
Starting your presentation	
When … it's important to …	☐
The first thing when … is to …	☐
There are a number of points to consider when …	☐
Mentioning and sequencing the points	
First of all, there's …	☐
For example …	☐
Secondly / The second point to remember is …	☐
Something else is …	☐
The final point is …	☐
Adding information	
It's also important to say …	☐
In addition to that …	☐
You also need to consider …	☐

3 What is Erica's question at the end? Do you think it's a good question? How would you answer it?

4 Now work in pairs and take turns to give a presentation. Each of you chooses from the two other topics below (not topic A). Remember to prepare for it with notes and then present to your partner. At the end, your partner asks you a question.

Speaking Success
- Start your talk by saying what you're going to talk about.
- Separate each point clearly.
- Say why each point is relevant.
- Give an example to support each point.

A WHAT IS IMPORTANT WHEN …?
Placing a newspaper advert
- The target reader
- Where the advert appears
-

B WHAT IS IMPORTANT WHEN …?
Arranging in-house training
- Training needs of staff
- The trainer
-

C WHAT IS IMPORTANT WHEN …?
Selecting applicants for a job
- Personal qualities
- Previous experience
-

5 When you practise making presentations, evaluate your own or each other's performance with this checklist.

Did you …
- spend time preparing and making notes? ☐
- introduce the topic? ☐
- mention the two points? ☐
- add your own points? ☐
- answer the other student's question? ☐

Learning Tip
Record the presentation. Listen afterwards. Which of the useful expressions in exercise 3 did you use?

Student's Book pages 54 and 55

Tracks 23, 24 (CD1)

1 Students study the topics sheet and discuss which one they think would be the best to choose.

2 5.5 Students need time to read the expressions first before listening.

Answers
There are a number of points to consider when …
First of all, there's …
For example …
The second point to remember is …
You also need to consider …
Something else is …

5.5 Listening script

T= Teacher   P = Pierre   E = Erica

P OK. So there are a number of points to consider when placing a newspaper advert because you want it to be as effective as possible. First of all, there's the reader to consider. You need to know who you are trying to reach. So, for example, if your product is for teenagers, you need to put your advert into the type of newspapers or magazines they'll read. Right, the second point to remember is that once you've chosen the best newspaper, you also need to consider where it will appear. Obviously, the front page is good but it's the most expensive place. That's also true for the back page. So look at the paper and decide which parts are most interesting to readers. Maybe it's the sports pages or perhaps it will be in the TV section. Again, this will help you reach the right kind of reader. Something else is the appearance of the advertisement. You need something to get the reader's attention like bright colours, perhaps a photograph or some of the words need to be very large. I think that all helps …

Ex Thank you. Now, Erica, can you ask Pierre your question about his talk?

T Yes, people say that newspaper advertising isn't as effective as, say, a TV commercial. Do you agree with this?

P Well, I think that it's true that TV commercials are sometimes very effective, but newspaper advertising can also be …

3 Discuss the questions as a class.

Answers
Erica's question at the end is *People say that newspaper advertising isn't as effective as, say, a TV commercial. Do you agree with this?*
Erica's question is good because she starts with a statement and then asks Pierre to comment. Ask students to suggest possible answers, eg *It's probably true that TV commercials are more effective because you have the person's attention, but on the other hand they're much more expensive.*

4 Refer students to the Speaking Success tip. The students prepare their topics and giving their presentations to each other. Remind the listening student to ask a question at the end.

5 Once they have both given their presentations, give feedback and ask students to use the evaluation checklist. Then repeat the task so that students can improve on their performance. They could work with another partner for variety.

Overview

6.1　Business topic: Recruitment

READING	**Employment news**
VOCABULARY	**Hiring and firing**
LISTENING	**Employment case studies**
SPEAKING	**Employment issues**
GRAMMAR	**Passives**

6.2　Business skills: Emailing

READING	**Clicking the habit**
VOCABULARY	**Emailing terms**
READING	**Internal communication and emails**
WRITING	**An email**

6.3　Learning strategies: Linking ideas

Missing sentences

Linking devices

PHOTOCOPIABLE

© 2009 Heinle, Cengage Learning

Useful language from Module 6

Wordlist

address	dismiss	lay off	save
email	document	link	send
attach	email	log on to	sender
back up	employ	make redundant	shut down
break	file	mouse	take someone on
button	fire	recruit	take voluntary
check	fire off	register	redundancy
click on	give notice	reply	type
computer	hire	resign	username
copy	icon	restart	walk out
delete	inbox	sack	website

Expressions

I'd be grateful if …
I'm afraid …
Please …
Please give me …
The reason is …
We appreciate …
Why don't you … ?
With regard to …
Would all staff note … ?
Would you like me to … ?

6.1 Recruitment

READING
Employment news

1 Find someone in your class who ...

Name

- has had a part-time job
- has had more than three jobs
- has only spent one week in a job
- has lost a job
- has had the same job twice
- has taken redundancy

2 Read the three news stories and match each extract A, B or C to a person described below. In 1 and 5 there are two correct answers. Underline the words in the text which give you the answer.

Which person ...

1 has stopped working? _____ _____
2 has started working? _____
3 doesn't need to work? _____
4 has lost a job? _____
5 didn't speak to their employer face-to-face? _____ _____

Text A

UK worker fired by text message

AP London: Katy Tanner's cell phone beeped with a startling message – you're fired.
Tanner, 21, had a migraine headache and took a sick day last week from her job at Blue Banana, a chain body-piercing studio in Cardiff, Wales, she said on Monday. She turned on her cell phone the next day to discover she'd been terminated from her sales position. 'We've reviewed your sales figures and they're not really up to the level we need,' shop manager Alex Barlett wrote in the message. 'As a result, we will not require your services any more. Thank you for your time with us.'

Text B

Don't call us; we'll call you!

When most people apply for a job they expect to go in for an interview. But not Jenny Jamieson. When a company rang her to arrange an interview they heard her voicemail and she was hired. Jenny came from a singing family and was trained in speech and music. She is now the voice of the company on all its automated messages and call centre systems. 'I suppose I'm always cheerful and smile a lot and I think people hear that on the phone,' says Jenny.

Text C

Car Plant Workers Win Lottery

Harry Lane was one of six employees at a UK car plant who received their £9.5 million winnings from last Saturday night's lottery and announced they wouldn't be going back to work. 61-year-old Harry said, 'I've been retired for two days now. I thought I'd have to work for another four years but this is like a dream!'
Harry's only plans so far are to pay off the rest of his mortgage and take his grandchildren on holiday. No one at his old factory was available to comment on how they would be replacing the six workers.

3 Discuss with your partner.
- Do you think Katy Tanner's employer acted correctly?
- Would you do the same as Harry Lane?

VOCABULARY
Hiring and firing

4 Put these verbs for talking about hiring and firing in the table.

hire   recruit   give notice   dismiss   walk out   sack   fire   lay off   resign
take voluntary redundancy   employ   take someone on   make redundant

give a job	take someone's job away	leave a job
take someone on		

LISTENING
Employment case studies

5 6.1 Listen to five speakers describing what happened to them at work. Match the speakers to actions A–G.

Speaker 1 _____
Speaker 2 _____
Speaker 3 _____
Speaker 4 _____
Speaker 5 _____

A walked out of the job
B was made redundant
C took someone on
D was fired
E gave notice
F was hired part-time
G took voluntary redundancy

SPEAKING
Employment issues

6 Work in pairs. Take turns to ask and answer the questions about employment.

1 Do you think it is unethical to lie about your qualifications on your CV?
2 When a member of staff has a problem at work, how important is it for the manager to discuss the problem before making a final decision?
3 How can good communication between managers and staff avoid potential problems at work?
4 If someone gives their notice, what do you think is a reasonable period? One week? Two months? What will it depend upon?
5 What is important to find out before you take a new member of staff on?
6 What are reasonable grounds for firing someone? How much warning should they be given in such situations?
7 Is it ever right to walk out of a job without giving any notice?

Student's Book pages 56 and 57

Employment news

READING

1 With larger classes, this activity will work better if students stand and have room to move around the classroom. They interview different students and write the name of a student who answers yes. With smaller or one-to-one classes, simply discuss and find out if your students have experienced any of the listed points.

2 Students read the three news stories and write the correct letter (A, B or C) next to sentences 1–5.

Answers
1 A, C   2 B   3 C   4 A   5 A, B

Alternative
Put students into groups of three with a letter each: A, B or C. Each student reads the text with their letter and then closes their book. They then summarise the news story they have read to the two other people in their group. Afterwards students can read all the texts and answer questions 1–5.

3 Students discuss the two questions about texts A and C in pairs and then report their conclusions back to the rest of the class.

Hiring and firing

VOCABULARY

4 Students categorise the verbs to talk about hiring and firing. Students may need to refer to dictionaries.

Answers
give a job: *hire, recruit, employ*

take someone's job away: *dismiss, sack, fire, lay off, make redundant*

leave a job: *give notice, walk out, resign, take voluntary redundancy*

Employment case studies

LISTENING Track 25 (CD1)

5 6.1 Give students time to read the task and get them to note the vocabulary from exercise 4 in A–G. Students could check their answers afterwards by reading the listening script on page 139.

Answers

Speaker 1: E
Speaker 2: G
Speaker 3: C
Speaker 4: A
Speaker 5: B

6.1 Listening script

S = Speaker

S1 I'd really had enough. The people there were great and I really liked my supervisor but it was just too boring. I only started in order to make a bit of extra money when I was a student. I didn't intend to stay this long and especially not after I finished my degree. So they said they were sad to see me go but they understood. Anyway, I told them when I wanted to leave, but they said I didn't need to worry about what it said in my contract, so I didn't actually have to work the full four weeks …

S2 Someone had to go. We haven't been getting the orders for a while so it was clear that they'd be laying people off sooner or later. Anyway, I thought rather than wait I'd go now and take the money. It was a good deal and it gives me a few months to find another job.

S3 Well, it's a good position and suits anyone who doesn't want to work every day of the week. We had three applicants but it was obvious who was right. I think Samantha will be perfect. She's keen and flexible which works well for both sides. And I think she can work at weekends, too, so that'll come in useful. Especially around Christmas time.

S4 I couldn't believe it. OK, so I've been late a couple of times but my boss said it wasn't a problem as long as I made up the extra hours in the evening. And then someone, and I can guess who, reported me. You know, that one who works in accounts who's always gossiping about other people. She said I'd been taking stationery from the cupboard and using it for personal correspondence. The manager asked me to come into the office so I could see what was coming. I wasn't going to wait around and get a lecture. I was through that door before anyone could stop me.

S5 The first thing I'm going to do is take the family on a nice long holiday while we can still afford it. Then I'll start thinking about what I'll do next when I get home. There's plenty of time, though for someone of my age I'm not sure what I'll get. Maybe I'll just work part-time until my pension begins. It's only seven years. Pity really. I would have liked to have stayed on 'til retirement. Mind you, it's worse for some of the others. They've got another twenty years to go. I mean, where will they get another job round here …

Employment issues

SPEAKING

6 Put students into pairs. The questions they ask each other will recycle some of the vocabulary in this section.

Possible answers

1 Many people will respond that it is unethical, however, it is also a cultural issue since people from some countries would take the attitude that if it gets you the job then it is acceptable. It may also be the case that an applicant doesn't have the right qualification but is still able to do the job well.

2 You would expect that all managers should talk to the person in question about an issue and also to anyone involved such as colleagues of the person.

3 Good communication can avoid problems before they get out of control. Staff problems can be caused by problems at home or difficulties with other members of the team. By regularly talking to staff a manager might be able to predict issues even before they arise and take action.

4 This will often depend on the level of the post. Senior managers may often have three to six months as a notice period whereas the basic employee may only have as little as a week in which to find a new job.

5 Responses will include qualifications, references, character and personality, how they work with others, reasons for leaving the other job, etc.

6 Many companies have a policy of one verbal warning, a written warning and finally the employee is fired. If your students work, find out from them what is normal in their company. Also discuss reasons for firing. For example, are issues such as sexual harassment, lateness or being caught using the Internet for personal use grounds for sacking?

7 Students might feel that if a company has not been honest with them that it is appropriate to leave.

GRAMMAR

Passives

1 Underline the passive form of the verb in these sentences.

0　300 people <u>have been made redundant</u> in a series of cutbacks.
1　He's employed by a number of different companies.
2　He must have been asked to leave after what he did.
3　It is hoped that new investment in the region will generate employment.
4　The news is that they are being made redundant.
5　Michael Jarvis and Kaleigh Macdonald's case is to be looked at by the European court.
6　A number of people were taken on with short-term contracts.
7　This time it's a warning but next time she'll be fired.

2 Now match them to these tenses and verb forms.

Present simple 1
Present continuous _____
Present perfect _____
Past simple _____
Will (future) _____
Present infinitive _____
It + passive _____
Modal _____

3 Complete sentences 1–8 with the passive form using the verb in brackets.

1　If we catch an employee stealing, they _____ (give) a verbal warning.
2　At present, the policy on dismissal _____ (review).
3　I _____ (offer) a redundancy package – I simply can't refuse it!
4　The company _____ (set up) by the family's great-grandfather.
5　The new performance-related bonus means that we _____ (give) a further 10% extra every month.
6　I'm not sure what happened exactly. The incident needs _____ (look) at quite carefully.
7　It _____ (hope) by the whole board that you will accept our generous offer.
8　It isn't like her to be late. She must _____ (delay) at the airport.

4 Complete these sentences about yourself using the passive form. Tell your partner.

• I'm employed by …
• Currently, the main project being worked on is …
• I've recently been trained to …
• The company was set up by …
• If an employee at my company works hard, they'll be …

5 Complete this report by underlining the correct form, active or passive.

Report on the dismissal of Ludwiga Chuhova

Introduction

The aim of this report is (1) *to assess / to be assessed* whether Ms Chuhova (2) *unfairly dismissed / was unfairly dismissed* and if the correct procedure (3) *followed / was followed* by her line manager.

Findings

First of all, it (4) *has found / has been found* that Ms Chuhova (5) *had failed / had been failed* to arrive for work on three occasions.
On the first occasion, when the manager gave a verbal warning, she (6) *reports / is reported* to have said that it was none of his business. On the second occasion, the line manager (7) *gave / was given* her a written warning. When she failed to arrive for work a third time, she (8) *dismissed / was dismissed* with immediate effect.

Conclusions and recommendations

In conclusion, the manager (9) *appears / is appeared* to have followed the correct course of action. However, it (10) *recommends / is recommended* that in the future, any disciplinary procedures (11) *should carry out / should be carried out* in the presence of one other person. This (12) *will help / will be helped* to avoid any similar situations.

6 Do you have disciplinary procedures that must be followed where you work? Are they similar to those outlined in the report?

Student's Book pages 58 and 59

Passives

GRAMMAR

1　Ask students to underline the passive forms in sentences 1–7.

Answers
1　's employed.
2　must have been asked
3　is hoped
4　are being made redundant
5　is to be looked at
6　were taken on
7　'll be fired

2　Students match the tenses to the verb forms in exercise 1.

Answers
Present continuous 4
Present perfect 0
Past simple 6
Will (future) 7
Present infinitive 5
It + passive 3
Modal 2

3　Students complete 1–8.

Answers
1　are given
2　is being reviewed
3　've been offered
4　was set up
5　will be given
6　to be looked at
7　is hoped
8　have been delayed

4　Students who are in work will be able to complete these sentences which all contain the passive form.

Alternative
For pre-work learners, write the following on the board so that students can describe their place of study.

The college/school was originally founded by …
I've recently been taught by …
Currently, the most popular course being applied for is …
If a student works hard at my college/school, he or she'll be …
Exams need to be taken … (when?)

5 Emphasise the frequent use of the passive in reports. Students underline the correct form.

Answers
1 to assess
2 was unfairly dismissed
3 was followed
4 has been found
5 had failed
6 is reported
7 gave
8 was dismissed
9 appears
10 is recommended
11 should be carried out
12 will help

6 Begin by summarising the disciplinary procedure in the report on the board:
1 Give the employee a verbal warning.
2 Give the employee a written warning.
3 The employee is dismissed.

Students in work can discuss whether their employer's disciplinary procedures are similar. Pre-work learners can comment on whether they think this procedure is too lenient or not tough enough. Would they change it?

Photocopiable activity 6.1
See page 166.

BUSINESS SKILLS

6.2 Emailing

READING

1 Are you an email addict? Complete this quiz and find out.

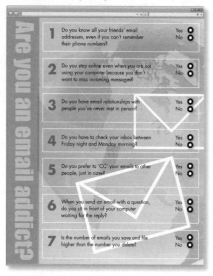

Are you an email addict?

1 Do you know all your friends' email addresses, even if you can't remember their phone numbers? — Yes / No

2 Do you stay online even when you are not using your computer because you don't want to miss incoming messages? — Yes / No

3 Do you have email relationships with people you've never met in person? — Yes / No

4 Do you have to check your inbox between Friday night and Monday morning? — Yes / No

5 Do you prefer to 'CC' your emails to other people, just in case? — Yes / No

6 When you send an email with a question, do you sit in front of your computer waiting for the reply? — Yes / No

7 Is the number of emails you save and file higher than the number you delete? — Yes / No

2 Read the article on page 61 and write in the correct letter, A–F, for the missing sentences.

A This is where we first find out about decisions that have been made, deals struck and the direction being taken.

B In the past few months, 290 employees at a government department have been sacked via their office intranet, while a car equipment firm laid off the workforce by email.

C Then suddenly you send an email to the wrong person.

D They are typical of the average employee who sends 34 emails a day.

E Sending mail CC has only made it worse.

F Two letters were attached, one saying her contract had been cancelled, the other that she should return any work items.

Clicking the habit

Email makes many things so much easier – including making someone redundant. (1) _____ In the case of Helen Saxon-Jones, she was checking her inbox from home one day when she read the subject line: 'This email is only to be opened during office hours'. But she clicked on it anyway. (2) _____. Unable to believe it, the 29-year-old, who had been working as a project development officer with a charity, took the case to a tribunal. She finally received £12,000 in compensation from her former employer.

But these bosses who dismiss workers by email aren't necessarily evil, cowardly people – they're mostly people just like you and me who have developed the habit of using email too much. (3) _____ They meet people and exchange email addresses rather than phone numbers. They email CVs to prospective employers. In a survey of workers last week, almost half admitted they email the person sitting next to them to avoid making verbal contact, and one in five of us uses email just to gossip about work colleagues.

Regardless of the field in which you work, it is a safe bet to guess that your first course of action on any given workday is to log on to your PC and begin checking your inbox. (4) _____ We send a question and become offended if the recipient does not respond within hours. We have become slaves to the inbox, dependent on a constant flow of typed communication.

So type-type-type, even when it is unnecessary. Workers type up their every thought and send off emails with tremendous inaccuracy or complete pointlessness. (5) _____ We are copied in on emails that do not directly affect us in the vague interests of keeping everyone 'in the loop'.

Email allows us to continue to work at home. Constant access leads to a compulsion to keep the communication going. You're at home, and there's nothing good on TV, so you decide to have a glass of wine and do a little work. As you review your inbox, you start firing off responses. (6) _____ You don't want them to read it and the next thing you know you're sending even more emails to try and undo the damage. Another round of emails has begun!

VOCABULARY Emailing terms

3 Underline one incorrect word in each group.

0 check your: button, inbox, email

1 click on: a link, a computer, an icon

2 delete, save, click: an email

3 send, copy, shut down: an email to (someone)

4 log on to a: mouse, computer, website

5 restart, delete, register: the computer

6 back up, save, break : a document

7 fire off, send, dismiss: a reply

8 attach a : sender, file, document

9 type in your: username, icon, address

Now look at the words you underlined. Can you use them in another phrase?

Click on this button to restart.

Student's Book pages 60 and 61

Clicking the habit

READING

1 Students can begin by working alone and completing the quiz with their own answers. Afterwards, they can compare their answers with a partner's. Find out who ticked the most Yes answers in the class.

2 When students look at the article, you might wish to explain that the headline is a play on words referring to the phrase, 'kick the habit', meaning to try and give up an addiction like smoking. Students complete the article with sentences A–F.

Answers
1 B   2 F   3 D   4 A   5 E   6 C

Extension
Discuss with the students how true they think the article is.

Emailing terms

VOCABULARY

3 Make sure students look for the incorrect, not the correct word.

Answers
1 a computer
2 click
3 shut down
4 mouse
5 delete
6 break
7 dismiss
8 sender
9 icon

Students can work together to try and make sentences with the underlined words.

Possible answers

1 Switch on the computer with this button here.
2 Double click on the icon.
3 Shut down the computer and restart it.
4 Use the mouse to move the cursor.
5 I deleted the email by mistake.
6 Put a page break in here.
7 Our company dismiss people who send personal emails.
8 This email doesn't say who the sender is.
9 Run the game by clicking on the icon.

Learning Tip

Encourage students to get into the habit of writing their own sentences with any new vocabulary. The sentences should be personalised, and, if possible, relevant to their work.

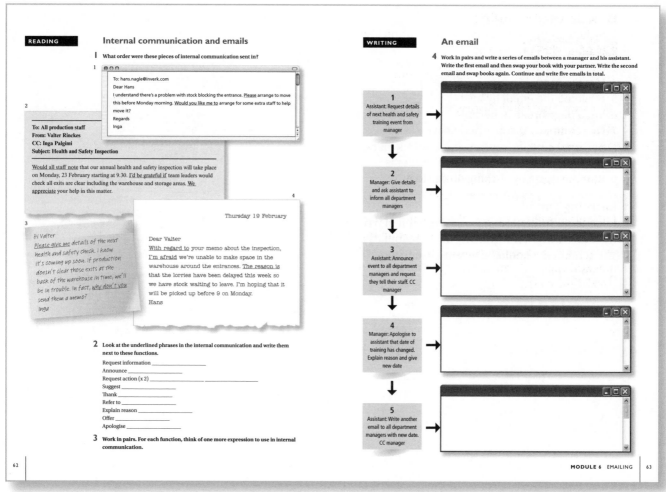

Student's Book pages 62 and 63

Internal communication and emails

READING

I Students look at a range of internal communication including an email, a memo and two notes. The basic situation is that a health and safety inspection is scheduled, and stock blocking the exits to and from the warehouse will break health and safety rules.

Answer
The order they were each sent is 3, 2, 4, 1.

Extension
Ask students to comment on the tone and register of each communication. Which is the most/least formal? Is the tone friendly or unfriendly?

Possible comments
The email in 1 from Inga to Hans is very direct and she is clearly not happy with him. Although she uses the phrase *Would you like me to arrange...*, she is not really offering but putting Hans in a position where he has to do something. The memo in 2 uses a semi-formal tone that you would expect in many types of business communication. The two notes in 3 and 4 are less

formal though Hans' note still uses some formal expressions such as *With regard to ...*

2 Students match the expressions to their functions.

Answers
Request information: *Please give me ...*
Announce: *Would all staff note ...*
Request action: *Please / I'd be grateful if ...*
Suggest: *Why don't you ...*
Thank: *We appreciate ...*
Refer to: *With regard to ...*
Explain reason: *The reason is ...*
Offer: *Would you like me to ...*
Apologise: *I'm afraid ...*

3 Students work in pairs to think of more expressions.

Possible answers
Request information: *I'd like ...*
Announce: *Please note ...*
Request action: *I'd like to request that ...*
Suggest: *How about ...*
Thank: *We thank you for ...*
Refer to: *With reference to ...*
Explain reason: *This is because ...*
Offer: *Can I ...*
Apologise: *I am sorry but ...*

An email

WRITING

4 Students will need to use some of their expressions and phrases from exercises 2 and 3 to complete this series of emails. Students work in pairs as for any other roleplay, but in this type of writing roleplay they play both parts. The idea behind swapping emails with another student is that certain aspects of the correspondence will change during the course of the communication. Set a time limit (perhaps two minutes per email) so students practise writing quickly and fluently. At the end, they should read back through their work and make any correction or think about how they could have improved the emails.

Possible answers

1
> Dear [name]
>
> Would you please send me details of the next health and safety training event? I'm aware that it is due in the near future.
>
> Regards
>
> [name]

2
> Dear [name]
>
> Thanks for reminding me. The training event takes place on the 3rd September from 9–5 in the conference rooms. Please inform all department managers and forward the attached documents which are to be read before the event.
>
> Thanks
>
> [name]

3
> Dear Department Managers
>
> Would you all please note that the next health and safety training event takes place on the 3rd September from 9–5 in the conference rooms. As you know this is a legal requirement. Please also find attached documents which you should be familiar with before the event.
>
> Thanks for your cooperation.
>
> [name]

4
> Dear [name]
>
> Thanks for informing the managers. Unfortunately, the training event has been postponed. The reason is the trainer is unavailable. He has suggested the 23rd September, so can you let all managers know?
>
> Sorry for the inconvenience.
>
> [name]

5
> Dear Department Managers
>
> Following my previous email, I am writing to inform you of a change in date to the health and safety training event. Due to the unavailability of the trainer on the 3rd September, the event will now take place on the 23rd. All other details remain the same.
>
> Apologies for any inconvenience caused.
>
> [name]

Photocopiable activity 6.2
See page 167.

LEARNING STRATEGIES

6.3 Reading: Linking ideas

In this section you will choose the correct sentences to fill gaps in a reading text. The first gap is given as an example so you have to fill five gaps.

1 Read the Reading Success tip box and look at sentences A–G in the question on page 65. Underline any pronouns.

2 Three of the target sentences (A, C and G) do not include pronouns. In this case, you need to decide which are the 'key words' and how they can help you to understand the text.

Reading Success

You will need to pay special attention to words which link the text together. These include words which refer to other words, for example pronouns: *this, these, that, those, he, she, they, his, hers, us, them, which …*

A There are some obvious signs of the second reason.
C Larry decided that the best solution was to get help from the organisation.
G The next conference is due to take place at the peaceful Dolphin Beach Resort on the Gulf of Mexico.

For example, in sentence A, you need to ask:
- Where in the text does the writer give 'reasons'?
- What was the first reason?
- What are the 'obvious signs'?

What could you ask about the key words in sentences C and G?

3 Do the activity below. Afterwards, compare and discuss the reasons for your answers.
- Read the article below about health at work.
- Choose the best sentence to fill each of the gaps.
- For each gap (1–5), mark one letter (A–G).
- Do not use any letter more than once.
- There is one extra sentence.

Too much work is a health hazard

If you constantly try to be the best of the best, stop it. Now. You could be well on the way to giving yourself future health problems. For example, take Larry, a US consultant, who travelled non-stop, worked 60 to 80-hour weeks and still attended meetings at weekends. (0) .... 'But I really got a kick out of it.' A period of intensive care in hospital convinced him to quit and adjust his work-life balance. (1) .... Headaches, high blood pressure and exhaustion are all the typical warnings that your body gives out. If your boss is irritable and guilty of confused thinking, prepare for a promotion. (2) .... A recent survey found that three quarters of UK workers cannot switch off when they leave the office.

Of course, not all our unhappiness at work is due to long hours or ill-health. There are many other good reasons to be unhappy about work. Research by Investors in People has found, for example, that 49% of employees are frustrated by their career progression. (3) .... More than a third say that their managers fail to set clear development goals or provide regular career reviews.

So how do you determine whether you are stressed out by your boss's careless attitude or because, like Larry, you are simply working too hard? (4) .... Do you take work on holiday and hide the fact from others such as your wife and children? If you answer 'yes', then you have probably crossed the line between everyday hard work and workaholism. This is just one of twenty questions that the organisation Workaholics asks potential members on its website.

The organisation, which was set up by a New York corporate financial planner and teacher in 1983, now has 50 branches across the world. There are no joining fees and the only requirement for membership is the desire to stop working compulsively. Members can attend a conference every two years and share their experiences with each other in a 'beautiful setting'. (5) .... If Florida seems a little too far to travel for this, then the 'Workaholics Anonymous Book of Recovery' is available at $15, including stories of recovery by members, a step-by-step study guide and helpful literature to support members in their recovery journey.

A There are some obvious signs of the second reason.
B Larry could have avoided this by looking out for the signs of burn-out or in his case something worse.
C Larry decided that the best solution was to get help from the organisation.
D He or she is probably too stressed and could be redundant very soon.
E 'Occasionally it occurred to me how stressful the job was,' he says.
F 46% of them say lack of management support is a barrier to success.
G The next conference is due to take place at the peaceful Dolphin Beach Resort on the Gulf of Mexico.

Student's Book pages 64 and 65

1 Refer students to the Reading Success tip on looking for words which link the text together. Tell them that pronouns often provide helpful clues as to where the sentence goes. They might refer back to a noun in the previous sentence or refer forward to the next sentence. This also explains why we often advise students to read the whole text and not stop reading as soon as they reach the first gap. Note that A, C and G don't contain any pronouns (see the next exercise).

Answers
(pronouns in bold)

B Larry could have avoided **this** by looking out for the signs of burnout or in **his** case something worse.
D **He** or **she** is probably too stressed and could be redundant very soon.
E 'Occasionally **it** occurred to **me** how stressful the job was,' **he** says.
F 46% of **them** say lack of management support is a barrier to success.

2 If the sentence contains key words or full nouns then it also suggests that sentences in the text either before or after might contain referring pronouns. When students have read the suggested questions that they might ask for sentence A, ask them to suggest questions for C and G.

Possible questions
For C: Which organisation?
For G: When was the previous conference? Which country or part of the world is the Dolphin Beach Resort in?

3 Students complete the activity.

Answers
1 B ('this' refers back to 'a period of intensive care in hospital')
2 D ('he or she' refers back to 'your boss')
3 F ('them' refers back to 'employees')
4 A (The first reason is in the previous sentence: 'your boss's careless attitude'. The second reason is 'you are simply working too hard.')

5 G (The previous sentence mentions conferences for the first time in the article. The other less obvious clue is that the following sentence says the next conference is in Florida, the west side of which is on the Gulf of Mexico.)

Overview

7.1   Business topic: Sales

READING   **Not sold on sales?**

VOCABULARY   **Sales terms**

READING   **The worst job in the world?**

VOCABULARY   **Describing jobs**

GRAMMAR   **Comparatives and superlatives**

SPEAKING   **Comparing jobs**

7.2   Business skills: Selling

READING   **How to sell ...**

LISTENING   **Selling**

SPEAKING   **A sales conversation**

READING   **A proposal**

WRITING   **A fax**

7.3   Learning strategies: Extracting key information

Matching statements to texts

PHOTOCOPIABLE

© 2009 Heinle, Cengage Learning

Useful language from Module 7

Wordlist

air	cold calling	jolly (informal)	sales pitch
boring	door-to-door	myth	varied
buzz	selling	repetitive	well-paid
challenging	frustrating	responsible	

Expressions

As an interesting alternative, you might wish to consider ...

Further to your request ...

I know it's proved much more popular than ...

I look forward to hearing from you.

I'd like to mention that I can also ...

Is there anything I can help you with at the moment?

It has the following features ...

It's a huge improvement on ...

I was wondering if you'd mind answering a few questions about ...

I would suggest a prompt decision ...

Perhaps ... could be useful?

Please consider this possibility and note ...

Please note ...

Shall I put you down for ...?

So is ... something you might be interested in?

Thank you for your order ...

What did you have in mind exactly?

MODULE 7   BUSINESS TOPIC

7.1   Sales

READING

1   Work in pairs. Compare the jobs in each of the following pairs. What are the similarities and differences? Say which you would prefer to do and why.

- doctor / vet
- manager of a company / manager of a charity
- fighter pilot / airline pilot
- school teacher / university lecturer
- politician / journalist

2   Read the article on page 67. Find out why more people prefer a career in marketing than in sales. Complete the table below with reasons from the text.

Reasons for choosing marketing	Reasons for choosing sales

3   Read the text again and answer these questions.

1   In the first paragraph, the writer says it's easier to start conversations at dinner parties
   A if you are in sales.
   B if you are in marketing.
   C if you are a fighter pilot.
   D if you lie.

2   According to the writer, the truth is that
   A marketing is a better profession.
   B sales is actually more glamorous than marketing.
   C more people are in sales than marketing.
   D there are more graduates in marketing.

3   One reason Ross Snowdon likes sales more than marketing is because
   A it's better paid.
   B you see real results.
   C you meet more people.
   D you can work on your own.

4   It's difficult to attract graduates into sales because
   A many aren't suited to it.
   B they aren't passionate.
   C they don't have the right qualifications.
   D of a false perception.

Not sold on sales?

'Hi. I work in sales.' Not a great conversation opener, is it? Not like being a fighter pilot or a director of Médecins sans Frontières, for example. Unfortunately, a job in sales can't quite shake off its unglamorous image or associations with something rather dishonest. This all means recruitment problems for graduate employees. On the other hand, marketing – a less direct way of selling a product – is rather more popular as a career choice,

and sounds better at dinner parties.

Why? Susan Stevens, head of HR at Toshiba, believes that marketing 'retains an air of glamour' and that graduates 'expect to work on creative campaigns with PRs and lots of jollies'. But, on the other hand, sales means 'door-to-door work and cold calling'. Yet this image is misleading. Sales professionals in the UK outnumber people in marketing by about 200,000. This is partly because those who do

fall into sales work realise it isn't anything like as awful as the myths suggest.

Stevens says that Toshiba recently had to market its graduate scheme as a sales and marketing programme because 'we knew sales alone wouldn't attract people'. The gamble paid off. Last year the majority of recruits chose sales, including Ross Snowdon, a marketing graduate. 'Unlike marketing, sales is tangible. It has direct impact on a company's results. It's all about meeting people and communicating with different personalities.'

Part of the reason why graduates are often not interested in sales is because it isn't seen as a profession. Clarissa Gent, a chemistry graduate and sales manager at Rackspace Managed Hosting, an IT support firm, says: 'Careers departments don't talk about sales and there is a lack of education about the different levels you can go to with it. I always thought marketing seemed more attractive, but it wasn't the dynamic world I'd imagined. Then I talked to people in sales and realised that it is possible to be passionate about it. It soon became apparent that I was much more suited to sales. Now I speak to customers every day in the buzz of a target-driven environment. It's fantastic.'

Tom Moody, a commercial director for Proctor and Gamble, says that sales can be 'managing millions of pounds of business and making sure the customer's happy. It's incredibly rewarding.' Now there's a convincing sales pitch if I ever heard one!

VOCABULARY   **Sales terms**

4   Match these words (1–7) from the text to their definitions (A–G).

1	sales pitch	A	Making an unexpected phone call or visit to sell something.
2	door-to-door selling	B	Excitement.
3	a buzz	C	Business trips with lots of free entertainment.
4	a myth	D	Knocking on doors all day to sell.
5	cold calling	E	Making a speech to convince people to buy something.
6	an air	F	Something people incorrectly believe to be true.
7	jollies (informal)	G	Feeling or attitude.

66   **MODULE 7**   SALES   67

Student's Book pages 66 and 67

Not sold on sales?

READING

1   Students begin by comparing the pairs of jobs. This will generate language for comparing and discussion of qualities and skills, which will be looked at in more detail during this module. A possible response to the first pair might be:

You need to be highly qualified to be a doctor or a vet. Both deal with health but obviously one deals only with people. I'd prefer to work with animals because they are less difficult!

2   This task encourages students to read the text for general meaning first. With a more experienced group you could begin by asking them to predict some of the differences between marketing and sales that might be in the article. Alternatively, ask the class whether they would prefer to work in sales or marketing and say why. Tell students to read and underline reasons for both, and then transfer these into the table. As students add these notes, they might start to think of some of their own ideas which could also be added to the table.

Answers

Reasons for choosing marketing
- sounds better at dinner parties
- has an air of glamour (whereas sales has an unglamorous image)
- (many graduates believe) you work on creative PR campaigns and go on lots of jollies
- marketing seems more attractive (than sales)

Reasons for choosing sales
- it isn't as bad as myths suggest
- unlike marketing, sales is tangible
- it has a direct impact on a company's results
- you meet people and communicate with different personalities
- in sales there's a buzz of a target-driven environment
- you can manage millions of pounds of business
- make customers happy
- it's incredibly rewarding

3   Students read the text for more detail to answer questions 1–4.

Answers
1 B   2 C   3 B   4 D

Sales terms

4 Students match the words to their definitions. Note that it will help if they see the words in context in the article, as well as checking in their dictionaries.

Answers
1 E   2 D   3 B   4 F   5 A   6 G   7 C

Extension 1
Ask students to write the seven words in their own sentences, or seven sentences with a gap where the word should go, eg *There's a real _____ about our latest product. Everyone's talking about it.* (Answer: *buzz*)

Students can test each other by reading out their sentences, but missing out the word so other students guess what it is.

Extension 2
If you have time or want to set homework, ask students to write the text for an advert for a Salesperson. Tell them to include the following information:
- type of person required
- qualities and skills
- what benefits and rewards the job will give the successful applicant.

Students can base some or all of their ideas on the information given in the text about sales.

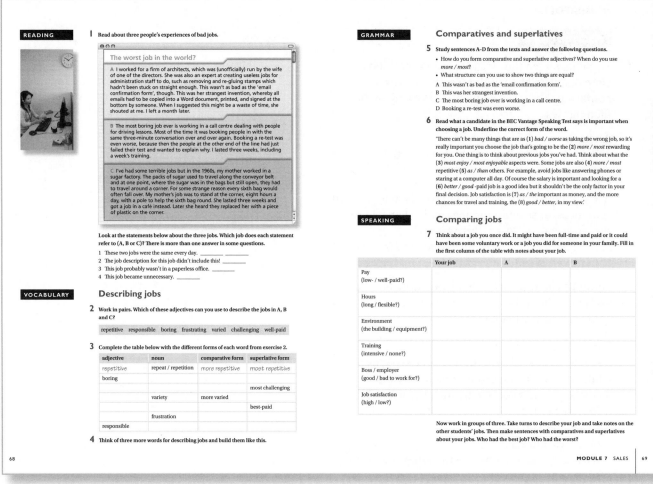

Student's Book pages 68 and 69

The worst job in the world?

READING

1 As a lead-in to the reading, students could discuss bad jobs in pairs or as a class. The three texts are taken from a blog where people have been invited to describe their worst job ever. Ask students which they think is the worst job of the three. Students then match the jobs in texts A, B and C to the sentences.

Answers
1 B,C   2 A   3 A   4 C

Describing jobs

VOCABULARY

2 Begin by telling students to work in pairs and make sure they know the meaning of the words. Students can help each other with the definitions or ask you if necessary. You could also ask students to say whether they think the words are usually positive, negative, or possibly both.

They then apply the adjectives to the three texts. In some cases there are no exact answers and students should explain why they have used a particular adjective.

Possible answers
Job A: frustrating, challenging
Job B: repetitive, boring
Job C: repetitive, boring, frustrating

Extension
Ask students to think of one job to match each adjective and explain their choices, eg *Being an engineer would be challenging because you need to solve lots of problems.*

3 This exercise requires students to put adjectives into different forms.

Answers

adjective	noun	comparative form	superlative form
boring	bore / boredom	more boring	most boring
challenging	challenge	more challenging	most challenging
varied	variety	more varied	most varied
well-paid	pay / payment	better-paid	best-paid
frustrating	frustration	more frustrating	most frustrating
responsible	responsibility	more responsible	most responsible

Pronunciation
Ask students to underline the word stress on any multi-syllable words. They can check in their dictionaries or you could read the words aloud.

Answers
re<u>peat</u>
re<u>pe</u>titive
repe<u>ti</u>tion
<u>bor</u>ing
<u>chall</u>enge
<u>chall</u>enging
<u>var</u>y
<u>var</u>ied
va<u>ri</u>ety
<u>pay</u>ment
frus<u>trate</u>
frus<u>tra</u>ting
frus<u>tra</u>tion
re<u>spon</u>sible
responsi<u>bil</u>ity

4 Students could work in groups to add more words and build them. Again, check they know where the word stress is and can say the word properly.

Examples
excite – exciting – excitement
popularise – popular – popularity
glamorise – glamorous – glamour

Comparatives and superlatives

GRAMMAR

5 Sentences A–D are taken from or based on the two previous texts in this module. Most students will be familiar with the basic rules for the comparative and superlative form but this task will consolidate and extend their understanding. Refer them to the grammar summary on page 129 if they need further help or to check their answers.

Answers
– You add *-er/-est* to form short comparative and superlative adjectives.
– You use *more/most* before longer adjectives.
– The structure *as* + adjective + *as* shows two things are equal.

6 Students check their understanding of the form by underlining the correct words.

Answers
1 bad
2 most
3 most enjoyable
4 more
5 than
6 better
7 as
8 better

Comparing jobs

SPEAKING

7 Students begin by working alone and writing notes about a job they have done. With pre-work learners the job could have been unpaid work or jobs round the house, eg under the category 'boss' they can even comment on their member of the family giving them the job.

Students then work in threes and describe and summarise the notes in their table while the other two listen and write down the key points. When they've completed their table, the group can work together to make sentences about the jobs. You could ask each group to produce a minimum of seven, if necessary. The group can then read them out to another group or a selection of the sentences to the whole class. They should also say who had the best or worst job. Finally, you could also decide who has had the worst job in the class.

Photocopiable activity 7.1
See page 168.

Student's Book page reproduction

BUSINESS SKILLS

7.2 Selling

READING

1 What are the qualities of a successful salesperson? Make a list of your ideas.

2 Read the guide to selling below and choose the best word A, B, C or D to fill gaps 1–15.

How to sell ...

It's not quite true that a great salesperson can sell anything to anyone. For a (1) _____, they might not need it – and sales is all about meeting needs. (2) _____, selling is one of those things that can happen to anyone, no (3) _____ what their job description, so here are the basics.

Step 1 Build trust
You need to (4) _____ trust with the person to whom you are selling. They don't have to be your best friend but essentially people don't buy from people they hate or distrust.

Step 2 Don't misunderstand the customer
Understand the needs of the other person. Then it's up to the salesperson to (5) _____ that the benefits of their goods or services match the requirements. Without that, you have no sale.

Step 3 Ask clever questions
Ask questions to find out what the customer's problems and issues are. Then think (6) _____ what the needs must be. It's often more (7) _____ than asking the obvious, 'What do you need?'

Step 4 Know your stuff
It (8) _____ without saying: know your product and understand the marketplace into (9) _____ you are selling.

Step 5 Don't overload people with (10) _____
You need to know every product specification but your customer doesn't. Essentially, he or she needs to know how it will make their life (11) _____. If later on they want the dimensions, they'll find it on your website.

Step 6 Salespeople are not necessarily born
The classic (12) _____ of a salesperson is someone who is outgoing. But like customers who come in all personality types, sales people can (13) _____. The main thing is to be able to reflect and react to a customer's personality.

Step 7 Be prepared to fail
It doesn't matter how good you are, you will get (14) _____. Sales is full of knockbacks so don't get hung up on it. (15) _____ on to the next customer.

1 A beginning	B start	C customer	D first
2 A However	B Although	C Because	D Whatever
3 A much	B more	C way	D matter
4 A set up	B find	C establish	D know
5 A perform	B compare	C present	D demonstrate
6 A along	B through	C out	D across
7 A clear	B efficient	C effective	D better
8 A goes	B moves	C does	D makes
9 A what	B which	C whom	D where
10 A details	B offers	C discounts	D prices
11 A good	B better	C well	D best
12 A vision	B look	C focus	D image
13 A change	B vary	C listen	D buy
14 A sent back	B recruited	C turned down	D contracts
15 A Phone	B Try	C Move	D Contact

Selling

LISTENING

3 7.1 Listen to five salespeople and their customers. In each case the salesperson is either following a step from the article on 'How to sell' or failing to follow it. Write the number of the step next to the salesperson and write what you think they are selling.

	Step	Product or service?
Salesperson 1	____	____
Salesperson 2	____	____
Salesperson 3	____	____
Salesperson 4	____	____
Salesperson 5	____	____

4 7.1 Listen again and complete the notes about each salesperson's product or services.

Demand falls in (4) _____ but July is better. The client might be interested in advertising on the (2) _____

The XR5 is a huge improvement on the (3) _____ model:
– backseat airbags
– Travels 0 to 70 in (4) _____
– air conditioning

Leather Diaries
– Available in black and (6) _____ as well as brown.
– Customer wants to know price for putting company (7) _____ on the front.

BEAVIS SUPPLIES
Ray would like to change the (5) _____ on the old letterheads.

Points to mention in each call:
– Warm and Cosy
– Ask questions about person's (8) _____
– Suggest (9) _____ visits to advise on home improvements

5 7.1 Listen for the expressions below. Write the number of the listening (1–5) in which you hear each expression.

A I know it's proved much more popular than ... _____
B What did you have in mind exactly? _____
C So is ... something you might be interested in? _____
D I was wondering if you'd mind answering a few questions about ... _____
E Perhaps ... could be useful? _____
F Is there anything I can help you with at the moment? _____
G Shall I put you down for ...? _____
H It's a huge improvement on ... _____

6 Match the expressions A–H in exercise 5 to the categories below. Write one letter on each line.

Establish customer needs: _____	Suggest possible requirements: _____	Compare: _____	Close the sale: _____

SPEAKING

A sales conversation

7 Choose an object in the classroom. Work in pairs and take turns to sell your objects to each other. Follow the flow chart in exercise 6.

Student's Book pages 70 and 71

How to sell ...

READING

1 Discuss the question as a class. Students can also refer back to the reading in the previous section.

Possible answers
- persuasiveness
- knowledgeable
- trustworthy
- believes in the product or service
- never gives up

2 Students choose the best word to complete the 'How to sell ...' text.

Answers
1 B 2 A 3 D 4 C 5 D 6 B 7 C 8 A
9 B 10 A 11 B 12 D 13 B 14 C 15 C

Extension 1
Once students have completed the text in exercise 2 and checked their answers, give them time to study the text and think about the advice. Discuss whether they agree with all the advice, eg some people may disagree that all salespeople should be prepared to fail and that they should always succeed.

Extension 2
Another activity to make students read more closely is to ask students to number the steps in order of importance (1 = most important advice, 7 = least important). They then compare their order with other students and give reasons.

Selling

LISTENING Track 26 (CD1)

3 7.1 Students might need to listen twice at this stage, firstly to note down which step the salesperson is or isn't following, and then to listen for exactly what is being sold.

Answers
Salesperson 1: 3 – advertising
Salesperson 2: 4 or 5 – car
Salesperson 3: 1 or 6 – stationery
Salesperson 4: 4 – personal organisers
Salesperson 5: 7 – home improvements/insulation

7.1 Listening script

C = Customer   S = Salesperson

Salesperson 1

C Well, June is always a little difficult because demand falls and we have to wait until July again before things pick up.

S So is extra advertising something you might be interested in?

C Maybe, though we have tried that before. You know, in local magazines and so on.

S Perhaps radio or a mailshot could be useful?

C Local radio's an interesting idea. I haven't thought about it, really.

Salesperson 2

This is our latest XR5. It's a huge improvement on the previous 2007 model because they've updated it with a number of key features such as backseat airbags for the kids, half a cubic metre extra in the back for luggage, and the braking system is state-of-the-art. It'll do zero to 70 in five seconds and of course there's air conditioning. The dashboard is particularly interesting because it will tell you when the tyres need more air pressure or if it's due a service check-up …

Salesperson 3

C Hello.

S Hello, Ray. It's Ivan from Beavis Supplies.

C Oh hi, Ivan. How are you? It's been a long time.

S Yes, I'm afraid I've been off sick for a couple of weeks.

C Oh, I'm sorry to hear that.

S Well, I'm OK now. How are things with you?

C Pretty good. We're busy.

S That's good. So is there anything I can help you with at the moment?

C As a matter of fact, I need some letterheads fairly soon.

S So shall I put you down for your usual order?

C Actually, I was thinking we could do something with the design.

S Sure, what did you have in mind exactly?

Salesperson 4

S Erm, well yes, err this is quite good. It has a diary section here, you know from January to February. And, err, I think at the back there's an address book … oh, I thought there was. Maybe there used to be. Anyway …

C Is this cover leather?

S Err yes (?) Well, yes, it feels like leather. I know we can get them in black and red as well as brown. I know it's proved much more popular than the old plastic sort.

C And how much does it cost to put our logo on the front?

S Logo? Sure. Right. Yes, that would look good, wouldn't it? Well, let me ring the office and maybe they can give me, I mean give you, a price on that … one moment …

Salesperson 5

C1 Hello?

S Hello, is that Mr Hawkes?

C1 Yes, who's this?

S Hello, Mr Hawkes, this is Martin calling from Warm and Cosy. Mr Hawkes, I was wondering if you'd mind answering a few questions about your home this evening.

C1 Why?

S Well, it happens that a representative from Warm and Cosy will be in your area tomorrow and he'll be available to advise you on any home improvements you might be thinking of …

C2 Hello?

S Hello, is that Mrs Jones?

C2 Yes, speaking.

S Hello, Mrs Jones, this is Martin calling from Warm and Cosy and I was wondering …

4 🔘 7.1 Students listen for specific words.

Answers

1 June
2 radio
3 2007
4 five seconds
5 design
6 red
7 logo
8 house
9 a representative

5 🔘 7.1 Play the recording again and ask students to write the number of the listening next to each expression as they hear it.

Answers

A 4 B 3 C 1 D 5 E 1 F 3 G 3 H 2

6 Students match the expressions to one of the four stages of selling shown in the flowchart.

Answers

Establish customer needs: B, D, F
Suggest possible requirements: C, E
Compare: A, H
Close the sale: G

A sales conversation

SPEAKING

7 Students can choose any object from the classroom, or, if they work for a company, they can sell their own product or service. They will need to begin by asking their partner about their needs related to the object, eg if it is a pen, they might ask, *I was wondering if you'd mind answering a few questions about your stationery needs*, and then suggest, *Perhaps a new type of pen might be useful …*

After the activity, ask students to comment on who was effective as a salesperson. Find out if they followed any of the steps in the article on page 70.

Photocopiable activity 7.2
See page 169.

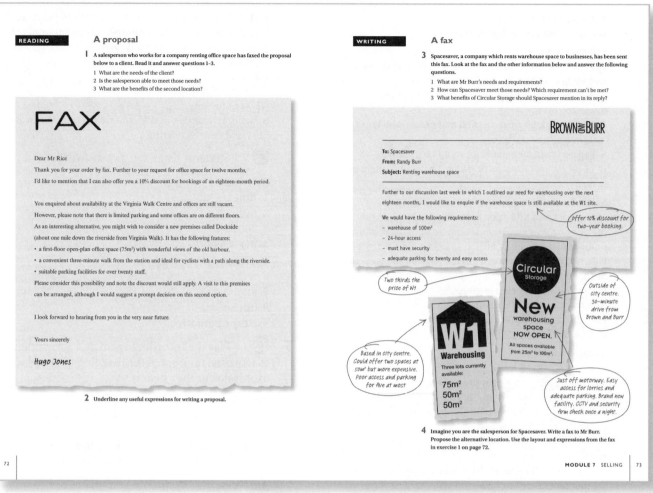

A proposal

READING

I   Ask students to read the fax quickly and answer questions 1–3. The purpose of this fax is to present students with a model version for the proposal will write for exercise 3.

Answers

1 The client needs office space for twelve months.
2 The salesperson can meet those needs and also wants to try and sell a little more in addition.
3 The second location offered has these benefits:
  – offices on the same floor
  – wonderful views
  – more convenient than the other location for transport
  – suitable parking facilities

2   Students should underline and make a record of useful expressions to use when writing a proposal.

Possible answers
  – Thank you for your order …
  – Further to your request …
  – I'd like to mention that I can also …
  – please note …
  – As an interesting alternative, you might wish to consider …

  – It has the following features …
  – Please consider this possibility and note …
  – I would suggest a prompt decision …
  – I look forward to hearing from you.

It's helpful if students always look for and underline useful expressions from any form of correspondence. Also draw students' attention to the use of bullet points in the middle of the fax. Point out that bullet points are perfectly acceptable in business writing but shouldn't be overused.

A fax

WRITING

3   Students are asked to study information including handwritten notes. Ask students to underline any information which answers questions 1–3.

Answers

1 Mr Burr needs warehousing for 18 months. He needs 100 square metres in space, security and parking for at least twenty people, as well as good access.

2 Spacesaver can meet those needs if Mr Burr takes two spaces of 50 square metres (although this is expensive). However, parking and access are poor.

3 Spacesaver is more positive about the warehouse at Circular Storage because there is 100 square metres' space. It's also cheaper and has good access and parking as well as security. The only drawback is that the warehouse isn't as central so the proposal to Mr Burr will have to convince him that the benefits outweigh this problem.

4 Students write their own fax using all the information in exercise 3. Point out that the fax follows the structure indicated by the three questions in exercise 1. In other words, it refers to the needs of the client. Explain that these needs can be met and then propose the second location by stressing its benefits. Students should then use the fax proposal on page 72 as a basic model to follow.

Possible answer

Dear Mr Burr

Further to your enquiry about the warehousing at the W1 site, I am delighted to say this space is still available. However, with regard to your additional requirements please note that you would have to rent two separate spaces of 50 square metres and the warehouse has limited parking for five cars only and limited access.

As an alternative, you might wish to consider a new storage option called Circular Storage that has recently become available to Spacesaver. While it is a little further from the centre of the city than W1, it has the following features:
— easy access for lorries and adequate parking for twenty
— security with CCTV
— space availability of 100 square metres (and more if required)

Please also note that it would be two-thirds the price of W1, and the 10% discount for a two-year booking would still apply. A visit to these premises can be arranged, although I would like to suggest a prompt decision on this second option.

I look forward to hearing from you in the very near future.

Yours sincerely

Extension
Ask students to swap their proposals and check that their partner has done the following:
- referred to the customer's needs
- included information from the handwritten notes
- used fixed expressions and a semi-formal business tone
- stressed the benefits of the second location.

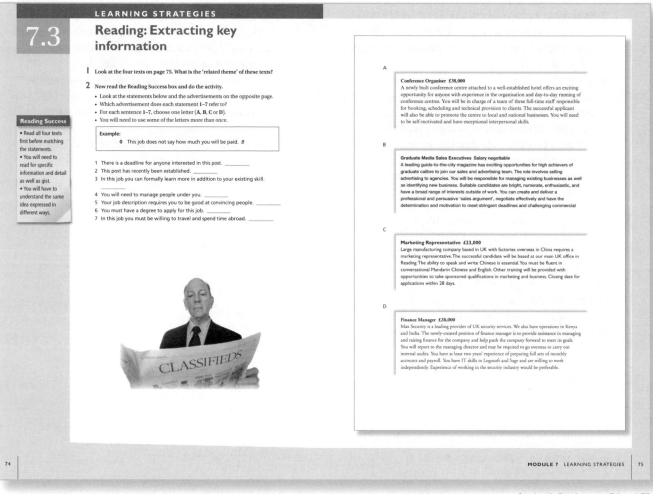

Student's Book pages 74 and 75

1 Students should read the texts briefly to answer the question.

Answer
They are all job adverts.

2 Refer students to the Reading Success tip and tell them to follow the guidelines when answering questions 1–7.

Answers
1 C   2 D   3 C   4 A   5 B   6 B   7 D

Extension 1
To provide more practice with this kind of task and to develop reading skills, cut out a number of job adverts from a newspaper or on the Internet. Put students into groups of three and give them four adverts. They then swap their adverts and sentences with another group and try to match them. Note that you could do the same with any short texts on a similar theme.

Extension 2
For further practice with writing letters, ask students to choose one of the adverts and write a letter of application for the position. It may be helpful to refer them back to the work they did in Unit 2 on this topic.

Overview

8.1 Business topic: Training

READING   **Training courses**

LISTENING   **Assessing training needs**

SPEAKING   **Giving reasons for and against**

GRAMMAR   ***-ing* form and infinitive**

SPEAKING   **Discussing training needs**

8.2 Business skills: Showing you're listening

READING   **The importance of listening**

LISTENING   **Good and bad listeners**

SPEAKING   **Showing you're listening**

VOCABULARY   **Linking phrases**

LISTENING   **Responding to a letter of complaint**

WRITING   **A letter of complaint**

8.3 Learning strategies: Short monologues

Matching speakers to opinions

PHOTOCOPIABLE

© 2009 Heinle, Cengage Learning

Useful language from Module 8

Wordlist

achieve results	databases	joint responsibility	presentation skills
action	duration	key factors	role
avoid interruption	effective	lead a project	single user
coach	enrol	leader	spreadsheets
complaint	face-to-face training	meet objectives	strengthen/ maintain the team
course	formulate a response	negotiating	
cross-cultural awareness		network	team building
		powerpoint	

Expressions

Another good reason is …

I don't think …

It's great because …

One advantage is that …

One argument against that idea is …

One big disadvantage with that is …

The other thing (reason) is that …

The problem is that …

You're right but I also think …

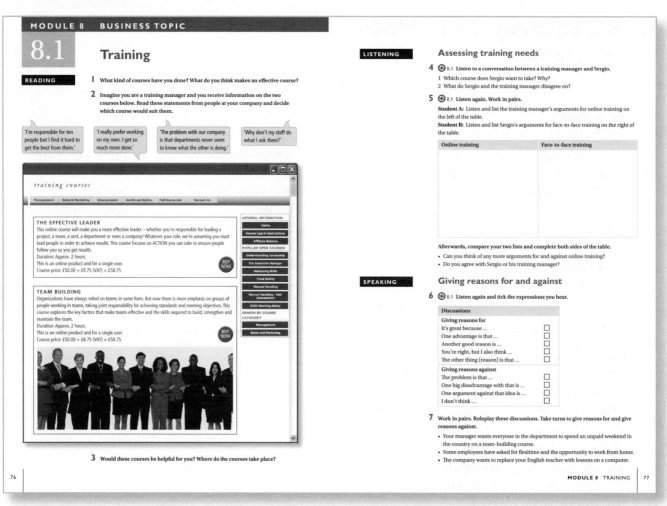

Training courses

READING

1 Discuss the questions as a class. Brainstorm reasons for an effective course.

Possible reasons
- the teacher
- the other people on the course
- the facilities
- the approach / methods
- how much it responds to your needs
- the extras (lunch, comfort, etc)

Extension
If any of your students have done courses by distance learning or online, ask them to describe how it worked and what the experience was like. How did it compare to face-to-face training?

2 Begin by asking students to read about the two courses and then consider each of the four statements.

Answers
- The people in the first and fourth statement would probably benefit from the Effective Leader course because they are both having problems with their staff.
- The other people in the second and third statement refer to situations where people are not working well with others.

3 Students discuss the two courses and say if they think they would be useful for them. Students should note that these courses take place online. We know this because of the words: 'This is an online product and for a single user.'

Assessing training needs

LISTENING Track I (CD2)

4 8.1 Students listen and take brief notes.

Answers
1 Sergio wants to take both of the courses because they will help him with his new role.
2 They disagree on whether online training is as effective as face-to-face training.

8.1 Listening script

M = Manager   S = Sergio

M Come in … oh hello, Sergio.

S Hi. Sorry for being late. Someone needed to speak to me. Anyway, I've looked at those courses you suggested doing …

M And?

S Yes, they both look good. I'm interested in doing both of them.

M Good. I thought they might help with your new role.

S Yes, well. It involves telling people what to do but I'm also working with other managers too.

M OK. So would you like to enrol for both of them?

S Yes, but I can't afford to take any more time off this month. I'm already behind.

M But these are online. You don't need to go away.

S What do you mean?

M Online means you train by using the Internet. I think you receive articles to read and you have a tutor who contacts you by email.

S Oh, I see. I remember doing something similar by post. I got books to read and had some exercises.

M Yes, like that but on the Internet. It's great because you don't have to go away and you arrange things around your work.

S The problem is that I'd prefer to have a course with other people in a room. You get lots of new ideas that way. Especially on a course called Team Building. If I do it online, I won't have the opportunity for networking with people. And you can ask the tutor questions.

M You're right, but I also think many online courses even have a place where you communicate with other people on the course.

S Hmm. But I don't think it is the same. Besides, if I'm working at my desk I always stop to answer the phone or someone asks me to do something.

M Well, why not do it from home?

S I don't understand …

M Take an afternoon off and use your computer from home. That way no one can interrupt you. The other thing is that if you want to do both courses it's cheaper if you do them online …

5 💿 8.1 Students listen again but, working in pairs, they listen out for information for one of the speakers only. They then share their notes to complete the table.

Alternative

You can ask students to listen and take notes on both views. This is obviously appropriate for a one-to-one class. In this case you might need to play the listening twice.

Answers

Online training:
– you don't need to go away
– you arrange things around your work
– you can communicate with other people on the course
– you can do it from home
– it's cheaper

Face-to-face training:
– you get new ideas from other people on the course
– networking
– you can ask the tutor questions

Afterwards, students discuss the arguments and think of some more, eg doing a face-to-face course allows you to go away and concentrate on the course rather than being interrupted. However, providers of online courses would say that Sergio's arguments for face-to-face are in fact responded to online, eg you can network or email the tutor questions. End the discussion by finding out which students in your class agree or disagree with Sergio.

Giving reasons for and against

SPEAKING Track 1 (CD2)

6 💿 8.1 Students listen again for the expressions.

Answers
It's great because …
You're right, but I also think …
The other thing (reason) is that …
The problem is that …
I don't think …

7 Students can roleplay these discussions in pairs, or you could put them into small groups of three or four. Set a time limit of three minutes for each issue and make sure students use the expressions. They could tick each expression as they use it to ensure all nine are said.

GRAMMAR

-ing form and infinitive

1 Look at what Sergio says in listening 8.1.

Sorry for being late. Someone needed to speak to me. Anyway, I've looked at those courses you suggested doing …

Match the underlined verbs to the explanations 1–3:

1 Use the *-ing* form after a preposition.
2 Some verbs are followed by the *-ing* form.
3 Some verbs are followed by the infinitive form.

2 Complete these sentences from the conversation between Sergio and his training manager. Write the verb in brackets as an *-ing* form or infinitive.

1 I'm interested in _____ (do) both of them.
2 It involves _____ (tell) people what to do …
3 So would you like _____ (enrol) for both of them?
4 Yes, but I can't afford _____ (take) any more time off this month.
5 Online means you train by _____ (use) the Internet.
6 Oh, I see. I remember _____ (do) something similar by post.
7 The problem is that I'd prefer _____ (have) a course with other people in a room.
8 If I do it online, I won't have the opportunity for _____ (network) with people.
9 If I'm working at my desk I always stop _____ (answer) the phone …
10 The other thing is that if you want _____ (do) both courses it's cheaper …

3 Some verbs can be followed either by an *-ing* form or an infinitive. Look at these pairs of sentences and decide if there is a big difference in meaning.

1 A: Would you like to play tennis?
  B: Do you like playing tennis?
2 A: Do you like to eat out?
  B: Do you like eating out?
3 A: They've started to advertise for a new receptionist.
  B: They've started advertising for a new receptionist.
4 A: I stopped working there years ago.
  B: I stopped to work on this new project.
5 A: We prefer to stay at home during the week.
  B: We prefer staying at home during the week.

4 Read this conversation. Underline the correct word.

Manager Hi, Sergio. Take a seat. (1) *Would / Do* you like to have coffee?
Sergio That would be nice. Two sugars, please.
Manager Oh I'm sorry. I didn't remember (2) *to ask / asking* for any this week. I only have milk, I'm afraid.
Sergio No problem. I'll have it black, please.
Manager Really? I (3) *can't stand / hate* to drink it without milk. Anyway, about your course. We've (4) *arranged / recommended* sending you away for a few days rather than doing it online. Is that OK with you?
Sergio Sure. I always (5) *prefer / enjoy* to work with a group of people rather than on my own …

SPEAKING

Discussing training needs

5 Work in pairs and roleplay this situation.

Student A: You are a training manager. You sent the memo below to all staff. Meet with an employee to discuss which courses will be useful for him or her to attend. Use some of these phrases:
Which courses would you like …?
Would you prefer …?
Do you want …?
Are you interested in …?
How good are you at …?
How much of your job involves …?

Student B: Read this memo from your training manager and discuss which courses might be suitable. Try to use some of these phrases:
I'd like … / I wouldn't like …
I'm (not) interested in …
I'm quite good at …
I can't afford …
My job involves …

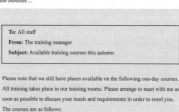

To: All staff
From: The training manager
Subject: Available training courses this autumn

Please note that we still have places available on the following one-day courses. All training takes place in our training rooms. Please arrange to meet with me as soon as possible to discuss your needs and requirements in order to enrol you.

The courses are as follows:
• effective selling
• presentation skills
• negotiating by phone
• cross-cultural awareness
• team building
• leading a project
• spreadsheets and databases
• computer skills 1 & 2 (building and maintaining a website)

78   MODULE 8 TRAINING   79

Student's Book pages 78 and 79

-ing form and infinitive

GRAMMAR

1 The grammar in this section uses the conversation between Sergio and his training manager as the context. In this exercise, students match the underlined use of the *-ing* forms or the infinitive to explanations 1–3.

Answers
1 for being
2 suggested doing
3 needed to speak

2 Ask students to complete sentences 1–10. They might find it helpful to look at the grammar summary on page 130 which includes lists of verbs followed by the infinitive or the *-ing* form. Note that the verb *stop* in sentence 9 can be followed by either but the meaning will change. This issue is addressed in exercise 3. You could play the listening again for students to check their answers, or they could read the listening script on page 140.

Answers
1 doing
2 telling
3 to enrol
4 to take
5 using
6 doing
7 to have
8 networking
9 to answer
10 to do

3 Students compare the sentences and decide whether there's a big or small difference in meaning. Ask them to try and say why when you check the answers.

Answers
1 Big difference: A is an invitation to play tennis in the future. B is a question about the person's general interests. Also point out to students that when they see the verb *would* in this kind of question, the next verb will be in the infinitive.

2 Little difference. *Like* can be followed by either form and for these two questions, the answer will be the same.

3 Little difference.

4 Big difference: A refers to the end of a continued activity. B implies that one activity was interrupted in favour of another.

5 Little difference.

4 Students check their understanding by underlining the correct word.

Answers

1 Would

2 to ask

3 hate

4 recommended

5 prefer

Extension

You could give students more practice by asking students to prepare sentences about themselves with these words. Write them on the board:

I always prefer ...

My dream is that one day, I'd like to ...

One thing I can't stand is ...

On my way to work/college today I remembered to ...

When I was younger I remember ...

Students then say their sentences to their partner.

Photocopiable activity 8.1

See page 170.

Discussing training needs

SPEAKING

5 Students work in pairs but give them time to read the details in the memo. They should also think about how they will use the phrases in the roleplay because they will need to use *-ing* forms and infinitives.

Allow plenty of time for the discussion. Monitor and give feedback on any correct and incorrect uses of the forms. Afterwards, students could swap their roles and repeat the situation.

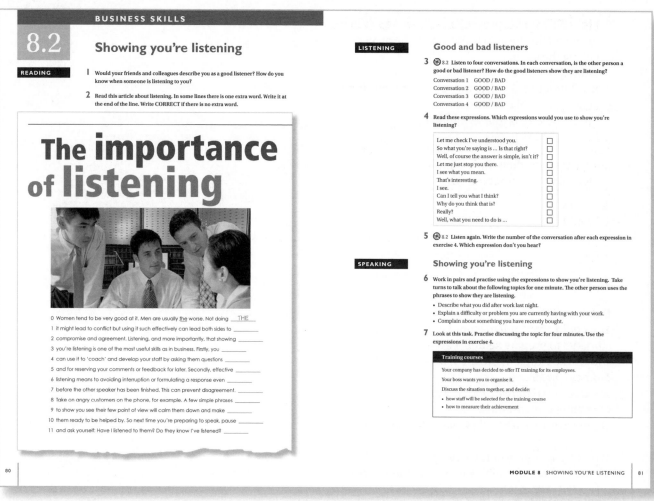

Student's Book pages 80 and 81

The importance of listening

READING

1 If the students know each other quite well, they could comment on each other and say if they think their colleague is a good listener.

Extension

Ask students to describe a friend or person at work or their place of study who they consider to be a good listener. Find out why students think this.

2 Students read the article and correct it.

Answers

1 SUCH	7 BEEN
2 THAT	8 ON
3 AS	9 FEW
4 CORRECT	10 BY
5 FOR	11 CORRECT
6 TO	

Extension

Discuss the views in the article. Do your students agree that women are better than men at listening? What are the ways the article says you can show you are listening? (By asking questions and reserving feedback for later, avoiding interruption and using certain phrases.) Ask students to suggest language or phrases that they might use in English.

Good and bad listeners

LISTENING   Track 2 (CD2)

3 🔘 8.2 As students listen, they should also note the language and expressions used.

Answers

Conversation 1: Good. The person asks questions and uses encouraging words like '*Really?*'

Conversation 2: Bad. The person interrupts and gives an opinion straightaway.

Conversation 3: Bad. The person says what to do without finding out how the other person feels.

Conversation 4: Good. The person checks and shows understanding.

8.2 Listening script

Conversation 1

A So what happened?

B Well, we all went out. We had the restaurant booked for eight. Anyway, everyone seemed to be having a good time, but it all went wrong in the end.

A Really?

B We had dinner and then of course they wanted to discuss the final part of the deal. I'd wanted to leave it until the morning but they were keen to finish things off.

A I see. Why do you think that is?

B I guess they were under pressure from their bosses to get a deal and go home …

Conversation 2

A Hello, Grainger and co.

B Hello, I have a problem with a coffee maker that you produce. Can I speak to …

A Sorry, let me just stop you there. Can I have your name first, please?

B It's Dana Lund.

A Well, what you need to do, Mr Lund, is to take it back to the place of purchase first. We only deal with online purchases …

B But I bought it from your website!

Conversation 3

A So I'm not really sure how I'm going to handle this one. I don't think they really believe I know how to run a project.

B Well of course the answer is simple, isn't it? You just have to let them know that you're the boss. They're paid to listen to you. If they don't like it they can leave.

A I know, but I want to work in a good atmosphere where people feel motivated …

B I know you do, but can I tell you what I think? I think …

Conversation 4

A OK. So that brings me to the end. Are there any questions?

B Sorry. Let me check I've understood you.

A Sure. Go ahead.

B So what you're saying is that we can virtually halve our costs if we restructure in this way. Is that right?

A That's right. It won't be pleasant. It will mean job losses but I don't think we have a choice.

B Yes. I see what you mean.

A Of course, if anyone has any other ways of approaching this, then let's hear them …

4 Students tick useful expressions to show they're listening.

Answers

Let me check I've understood you.

So what you're saying is … Is that right?

I see what you mean.

That's interesting.

I see.

Why do you think that is?

Really?

Pronunciation

Ask students to notice the intonation on these expressions from the list:

Really?

Is that right?

The intonation rises at the end in both cases. Drill and practise this with the class.

5 8.2 Play the four conversations again. Students write the number of the conversation (1, 2, 3 or 4) after each expression. One expression isn't used.

Answer

Let me check I've understood you. **4**

So what you're saying is … Is that right? **4**

Well of course the answer is simple, isn't it? **3**

Let me just stop you there … **2**

I see what you mean. **4**

That's interesting. **(not used)**

I see. **1**

Can I tell you what I think? **3**

Why do you think that is? **1**

Really? **1**

Well what you need to do is … **2**

Showing you're listening

SPEAKING

6 Students might want to take a few minutes to make notes on each of the topics. When they start speaking, their partner needs to use phrases to show they're listening.

Extension

To change the format slightly and add some fun, the listening student can decide whether to be a good or bad listener. If they choose to be a bad listener, they can try to interrupt and say what they think all the time. This makes it harder for the speaker but presents them with a very real problem when dealing with a bad listener.

7 Explain that even when you aren't speaking, it's important to show you are listening and continue to be active during conversation.

Afterwards, you can give feedback on their listening skills as well as their performance in dealing with the topic. It might be helpful for students to repeat the task with a new partner.

VOCABULARY Linking phrases

1 You work for a training company and receive this letter. In which paragraph do you find out ...
- the purpose of the letter?
- what happened?
- what action the sender requires?

1st May

Dear Mr Le Fevre

Following the recent experiences of two of my staff with your training company, I have decided to send you some feedback based on their comments.

On the 25th April, they attended a two-day computer course in creating PowerPoint presentations. **However**, on the first day the trainer arrived 30 minutes late, which was followed by a further delay **due to** a room change. **As a result** of this nearly 90 minutes was missed. **In addition to** this, my staff inform me that the approach of the trainer was to let participants 'discover' solutions to problems rather than being told what to do.

Despite having been very satisfied with your services in the past I may have to reconsider sending staff in the future. I would be grateful to hear any comments you have to make either by phone or in writing.

I look forward to hearing from you.

Yours sincerely

A Heneage

Mrs A Heneage
Human Resources

Learning Tip
Underline any useful expressions in the letter which you would like to use in your own writing.

2 Look at the words in bold in the letter. Write them into this table.

Cause and effect	Contrasting	Additional information
because of	(4) _____	(6) _____
(1) _____	Nevertheless	Furthermore
(2) _____	(5) _____	Moreover
(3) _____	(verb + ... -ing)	

3 Complete sentences 1–6 with a suitable word or phrase from the table.

1 I am writing _____ a problem with a product I recently bought from you.
2 The advert contains misleading information. _____, it is unsuitable for children.
3 I have complained about this twice before. _____, you have continually taken no action to resolve the issue.
4 _____ having written to them, she has received no reply.
5 We will no longer use your services in the future. _____ we will be contacting our lawyers to discuss possible legal action.
6 _____ further increases in your prices, we are changing supplier.

82

LISTENING Responding to a letter of complaint

4 🔊 8.3 As a result of Mrs Heneage's letter, Mr Le Fevre calls Fred Perrot, who is in charge of computer training. Listen to the call and make notes about the reasons for the problems outlined in Mrs Heneage's letter.

5 Now complete Mr Le Fevre's reply to Mrs Heneage using the information in your notes from exercise 4.

Dear Mrs Heneage

With regard to your concerns about the PowerPoint course on (1) _____ _____, I have now spoken to my head of computer training and as a result I am in a position to respond.

Unfortunately, and due to circumstances beyond our control on that day, the head of training (2) _____. As a result (3) _____ and he was somewhat late. For this I apologise, but because of this delay (4) _____ .

Secondly, there was a room change which was due to the fact that (5) _____ _____.

Finally, our approach to training has always been based on a (6) '_____ _____ approach'.

Moreover, it has always received (7) _____.

Following this letter, I would like to suggest a meeting at your convenience to discuss any remaining issues and your future training needs ...

WRITING A letter of complaint

6 Work in pairs. You will write a letter to each other and then write the reply. You recently stayed at a hotel. Your partner is the manager. Read the notes on the problems.

- There was no record of the booking at reception – I waited 45 minutes.
- The meeting room was double-booked – had to meet clients in smaller room.
- The towels were not changed in the bathroom overnight – room service said this was hotel policy based on 'environmental reasons'.

Write a letter to the hotel manager (your partner). Write 120–140 words using appropriate linking words or expressions.

Swap letters with your partner. Now you are the hotel manager. Write a reply to the letter. Respond to each complaint, again using appropriate linking words or phrases.

Student's Book pages 82 and 83

Linking phrases

VOCABULARY

1 This initial task focuses students on the importance of structure in a letter and how to organise the paragraphs. Ask students to find out where the three pieces of information are and to summarise the purpose, what happened and what action is required.

Answers
- The purpose is always in the first paragraph of the letter. In this case the purpose is to complain.
- The explanation of what happened is in the second paragraph where more detail is generally given in a letter to support the first paragraph. In this case, the trainer was late and sessions were delayed. The two members of staff also didn't like the trainer's approach.
- The final paragraph should explain the action the sender requires. The sender wants to receive an explanation.

2 Point out to the students that the linking phrases in this section will be useful in all of their business writing, not only letters of complaint. Students categorise the linking phrases from the letter.

Answers

1 Following	4 However
2 due to	5 Despite*
3 As a result of	6 In addition to

*Note the verb construction that follows this linker.

3 Students complete the sentences. Note that there is more than one possible answer for some sentences.

Answers
1 as a result of / due to / following
2 Furthermore / Moreover
3 However / Nevertheless
4 Despite
5 Furthermore / Moreover
6 Following / As a result of / Due to

Photocopiable activity 8.2
See page 171.

Responding to a letter of complaint

LISTENING Track 3 (CD2)

4 🔊 8.3 Be prepared to play this listening twice as students need plenty of information in order to complete the letter in exercise 5. As a guide, tell students to note particular information such as dates, times and explanations by Fred Perrot.

8.3 Listening script

LF = Le Fevre   **P** = Perrot

LF Hello, Fred. It's Jean here.

P Hi, Jean.

LF Sorry to bother you but I've just received a letter from a client here. She isn't happy and I need to reply as soon as possible.

P Really? What's the problem?

LF Well, she's referring to a computer course in PowerPoint on the 25th April. Two people from her company Hollers and Fry were on the course.

P I think you mean on the 26th actually. The 25th was a Sunday.

LF Oh, OK. Anyway, you know about it?

P Well, I wasn't here. I was supposed to be but I had to take the day off work because of one of my children – she was sick. My wife was away so as a result I rang in early to see if we could get a replacement trainer. Anyway, we did and he was a little late. However, he's good. I know his work. And we added the lost time on to the end of each of the two days. Is that what they're complaining about?

LF Well, that's one thing. I didn't know you added the time back on. That's useful to know. And it's also because of a room change or something.

P OK. Well, that's because of them sending two people. Despite having told them the course was full and we could only take one of their people they still sent two. So rather than send one of them home we were able to switch training rooms and deal with it.

LF So that sounds like their fault. OK. And this last thing I'm less concerned about.

P What's that?

LF Oh, she says my staff inform me that the approach of the trainer was to let participants 'discover' solutions to problems rather than being told what to do.

P I'm sorry, Jean, but I'm always telling our computer trainers to follow a discovery approach. To do less talking and let trainees find out for themselves. And anyway, everyone else always gives us positive feedback because of this approach.

LF I know. I understand. Don't worry. That's all I need to know. I'm sure I can sort it out. Thanks, Fred.

P Bye.

5 Students use their notes to complete the letter. If students don't appear to have certain facts, you may need to play the listening again or let them check in the listening script on pages 140–141.

Answers

(allow for some variation)

1 the 26th April
2 was unavailable at short notice
3 we had to get a replacement trainer
4 we added the lost time on the end of the two days.
5 your company sent an extra person
6 discovery
7 positive feedback

A letter of complaint

WRITING

6 Students write their letter of complaint based on the notes and then swap roles to play the part of the hotel manager writing a reply. They should use the structure of the two letters in exercises 1 and 5, including any helpful expressions and linking phrases.

Possible answers

Dear Sir or Madam

Following my recent experience of your hotel, I have decided to send you some feedback in the hope that you can improve your services.

I arrived at reception at 6pm on 7th November to find there was no record of my booking. As a result of this I waited 45 minutes. The following day, my two clients and I were delayed due to the meeting room being double-booked. Eventually we were given another smaller room. Finally, towels were not changed overnight. Room service explained that this was because of the hotel's 'environmentally-friendly' policy. While I agree with the sentiment of this policy, I do not think that changing at least one towel is unreasonable.

Despite having been very satisfied with your services in the past I may have to reconsider using your hotel in the future. I would be grateful to hear any comments you have to make in writing.

Yours faithfully

Dear M ...

Thank you for your recent letter regarding your stay at our hotel. I regret that the experience did not achieve your normal expectations. I have now spoken to the staff involved and as a result I am in a position to comment.

Unfortunately, our online booking system has been undergoing some changes and this may have affected both your booking of a room and the meeting rooms. I apologise for any delays but please note that all our meeting rooms are equipped with the same level of services. With regard to the policy on towels, the hotel feels that it must play its part in working towards helping the environment and so we have recently considered a number of ways in which to achieve this. However, your comments on towels will be raised at our next meeting on this policy.

Following your letter therefore, I wish to apologise for any inconvenience caused. I would like to offer you a free two-day voucher, which can be used at this hotel in the future. We look forward to your next visit and any further feedback you have.

Best regards/Yours sincerely

LEARNING STRATEGIES

8.3　Listening: Short monologues

In this section you will practise understanding parts of conversations. This will test your ability to use key words to:
- understand the context
- identify the attitude of the speaker
- note important details.

When listening, it is important to think about the following.
1　What is the purpose of the speaker? What is his / her aim?
2　What is the role (job, position) of the speaker?
3　What opinion is he / she expressing?
4　What key vocabulary does he / she use?

I This is what the two speakers say in the recordings for questions 1 and 6. Try to answer the four questions above for each of the speakers below.

> Actually, it didn't tell me more than I already do. I suppose the parts on how to answer questions and working on convincing people was OK. But how to stand and when to use your hands seemed a bit excessive. And when he talked about visual aids I wondered if everyone else thought it was as pointless as me.

> Hi Joe. I'm just phoning to say I'll be in at three o'clock as planned. They had said there would be problems on the planes because of a strike but it seems to be OK now so I'll see you tomorrow.

Listening Success
- Listen for key words that give the context and meaning.

2 🔊 8.4 You will hear five short recordings. For each recording, decide which training course the speaker is referring to.
- Write one letter (A–H) next to the number of the recording.
- Do not use any letter more than once.

1	A　Managing teams
2	B　Using PowerPoint
3	C　Sales on the telephone
4	D　Effective presentations
5	E　Doing business with other cultures
	F　Report writing
	G　Marketing on the web
	H　Interviewing and staff selection

3 🔊 8.5 You will hear another five short recordings. Each speaker is on the phone. For each recording, decide what the main reason for the call is.
- Write one letter (A–H) next to the number of the recording.
- Do not use any letter more than once.

6	A　to complain
7	B　to explain a delay
8	C　to ask for information
9	D　to confirm arrangements
10	E　to report on plans
	F　to ask for confirmation
	G　to request help
	H　to speak to someone else

Student's Book pages 84 and 85

Tracks 4, 5 (CD2)

I Students try to answer the four questions listed, practising with the listening scripts for speakers 1 and 6.

Answers
(Views on key vocabulary may vary.)

1: Purpose: To describe a training course
　Role: A trainee on a course
　Opinion: Very critical
　Key vocabulary: the parts on how to answer questions / working on convincing people / how to stand / when to use your hands / bit excessive / visual aids / pointless

6: Purpose: To confirm arrangements
　Role: A colleague of Joe
　Opinion: Neutral / No opinion
　Key vocabulary: at three o'clock as planned / problems on planes / seems to be OK now / see you tomorrow

2 🔊 8.4, Refer students to the Listening Success tip before they begin the task. They should read the questions and predict the expressions they might hear.

Answers
1 D　2 F　3 A　4 H　5 E

3 🔊 8.5, Again, get students to read the questions and predict the expressions they might hear.

Answers
6 D　7 E　8 A　9 G　10 C

8.4 Listening script

Narrator One.
Speaker 1 Actually, it didn't tell me more than I already do. I suppose the parts on how to answer questions and working on convincing people was OK. But how to stand and when to use your hands seemed a bit excessive. And when he talked about visual aids I wondered if everyone else thought it was as pointless as me.

Narrator Two.
Speaker 2 We tend to cover areas such as planning and organisation. Then I give exercises on how to simplify your language, because so many of us seem to think that on paper we need to be more formal than when we speak. The trouble with that is that I find many people make quite simple information quite complicated.

Narrator Three.
Speaker 3 I really found the group activities useful. You know, we played some games and did roleplays to see what it was like to work with others and how to facilitate groups of people so they pull on each other's strengths and weaknesses.

Narrator Four.

Speaker 4 I've just started in HR so it'll be helpful in the future when departments contact me about finding people to join them. It's amazing how much you can tell about someone by the way they sit or their body language as well as asking the right questions. I also learnt about different methods of testing to assess characters and potential.

Narrator Five.

Speaker 5 You often think that people don't understand or wonder why teams don't get on. So it was interesting to think about how we all view the world in different ways. Even down to how we say hello and shake hands or bow. For example, did you know that it's rude to talk about business straight away in Brazil?

8.5 Listening script

Narrator Six.

Speaker 1 Hi Joe. I'm just phoning to say I'll be in at three o'clock as planned. They had said there would be problems on the planes because of a strike but it seems to be OK now so I'll see you tomorrow.

Narrator Seven.

Speaker 2 Hi. It's me. It's about the meeting you couldn't come to. Sorry your train was delayed, by the way. Anyway, just to say it was agreed we should start work on the 25th and Hamid thinks we'll make the schedule we talked about if we bring in one more person to act as site manager. I said I thought this would be OK as the budget allowed for it.

Narrator Eight.

Speaker 3 Good morning. I'm calling about your advert for a secretary that was in today's newspaper. I applied for that post two weeks ago and heard nothing back from you. I really think that if you didn't like my application you should have at least replied and let me know. Instead I discovered it in the paper!

Narrator Nine.

Speaker 4 I was wondering if you could call Lucy for me. I think I left the plans for the Royale Project at her office. If you have time, could you go round and pick them up because I'll need them for tomorrow. Sorry to bother you with it but I'm in our other office all today. I've been trying to call her all morning but she must be out. Can you try her this afternoon?

Narrator Ten.

Speaker 5 Hello, I'm calling about the overdraft facility you offer to customers with online banking. I was wondering how I can get it. Also, I'm not sure how to get an online account, so maybe you can tell me what I need to do.

Overview

9.1   Business topic: Branding

READING   **What's that smell?**

SPEAKING   **Discussing branding**

GRAMMAR   **Relative clauses**

9.2   Business skills: Getting through

LISTENING   **Getting through**

VOCABULARY   **Telephone words**

SPEAKING   **Making phone calls**

READING   **Email marketing**

SPEAKING   **Planning a newsletter**

WRITING   **Correcting and rewriting**

9.3   Learning strategies: Reports

A report

Understanding the task

Checking your written work

PHOTOCOPIABLE

© 2009 Heinle, Cengage Learning

Useful language from Module 9

Wordlist

(on) hold	displays	odour	subject line
aroma	distinguish (a	put through	suit
attachment	brand)	quality assurance	turnover
bear (with	fragrance	scent	unavailable
someone)	inbox	slogan	urgent
brand	jingle	smell	voicemail
brand identity	logo	spam	whiff
capitals	luxury	speech recognition	
consumers	obsession	technology	

Expressions

All of our operators are currently unavailable to answer your call.

Can I call you back?

Can I take your name, please?

Can you bear with me a second?

Could you connect me/put me through to ...?

Do you mind if we put the meeting back to Tuesday?

Hold on a moment.

I'm just going to put you on hold.

I'm just looking his number up on the computer.

I'm just putting you on hold for a moment.

Let me call you back later.

Let me read that back to you.

One moment, please.

Please hold.

Sorry, he's tied up with something at the moment. Can I help?

Sorry, the battery on my mobile is about to run out.

We'll bring the schedule forward by a week.

When would be convenient for you?

When would suit you?

MODULE 9   BUSINESS TOPIC

9.1   Branding

READING

1 What is your favourite brand of ...
- coffee?
- soap?
- clothes?

Tell your partner and explain why you choose that particular brand. Is your choice affected by the colour, packaging, advertising, price, logo? Do you ever buy a product or service because of its smell?

2 Read the article on page 87 and write in the correct letter, A–G, for the missing phrases.

A where the odour of waffle-cones were released into the air to encourage visitors to an out-of-the-way ice cream shop

B that his grandmother used to make

C which typically includes more than six smells

D whose recently-introduced cell phone keypad was lavender-scented

E when it began twelve years ago

F why so many companies are now associating brands with a scent

G who walk around reception will get a whiff of a chocolate chip cookie

SPEAKING

Discussing branding

3 Try to complete the sentences below about what you have read. Tell your partner what you think.
- One thing that interests me about this is ...
- One thing that surprises me is ...
- One thing that I find hard to believe is ...

4 What smell could you use to brand the following? You can use the suggestions in the pictures.
- your company's product or service
- your school or college
- a new range of clothing
- bicycles
- a language course

What's that smell?

David Van Epps opens his briefcase and touches several of the 72 bottles inside. 'Here's one you'll like,' he says, taking the top off one. He dips a paper strip inside and waves it under his nose, breathing in deeply. It smells of sugar and butter like the 'sugar cookies' (1) _____. It also makes him think of money: sugar cookies is only one of 1,480 fragrances sold by Van Epps' company ScentAir Technologies and used to improve brand identity.

Fragrance is as much a marketing tool these days as a logo, a slogan or a jingle. Sony puts its customers 'in the mood' for buying in its stores with the smell of vanilla and mandarin. At some Doubletree Hotels guests (2) _____. And Proctor and Gamble has experimented with ScentAir scents to attract shoppers to displays in stores, says Van Epps. 'What's better than having a brand people want to use because of fragrance?'

ScentAir first started putting that attitude into bottles (3) _____. ScentAir will charge as much as $25,000 to create a custom blend, (4) _____. This year turnover has quadrupled as more marketers use scents to distinguish their brands.

Once a client selects a scent, ScentAir puts the liquid aroma in a cartridge that fits inside a device with a fan which pushes the smell into the air. You control the strength with a dial. Monthly refills are $100 per device.

Some companies want to make shoppers wait around longer in the hope they will spot something to buy. It seems to have worked at the Hard Rock Hotel in Orlando, (5) _____. Sales jumped 45% in the first six months after a ScentAir device was installed. Westin Hotels and Resorts contacted ScentAir for a white tea fragrance to put in its 127 properties. Added to this, the hotels have just started selling white tea-scented items, including $36 candles.

Alan Hirsch of the Smell and Taste Treatment and Research Foundation in Chicago explains the reason (6) _____. 'Smell has a greater impact on purchasing than everything else combined. If something smells good, the product is perceived as good.' There's LG Electronics (7) _____, or the cherry smell from billboards advertising a new shampoo from L'Oreal. All we need now is a PC that can pick up aromas from websites.

86

Student's Book pages 86 and 87

What's that smell?

READING

1 Students discuss the questions in pairs before reporting back to the class. Encourage students to give specific examples of brands that they like or think are particularly effective.

2 Students complete the article with the phrases, A–G.

Answers
1 B 2 G 3 E 4 C 5 A 6 F 7 D

Extension

For more vocabulary and reading practice, ask students to underline:
1 any smells (they may need bilingual dictionaries to check understanding of these smells);
2 examples of how companies have used these smells;
3 synonyms for the word *smell*.

Answers
1 Sugar and butter, vanilla and mandarin, white tea, lavender, cherry.
2 In stores to put customers in the mood for buying, attract customers to displays, make shoppers wait longer, visit a hotel ice cream shop, to create the perception that the product is good, on mobile phone keypads and on billboards
3 odour, scent, fragrance, aroma

Discussing branding

SPEAKING

3 Students work alone to complete the three beginnings of sentences. Students then compare their views and continue discussing the article.

Possible answers
One thing that interests me about this is that smell can have such an effect on humans.
One thing that surprises me is that ScentAir's turnover has quadrupled as a result.

4 Put students into groups of three to discuss each of the five items. One person in each group should make notes on their decisions and which smells they will use. At the end, each group can report back to the class.

Photocopiable activity 9.1
See page 172.

GRAMMAR

Relative clauses

We often add information or more detail to the main clause of the sentence.
For example, the speaker may want to say what type of company he works for:

ScentAir is a company which sells scents.

Main clause | Relative clause

1 Complete the defining relative clauses in these sentences with a word from the box.

| when | where | why | which | who | whose |

1 The new product _____ goes on sale next month isn't ready yet.
2 The turnover was just under half a million _____ it was first founded in 1985. Now it's a hundred million.
3 The people _____ work for us are all highly qualified.
4 We like to think we're a supportive company _____ staff are loyal.
5 Let me explain some of the reasons _____ we're making these changes.
6 The company _____ I used to work is closing down, apparently.

2 Underline the two relative clauses in this extract from a report.

We're a Swedish company which has controlling shares in three subsidiaries and a large stake in one smaller division. It is recommended therefore that we focus our financial interests on the smaller subsidiary, which incidentally is also based in Sweden.

3 Work in pairs and answer these questions about relative clauses.

1 Which relative clause – defining or non-defining – adds necessary information?
2 Which relative clause – defining or non-defining – adds extra but non-essential information?
3 What punctuation do you need with a non-defining relative clause?
4 Look back at the relative clauses in the article *What's that smell?* Which are defining and which are non-defining?
5 In defining relative clauses you can replace *which* or *who* with another pronoun. What is the pronoun?

4 Add the second sentence to the first using the word in brackets.

0 (which) I work for a large multinational based in Sydney. We employ over three thousand people.
I work for a large multinational based in Sydney which employs over three thousand people.

1 (who) Let me introduce you to David. He's the director of our company.
_____

2 (where) This is the main factory. We produce car parts.
_____

3 (which) This is our latest product. It's also our biggest seller.
_____

4 (when) The company had a turnover of about a million euros in 2004. It was founded in 2004. _____

5 Complete the relative clauses to make sentences about you.

• I work for a company which ...
• I study at a college / school that ...
• The best kind of boss is someone who ...
• I first applied for this job / course when ...
• In the future I'd like to work in a country where ...
• ... is the reason why I'm studying English.

6 Combine the two sentences, using a non-defining relative clause.

0 David Van Epps sells over 1,480 fragrances. His favourite smell is chocolate chip cookie.
David Van Epps, whose favourite smell is chocolate chip cookie, sells over 1,480 fragrances.

1 My company has offices all over the world. It's based in Sydney.
_____

2 Mrs Sayers says she has an appointment with you. She's waiting in reception.
_____

3 The man called this morning to see if we had his briefcase. We found his briefcase last night.
_____

4 The report is in your in-tray. I've just finished it.
_____

READING

7 Read about luxury brands in China. Each line contains one mistake (including punctuation). Correct it.

Chinese luxury obsession

0 When that many people visit cities in China, they are still surprised to see the luxury [which]
00 brands who normally fill the fashion boutiques of New York and Paris. But in a
1 country which more and more young people have become big-spending consumers,
2 the world's top brands attract twenty- and thirty-somethings what, in a recent survey,
3 say they want to 'seize every opportunity to enjoy life.' Take Miss Yu, who's monthly
4 salary is 5,000 yuan working as a journalist. She regularly stops by the boutiques where,
5 you can find Louis Vuitton or Gucci. She explains the reason when: 'I think a bag worth 10,000 yuan
6 is more suitable for me than 100 bags at 100 yuan each.' And her fashion collection, whose includes
7 names such as Chanel, Burberry and Prada, is far from unique in a country why the proportion
8 of luxury goods purchased nowadays, is 40% compared to only 4% globally.

Student's Book pages 88 and 89

Relative clauses

GRAMMAR

Ask students to read the information about relative clauses. They could also refer to the grammary summary on page 130 for more detailed information.

1 Students complete the sentences with the correct relative pronoun. These pronouns should be familiar to students at this level.

Answers
1 which
2 when
3 who
4 whose
5 why
6 where

Extension
Write the following on the board and the relative pronouns in a jumbled list. Ask students to match the pronoun to what it refers to: (answers in brackets)

person (*who*)
thing/item (*which*)
possession (*whose*)
location (*where*)
reason (*why*)
time (*when*)

2 The aim of this exercise is to draw students' attention to the fact that there are two types of relative clauses (defining and non-defining).

Answer
We're a Swedish company <u>which has controlling shares in three subsidiaries and a large stake in one smaller division</u>. It is recommended therefore that we focus our financial interests on the smaller subsidiary, <u>which incidentally is also based in Sweden</u>.

3 Students analyse the key differences between the two clauses by referring back to exercise 2. They may also need to refer to and check their answers in the grammar summary on page 130.

Answers
1 defining
2 non-defining
3 commas
4 The sentences in the text on page 87 containing relative clauses are those which were completed with A–G in exercise 2 on page 86. If students seem unsure, tell them that if there is a comma it will be non-defining.

Defining:
... that his grandmother used to make
... who walk around reception will get a whiff of a chocolate chip cookie
... when it began 12 years ago
... why so many companies are now associating brands with a scent

Non-defining:
... which typically includes more than six smells
... where the odour of waffle-cones were released into the air to encourage visitors to an out-of-the way ice cream shop
... whose recently-introduced cell phone keypad was lavender-scented
5 that

4 Students study the example and complete sentences 1–4.

Answers
1 Let me introduce you to David who's the director of our company.
2 This is the main factory where we produce car parts.
3 This is our latest product which is also our biggest seller.
4 The company had a turnover of about a million euros in 2004 when it was founded in 2004.

5 Students personalise the grammar focus with sentences of their own.

Possible answers
I work for a company **which produces software**.
I study at a college **that specialises in business courses**.
The best kind of boss is someone **who doesn't interfere**.

Extension
Students could compare their sentences in pairs or groups.

6 Tell students to make the sentences non-defining. They should insert the clause in the middle of the sentence.

Answers
1 My company, which is based in Sydney, has offices all over the world.
2 Mrs Sayers, who's waiting in reception, says she has an appointment with you.
3 The man, whose briefcase we found last night, called this morning to see if we had it.
4 The report, which I've just finished, is in your in-tray.

Pronunciation
You could help students focus on the pronunciation of non-defining relative clauses at this stage by drilling the four sentences in exercise 6. Students need to note that there will be a slight pause where there are commas and that the intonation often rises before the first comma to indicate the speaker has more to say. You could mark the sentences on the board like this:

1 My company, / which is based in Sydney, /

has offices all over the world.

2 Mrs Sayers, / who's waiting in reception, /

says she has an appointment with you.

3 The man, / whose briefcase we found last night, /

called this morning to see if we had it.

4 The report, / which I've just finished, /

is in your in-tray.

Chinese luxury obsession

READING

7 This task requires students to read a text very carefully, and correct any pronouns or features of relative clauses (such as commas).

Answers
1 ~~which~~ where
2 ~~what~~ who
3 ~~who's~~ whose
4 where, (delete comma)
5 ~~when~~ why
6 ~~whose~~ which
7 ~~why~~ where
8 nowadays, (delete comma)

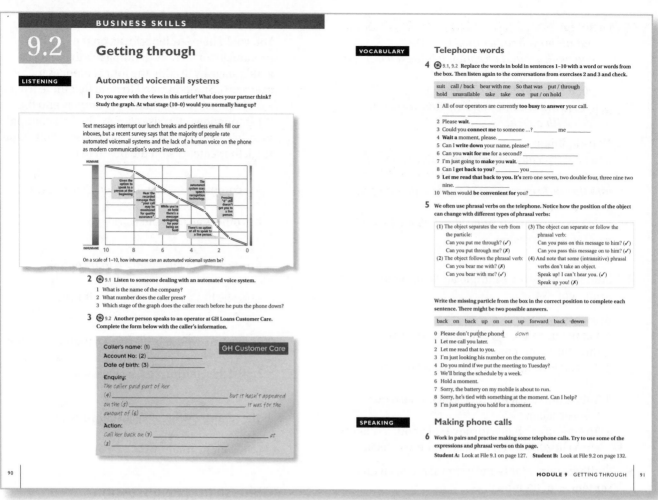

Student's Book pages 90 and 91

Automated voicemail systems

LISTENING Tracks 6, 7 (CD2)

I   Ask the students what they think is the worst invention of the modern age, eg the car, the mobile phone, etc. They then compare their ideas with the view in the article. Find out at which point on the scale (1–10) most students give up listening to an automated voice mail system. Also find out if their companies use them.

2   9.1 Play the recording of someone having to deal with an automated voicemail system.

Answers
1 GH Loans.
2 The caller presses 2 because he wants to speak to an operator.
3 The caller reaches 3 on the scale before he puts the phone down because the system uses speech recognition technology which requires him to answer 'Yes' or 'No'.

9.1 Listening script

C = Caller   M = Machine

C   Hello, I'd like to speak to …
M   Hello. Thank you for calling GH Loans Customer Care. You will now hear a number of options. Please press the

option you require. For a statement, press 1, for early repayment, press 2, for any other enquiry or to speak to one of our operators, press 3 … Thank you.
C   Hello, I'm calling about …
M   Thank you for calling GH Loans. Please note that your call may be monitored for quality assurance and training purposes.
M   We're sorry but all of our operators are currently unavailable to take your call. Please hold. Your call is important to us.
M   Hello. You're through to our loans department.
C   Could you put me through to someone …
M   To help us deal with your call quickly and efficiently, please answer the following questions with 'yes' or 'no'. Do you currently have an account with …

3   9.2 This second call successfully reaches an operator. Students listen and complete the information.

Answers
1 Abi Kaye
2 TI3662
3 21st April 1981
4 loan early last month
5 statement
6 five thousand euros
7 0172443929
8 four

9.2 Listening script

O = Operator   C = Caller

O Hello, you're through to Katrina. How can I help you this morning?

C Oh hello, it's with regard to a statement I received. I think there's been a mistake.

O OK. One moment, please. Can I take your name, please?

C Yes, it's Abi Kaye.

O Can you spell that for me?

C Sure. Abi. A-B-I. Kaye. K-A-Y-E.

O And do you have an account number?

C Yes. TI3662.

O Sorry. Was that T for Thailand, I as in India?

C That's correct.

O And for security can I have your date of birth?

C The 21st of April, 1981.

O That's fine, Ms Kaye. So how can I help you?

C Well, I paid off part of my loan early last month but I received a statement from you this morning and it isn't on the statement. Could you tell me if the payment has gone through?

O Right. I don't see it. Can you bear with me for a second? I'm just going to put you on hold.

C Sure.

O Hello. Sorry to keep you waiting. I'm afraid I can't find a record of it. How much was it for?

C Five thousand euros.

O I'll have to check this for you. Can I call you back?

C Yes, please.

O What's your number, Ms Kaye?

C Zero one seven, two double four, three nine two nine.

O So that was zero one seven, two double four, three nine two nine.

C That's right. What time do you think you'll call back because I have to go out now?

O When would suit you?

C At four.

O That's fine. Speak to you then. Goodbye.

C Bye.

Telephone words

VOCABULARY Tracks 6, 7 (CD2)

4 9.1, 9.2 Ask students to try to complete 1–10 before they listen. If your students have difficulties, you could play the conversations again to help them.

Answers
1 unavailable / take
2 hold
3 put / through
4 One
5 take
6 bear with me
7 put (you) on hold
8 call (you) back
9 So that was
10 suit

Pronunciation
Students often have problems saying the words *convenient, unavailable* and *suit* so you may want to drill these. It will also be helpful to drill the entire phrases from exercise 4. Make sure your students' intonation sounds friendly and polite.

5 Give students time to study the rules for phrasal verbs and how the position of the object can change in some cases. Once they have looked at this, let them complete 1–9. Note that they should also try to write two answers where possible.

Answers
1 Let me call you back later.
2 Let me read that back to you.
3 I'm just looking up his number on the computer. / I'm just looking his number up on the computer.
4 Do you mind if we put the meeting back to Tuesday? / Do you mind if we put back the meeting to Tuesday?
5 We'll bring the schedule forward by a week. / We'll bring forward the schedule by a week.
6 Hold on a moment.
7 Sorry, the battery on my mobile is about to run out.
8 Sorry, he's tied up with something at the moment. Can I help?
9 I'm just putting you on hold for a moment.

Making phone calls

SPEAKING

6 Students carry out similar roleplays to the situation in listening 9.2. Student A looks at File 9.1 on page 127 and Student B looks at File 9.2 on page 132. They take turns to call and must complete notes in a message.

Possible answers
Student A's message (File 9.1):

Caller: Mr/Ms Jakuczik
Message: He/She rang to postpone meeting with Mr Vathone on 24th in Hong Kong.
Account number: YE99-087
Call back at: 7pm (US time).

Student B's message (File 9.2):

Caller: Mr/Ms Jingshan
Message: He/She paid $3,760 into account, but it isn't on this month's statement.
Account number: HIE364 4756
Call back at: [students decide time] on 980 765 55 44

Photocopiable activity 9.2
See page 173.

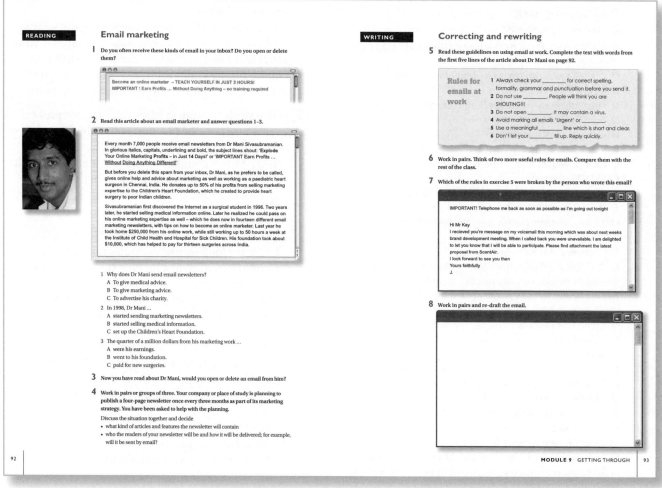

Student's Book pages 92 and 93

Email marketing

READING

I Discuss the questions as a class. Check that students know the word 'spam' which is often used to refer to unwanted emails. Students should also be familiar with the words 'junk email' which many email programs can now identify and prevent from arriving in your inbox.

2 Students read the article and answer questions 1–3.

Answers
1 B 2 B 3 A

3 Discuss the question with the class. Dr Mani is an interesting case in terms of unwanted emails because part of the money he makes from sending spam goes to charity. For this reason, students might have to think twice about deleting his emails.

4 It will be helpful if one student takes notes on what the newsletter will include and who will receive it. This information can be presented to the class at the end.

Extension

With pre-work learners on college courses or on courses where you have plenty of time for project work, it may be appropriate to set up a project where students produce a newsletter, possibly for their place of study. This lesson would be a good moment to introduce the concept and find out what students would like to include.

Correcting and rewriting

WRITING

5 Students will find the six missing words in the first five lines of the article on page 92.

Answers
1 email
2 capitals
3 spam (or) email newsletters
4 important
5 subject
6 inbox

6 Students try to add more tips to the six listed in exercise 5.

Possible answers
- With emails to people you don't know, use formal expressions such as *Dear ... , I am writing to ... , I look forward to ... .*
- Organise your emails into folders.
- Send many attachments in separate emails.
- Only cc emails to someone else when it's really necessary.

7 Students read the email and study the rules in exercise 5.

Answers
The person broke the following rules:
1 He/She didn't check for things like spelling, grammar and formality (eg *recieved* / *I look forward to see you then* / *Hi ...*).
2 and 4 He/She used capitals and marked it IMPORTANT!
5 The subject line wasn't short and clear.

8 Students re-draft the email in exercise 7 to improve it. It is up to the students to decide how well the two people (Mr Kay and J) already know each other. If in doubt, remind students that as a general rule it's best to use a semi-formal or neutral business register.

Possible answer

Dear Mr Kay

Further to your message regarding next week's brand development meeting, I can confirm that I will be able to attend. Please also find attached ScentAir's latest proposal, which we can discuss in more detail next week.

I look forward to seeing you.

Best regards

John Taylor

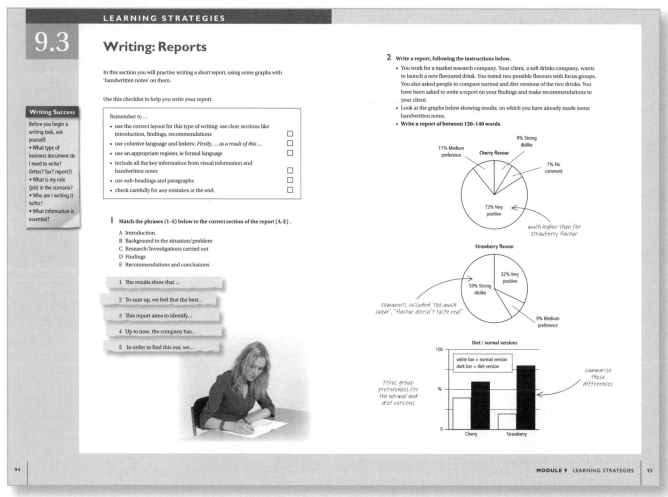

Student's Book pages 94 and 95

Begin by reading through the checklist with students. Remind them that reports are usually written in formal English and follow a clear structure. They often use bullet points and headings.

1 Students do the matching activity individually and then check their answers in pairs.

Answers

A – 3
B – 4
C – 5
D – 1
E – 2

2 Refer students to the Writing Success tip and ask them to answer the four questions in the tip with reference to the task on page 95.

Answers

- *What type of business document do I need to write?* A report.
- *What is my role (job) in the scenario?* A representative from a market research company carrying out research.
- *Who am I writing it for / to?* A soft drinks company.
- *What information from the visual material and handwritten notes is essential?* With the pie charts, students will need to summarise the main trends indicated rather than list every figure given. With the bar chart, students should summarise the overall indication of preferences and not worry about quoting exact percentages.

Students write their reports. If necessary, refer them back to the introduction to writing reports in Module 4 on pages 42 and 43. They will also find the checklist on page 94 helpful while they write or after they have completed their reports. They could then swap with a partner and use the checklist to mark their work.

Possible answer

Report on findings from focus group research

Introduction
The aim of this report is to make recommendations based on findings from ten focus groups.

Findings
Firstly, nearly three-quarters of responses to the cherry flavour were very positive with only 7% being neither positive nor negative about the product.

On the other hand, about two-thirds said they disliked the strawberry flavour because of the sugar and artificial taste.

Finally, with regard to the normal and diet versions, approximately 20% more people preferred the diet cherry version and nearly three times as many preferred the diet strawberry version.

Recommendations
Based on these findings, I would recommend that the company launches two types of cherry flavour drink (normal and diet). While I wouldn't suggest a normal strawberry version, the company could consider producing a diet version which was clearly more popular.

Overview

10.1   Business topic: Management

READING	**How Madonna managed success**
VOCABULARY	**Verb + noun combinations**
GRAMMAR	**Conditionals**
SPEAKING	**Case study**
WRITING	**A report on a meeting**

10.2   Business skills: Solving problems

LISTENING	**Problems and solutions**
SPEAKING	**Discussing problems**
VOCABULARY	**Managing projects**
VOCABULARY	**Cause and result**
WRITING	**An email**

10.3   Learning strategies: An interview

Predicting likely answers

Listening for speakers' feelings and opinions

PHOTOCOPIABLE

© 2009 Heinle, Cengage Learning

Useful language from Module 10

Wordlist

achieve success	in time	out of time	set targets
ahead of schedule	learn a great deal	over budget	succeed in business
behind schedule	miss opportunities	plan a strategy	under budget
develop an understanding	on schedule on time	recognise weaknesses	within budget

Expressions

Good idea. / I agree.

If I were you, I'd ...

If we do / did ... it will / would ...

I'm not so sure. / I don't think it'll work.

It'd have the advantage of ...

I was wondering if we ...

Let's start by ...

My other idea is to ...

One alternative is to ...

One solution would be to ...

On the other hand ... / The disadvantage might be ...

The main problem is ...

The main thing is to find a solution.

We can worry about ... later.

What are our options?

What if we were ...? / Would it make any difference if ...?

What would happen if we ...? / How about if ...?

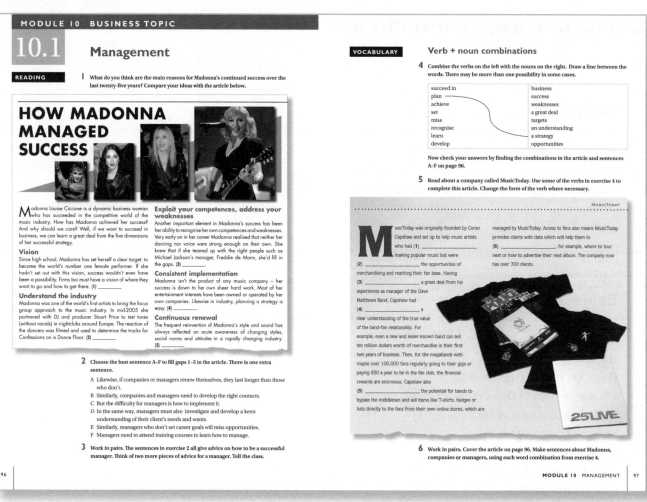

Student's Book pages 96 and 97

How Madonna managed success

READING

1 Assuming that most or all of your students will have heard of Madonna, you could begin by brainstorming reasons for her success with the rest of the class. Write their ideas on the board and then ask students to read the article to see if any of their ideas are mentioned.

2 Students complete the text with missing sentences. It could be helpful for students to refer back to the Learning Strategies on pages 64–65 with tips on answering this type of question. Students could underline any pronouns in sentences A–F to help them look for any forward or backward referencing.

Answers
1 E   2 D   3 B   4 C   5 A

3 Students in pairs think of more advice for would-be managers.

Possible answers
– Managers shouldn't ask staff to do things they aren't prepared to do themselves.
– Managers need to be open to new ideas and ways of doing things.

Verb + noun combinations

VOCABULARY

4 Students match the verbs and the nouns. They can refer to the article on page 96 while they match the words, or use it to check their work afterwards. They should also note down any other possible combinations.

Answers
(other possibilities are given in brackets)
succeed in business
achieve success (a great deal, targets)
set targets
miss opportunities (targets)
recognise weaknesses (success)
learn a great deal
develop an understanding (a strategy)

Extension

Ask students to think of more nouns that might collocate with each of the verbs, eg *succeed in life, plan a career, achieve goals, set goals, miss deadlines, recognise competences, learn from mistakes, develop contacts.*

5 Explain that MusicToday is a real company created to help musicians promote their work. Before students begin reading, you could ask them how a musician or group might promote their work, eg through selling T-shirts, appearing on TV, having a website, etc. Note that students will need to match some of the verbs with new nouns which don't appear in exercise 4.

Answers

1 succeeded in
2 missing
3 learned
4 developed
5 recognised
6 plan

Extension

Ask students to write five questions about MusicToday. They then get into pairs and close their books. They take turns to ask and answer each other's questions about their company and see how many they can answer from memory.

Example:
A: Who founded MusicToday?
B: Coran Capshaw.
A: Why did he set it up?
B: To help artists promote themselves and reach their fans.

6 With the word combinations from exercise 4, students create sentences to summarise the article, or they could use any prior knowledge they have of her to make sentences.

Possible answers

Madonna has succeeded in business because she reinvents herself.
She has always planned a strategy for each stage of her career.
She has achieved success through hard work and determination.
It's been important for her to set personal targets.
When she has missed opportunities, she's learnt from it.
She also recognises her weaknesses and brings in other people to help.
Madonna has learnt a great deal from others.
She realised early on that it's important to develop an understanding of the music industry.

Extension

Ask students to make sentences about what makes a successful manager using the verb + noun combinations, eg *Many managers succeed in business by constantly developing and learning.*

Photocopiable activity 10.1
See page 174.

GRAMMAR — Conditionals

1 Read sentences A–E. They are all examples of conditionals. Choose the best sentence to answer each question 1–5.

A If companies or managers renew themselves, they last longer.
B If I were you, I'd team up with a partner.
C If he'd set out with a vision, success would have been more likely.
D If you want personal success in the business world, you can learn a great deal from Madonna.
E If you set yourself career goals, you'll have greater opportunities.

1 Which sentence is about the past? _____ Did the action happen? Yes / No
2 Which sentence describes something that is generally true? _____
3 Which sentence refers to a future possibility? _____
4 Which sentence gives advice? _____
5 In which sentence is *will* replaced by another modal verb? _____

2 Complete this text by writing the verbs in brackets in the correct form to make conditionals. Add a modal verb if necessary.

Advice for new managers

1 Work to your strengths. If you _____ (not do) something, bring someone in on your team who can.

2 When everything becomes routine, it's time to ask, 'What _____ (happen) if we tried it a different way?'

3 If you _____ (want) everyone to like you all the time, you shouldn't have gone into management.

4 Don't give your people targets unless you _____ (know) they can be reached.

5 If you aren't prepared to take risks and fail, you _____ (not succeed).

6 If you _____ (know) the answer to every problem, then you wouldn't need a team. But without a team, you'd have no one to manage!

7 When you make a mistake, ask yourself what you _____ (do) differently if you'd known. This can be more important than getting it right first time.

Learning Tip
When we give advice, we often say *If I were you* instead of *If I was you*.

3 We often use *if* clauses and conditional forms to brainstorm and discuss new ideas. The sentences below are from a meeting. Choose the best ending A–G for each sentence 1–7.

1 If I were you, I'd …
2 What if we were …
3 Would it make any difference …
4 I was wondering if we …
5 What would happen if we …
6 How about if …
7 Unless we …

A to bring in some outside consultants?
B try this out, we won't know.
C redesign the website.
D changed our wholesaler?
E could change our approach.
F the price was lower?
G if we sold it via the website?

98

SPEAKING — Case study

4 You run a management consultancy which gives advice to businesses on how to remain successful and competitive. You have been approached by the music group Soundblaster who would like your consultancy's advice. Study this information about them and list their problems:

MUSIC REVIEW

Soundblaster: TALK TO THE WORLD

Record label: ANI
Star rating: ★☆☆☆☆

It was always going to be a tough challenge to equal the phenomenally successful *Hear to Believe* but after three years of waiting you would have expected something more original from Soundblaster's third studio album. *Talk to the World* will of course appeal to the band's core fans. It has the same funk guitar sounds and disco rhythms but by the end you feel they are still living in 2003 both in terms of music and appearance …

SALES OF MERCHANDISE ON LAST THREE TOURS

CD Sales

2001 Soundblaster I	3.5 million copies
2003 Hear to believe	5.1 million copies
2004 Soundblaster live	3.1 million copies
2007 Talk to the world	2.9 million copies

5 The band are now planning to record and launch a new CD. They want your consultancy to prepare a report on how they can improve on their success. Hold a brainstorming meeting with two colleagues, with the following agenda:

1 Define a clear target for Soundblaster.
2 How to develop the band's brand.
3 How to develop the band's music and attract new fans.
4 How to increase sales of music and merchandising such as T-shirts, posters, etc.
5 Prepare a presentation of your strategy for the band.

Work in groups of three. Read about your roles and start your meeting. Try to use some of the expressions in exercise 3 on page 98.

Student A: You are an expert in brand management. Look at File 10.1 on page 127.
Student B: You are an expert in market research. Look at File 10.2 on page 132.
Student C: You are an expert in product placement. Look at File 10.3 on page 131.

6 Join another group. Take turns to give your presentations and ask each other questions about your strategy.

WRITING — A report on a meeting

7 Write a report of what you decided in your meeting and recommend your strategy to the band.

MODULE 10 MANAGEMENT *99*

Student's Book pages 98 and 99

Conditionals

GRAMMAR

1 At this level, students are usually familiar with conditionals but may still have problems producing them. This first exercise reviews common uses and students will also find it helpful to refer to the grammar summary on page 130.

Answers
1 C / No, the action didn't happen.
2 A (Note that students might also answer D which is correct. However it contains a modal verb so is also the answer to 5.)
3 E
4 B (Students may wonder why we use 'were' and not 'was' in this sentence. In fact, both forms are possible, however we often use the 'were' form as part of an expression to give advice. Note that the Learning Tip refers to this and the structure reappears in exercise 3.)
5 D

Extension
If students are familiar with the terms zero, first, second and third conditional, ask them to categorise the sentences in exercise 1.

Answers
Zero: A, D
First: E
Second: B
Third: C

2 Students practise using the conditional forms in context.

Answers
1 can't do
2 would happen
3 'd wanted
4 know
5 won't succeed
6 knew
7 would have done

3 Students choose the best endings for sentence openers 1–7. This exercise draws students' attention to the fact that *if*-clauses or *conditionals* are used when speaking about problems or brainstorming ideas.

Answers
1 C 2 A 3 G 4 E 5 D 6 F 7 B

Extension

In the case study that follows in exercise 4, students can make use of the expressions in exercise 3. However, before they begin it will be helpful to provide some controlled practice with the expressions with *if* in 1–7. Write the following situations on the board and ask students to work in small groups and spend two minutes brainstorming ideas for each one. Students should try to use all the expressions.

- *Plan a special party for someone who has worked at the company for 25 years.*
- *Plan a team-building event for everyone to attend in your department.*
- *Plan a new website to promote your company or place of study.*

Case study

SPEAKING

4 This case study builds on the theme of management and the music industry. Students imagine they have been asked to ensure the continued success of a group called 'Soundblaster'. Initially students can work alone, in pairs or in the groups that they form in exercise 5. They will need 10–15 minutes to study the three pieces of information about the group and make a list of the problems and issues. Ask students to tell you which problems they have identified. Write these on the board so all the students are clear about what needs to be discussed.

Possible answers

The problems will include:
- their most recent album *Talk to the world* has received poor reviews by the music press
- according to the review the group sound similar to their previous albums
- the review also suggests they haven't changed their image or appearance
- since their second album, sales have fallen
- sales of merchandise have fallen.

Once you have written their ideas on the board, remind the class about the reading on Madonna which explained how she continued to develop her music and image in order to maintain her success. Explain that her ideas may be helpful for helping Soundblaster.

5 Students work in groups of three. If you have a group of four, two students can play the part of Student A. The group follows the agenda but each student has a particular area of expertise and refers to their notes in the Files on pages 127, 131 and 132. Also make students aware that they can put forward their own ideas as well as those in the book. As the meeting progresses, students should take notes and summarise their final strategy for Soundblaster at the end.

6 The groups present their ideas. With larger classes, one group can present to another but if you have time, each group can present their strategy to the class and the other students can ask them questions.

A report on a meeting

WRITING

7 Students write their reports in class or for homework. They should follow the format for writing reports and may find it useful to refer back to the guidance in Module 5 on page 53.

BUSINESS SKILLS

10.2 Solving problems

LISTENING

Problems and solutions

1 🔊 10.1 Listen to Linda telephoning her manager.
1 What is she in charge of?
2 What's the main problem?
3 What does she want her manager to do?

2 🔊 10.1 Listen again and complete the notes on the message pad.

Linda called from the (1) _____
There's a problem. The (2) _____ for the
(3) _____ of the building have arrived but
(4) _____ of them don't fit. They are
(5) _____ centimetres too wide. She thinks
the fault is with the (6) _____ not the
(7) _____ Please (8) _____
as soon as possible.

3 Study this flowchart showing ways to solve a problem.

1	2	3	4	5
What is the problem?	What is one possible solution?	What is another possible solution?	What are the pros and cons of each solution?	What is the best solution?

🔊 10.2 Roger calls Linda back to discuss possible solutions to the problem with the windows. Listen and answer the five questions in the flowchart above.

1 _____
2 _____
3 _____
4 Solution A: _____
   Solution B: _____
5 _____

4 🔊 10.2 Look at the list of expressions below for discussing and solving problems. Listen again and tick the expressions you hear.

Solving problems

Stating and prioritising	
The main problem is ...	☐
We can worry about ... later.	☐
The main thing is to find a solution.	☐
Let's start by ...	☐

Considering options	
What are our options?	☐
One solution would be to ...	☐
If we do / did ... it will / would ...	☐
My other idea is to ...	☐
It'd have the advantage of ...	☐
On the other hand ... /	
The disadvantage might be ...	☐
One alternative is to ...	☐

Agreeing / Disagreeing	
Good idea. / I agree.	☐
I'm not so sure. / I don't think it'll work.	☐

SPEAKING

Discussing problems

5 Work in pairs. Make a series of telephone calls to each other in order to solve these problems. Follow the flowchart on page 100 and practise using the expressions above.

Problem 1
The new office furniture has arrived but it doesn't fit together. You don't know if it's the fault of the designer or the manufacturer. You need the offices ready by tomorrow.

Problem 2
You want to promote your company more widely without increasing the advertising budget.

Problem 3
You need someone to manage the warehouse. You could either contact a recruitment agency or promote someone within the company.

Student's Book pages 100 and 101

Problems and solutions

LISTENING **Tracks 8, 9 (CD2)**

1 🔊 10.1 Before students begin listening, ask them to look at the photo of Linda and suggest what kind of work she does. Then play the recording to listen for the key points.

Answers
1 Linda is in charge of construction of a building.
2 The windows don't fit.
3 She wants her manager to call her back.

10.1 Listening script

Linda Hi, Roger. It's Linda. Sorry, it's really noisy here. I hope you can hear this. I'm at the site. It's going well but we have a problem. The windows have just arrived for the south side of the building. They'd be fine if it wasn't for the fact that four of them don't fit. They seem to be about one point five centimetres too wide for the spaces. I think it's a manufacturing fault but if I send them straight back, the manufacturer'll probably say it's the architect's fault. What do you think I should do? Can you call me back as soon as you get this. We can't afford any more mistakes. I don't know, Roger. If I'd known this project was going to cause this much trouble, I would have said forget it! Anyway, call me back on my mobile if you get this message.

2 🔊 10.1 Encourage students to predict the kind of information they have to listen for. They then listen again for more detail and complete the message.

Answers
1 site
2 windows
3 south side
4 four
5 1.5
6 manufacturer
7 architect
8 call her

3 🔊 10.2 Give students time to read the flowchart for solving problems. Ask students if this is how they would normally solve problems at work. Ask them to explain a recent problem they might have had which they had to solve.

Students listen to Roger's call. Roger and Linda's discussion follows the structure of the flowchart so students write down the answers to each stage.

Answers

1 The windows don't fit.
2 Send the windows back to the manufacturer
3 Make the space for the windows wider.
4 Solution A: it will take the manufacturer 16 weeks to redo them, and the architect will need to do more designs.
  Solution B: it's a bit expensive but the people on the site are being paid anyway so they can make the space wider.
5 The best solution is probably the second solution (to make the space wider).

Extension

Ask students to suggest some possible solutions to Linda's problem before listening to the call in the next exercise.

10.2 Listening script

Linda Linda speaking.
Roger Hi, Linda. It's me, Roger. Thanks for your message. I would have rung you straight back if I'd managed to get hold of the architect. He's in Madrid or something.
Linda So did you speak to the window people?
Roger Yes, and as you predicted they said if they'd received the right specifications from the plans in the first place, there wouldn't have been a problem.
Linda Well, I bet when you get the architect, he'll say it's their fault.
Roger Anyway, we can worry about whose fault it is later. The main thing is to find a solution. And quickly. What are our options?
Linda Well, if we send the windows back to the manufacturer it'll take about sixteen weeks to have them redone. That'll include the architect doing new designs.
Roger Sixteen weeks is ages. We'll go way behind schedule. The client would never agree.
Linda Yes, I know, so my other idea is to make the space for the windows wider by cutting into the area around the window. If we did this, it'd have the advantage of using our people already on site so I wouldn't be paying them for doing nothing. It's a bit expensive but I think it'd take about two weeks.
Roger Good idea. And what you save in time means it'll be cheaper overall. Look, before I give you the go-ahead on that, let me check with the architects to make sure there aren't any structural issues to consider...

4 10.2 Students listen again and tick the expressions they hear.

Answers

We can worry about ... later.
The main thing is to find a solution.
What are our options?
If we do/did ... it will/would ...
My other idea is to ...
It'd have the advantage of ...
Good idea. / I agree.

Discussing problems

SPEAKING

5 Students roleplay each of the three problems and practise using all the expressions in exercise 4. They should also try to follow the problem-solving flowchart in exercise 3.

Extension

Ask students to write down a problem they typically have at work or at home, eg ordering something online and the wrong item arriving. They then explain the problem to their partner who must help them to solve the problem.

Student's Book pages 102 and 103

Managing projects

VOCABULARY

1 The word combinations with prepositions are typically used when referring to projects by managers, and for discussing and solving problems.

Answers
in time (+)
on time (+)
within budget (+)
over budget (–)
under budget (+/–)
on schedule (+)
behind schedule (–)
ahead of schedule (+/–)

Extension

Ask students to write five sentences about a project they are currently working on or a problem they have, using some of the word combinations, eg *If we don't speed up on my current project, we'll run out of time and the client will go to someone else.*

2 Before doing the exercise, ask students to brainstorm what they think would need planning for a group going on tour. Write their ideas on the board.

Possible ideas
– Decide and book the venues.
– Print and sell the tickets.
– Make merchandise to sell to fans like T-shirts, hats, etc.
– Arrange transport.
– Employ a road crew.

Students then complete the email with the prepositions from the box. They may find it helpful to refer back to the preposition combinations in exercise 1.

Answers
1 over
2 on
3 in
4 in
5 ahead
6 behind
7 in
8 in
9 within

Cause and result

VOCABULARY

3 Students find more phrases for showing cause and result in the email on page 102.

Answers
further to / **following on from**
so that we are / **in order to be**
due to / because of / **as a result of**
therefore / **so**

An email

WRITING

4 Students choose appropriate expressions from exercise 3 to complete the new email. Note that more than one answer may be possible.

Answers
1 Further to / Following on from
2 due to / because of / as a result of
3 In order to / So that we
4 therefore / so
5 so

5 Students use the new information to change the Gantt Chart.

Answer

	Jan	Feb	March	April	May	June
Tickets printed	▬					
Tour dates announced		X(28th)				
Tickets go on sale			▬▬▬▬▬▬▬			
Plan/design merchandise			▬▬▬▬			
Merchandise to be delivered					▬	
Tour starts						X(1st)

6 Students write an email with the new information. Limit the word count to 50 words.

Possible answer

> Subject: Further changes to schedule for LJ tour.
> Further to my previous email, I can confirm that tickets need to be printed by January 31st. Please also note that the client has increased the merchandising budget in order to include hats and scarves. I appreciate your patience with these changes to the schedule.

Photocopiable activity 10.2
See page 175.

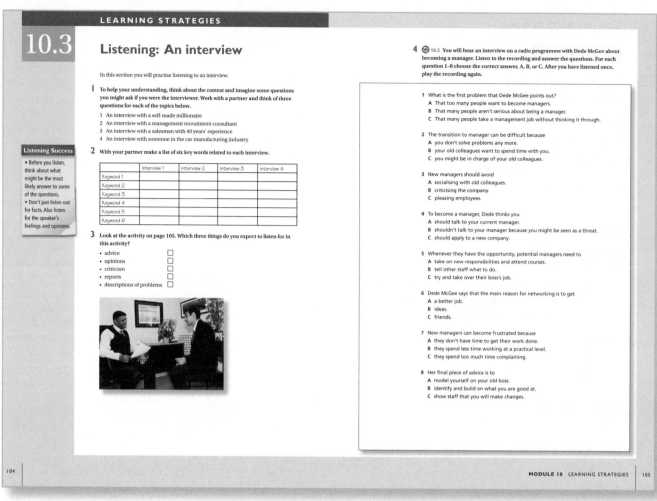

Student's Book pages 104 and 105

Track 10 (CD2)

1 Students read through the different interview topics and think of questions they might ask. They can work together in pairs and then exchange their ideas with other pairs

Possible answers

1 What was your first job?
What motivates you?
Have you ever lost a lot of money on a deal?

2 What qualities do you look for in a good manager?
Do you look for managers or do they come to you?
Have you ever recommended the wrong person for a job?

3 What is the secret of being a good salesman?
What was the first thing you sold?
What is the most difficult thing you have had to sell?

4 Have you seen many changes in the industry in your working life?
What are the main risks in the industry?
What is the future for the industry?

2 Students read through the interview topics again and, in pairs, make lists of key words for each topic.

3 Refer students to the Listening Success tip. In this particular task, students should be able to predict at least two of the answers fairly well based on their own views on management. Rather than listening only for specific information, students need to infer information in this listening task so it's important for them to understand the speaker's purpose.

Answer
The questions suggest the main speaker will probably give advice, opinions and describe problems.

4 🔘 10.3 Play the recording twice.

Answers
1 C   2 C   3 B   4 A   5 A   6 B   7 B   8 B

10.3 Listening script

P = Presenter   **D** = Dede

P OK. In the final part of today's programme we continue our series on career progression, and this week we're taking a special look at the move from regular member of staff working alongside everyone else to becoming a manager. In the studio today we've invited Dede McGee, a freelance HR consultant, to talk to us. Dede, thanks for coming in today. What's the problem here? Presumably most people jump at the opportunity to move into management, don't they?

D Well, no. Actually, people often feel they should take a management position but they don't really ask themselves if it's really what they want.

P How do you mean?

D Well, deciding whether you want to continue working on the front line or whether you'd rather take on a management position sounds like a straightforward, logical step. But in fact it means changing how you work, how you think and the way you judge your own success. For example, do you want to be part of the team which solves big technical challenges or do you suddenly want to be the person who is in charge of encouraging others to come up with those solutions? You might find you miss being with your old colleagues. And that's another problem. New managers have to be able to tell people who were once their workmates – or equals – what to do.

P Yes, that must be a big problem.

D Well, it can work as long as you accept that your relationship with your old colleagues can never be the same. The dynamics of the relationship have to change. For example, you won't have that chance to go for a drink after work and have a quiet moan about the company any more. When you become a manager you are saying I agree with the values and direction of the company and I will work to promote these. The other big mistake, of course, is trying to please everyone all of the time. You can't. You'll have to make decisions that members of the team might not always like. You know, managers shouldn't expect love!

P No. I see. OK. But imagine we have someone who has decided management is their next career goal. What should they do?

D Funnily enough, the one thing that people don't think of doing is to go and tell their immediate boss that they want to move up.

P Is that because they're scared that their boss will think they're trying to get his or her job?

D Maybe, but in fact your manager is the first person you should talk to. They're in the best position to help by telling you what you need to do to develop. Many companies can also give you the chance to try out management roles, for example, by taking more responsibility such as mentoring new staff or taking on the duties of your boss when he or she is away. My other golden rule is to say 'yes' to any courses or training that comes your way. If there's a course on leadership or finance, take it. It'll help your professional development but also it'll be noted by the company that you're keen. It's also all part of the networking process.

P What? So you mean knowing the right people to get the promotion? Or selling yourself?

D Well, I don't think I'd be quite that cynical. Obviously, you need to let people know you are interested and – yes – selling or promoting yourself is important for promotion, as it is for that matter to get on in any part of business. But what I really mean to say is that networking with managers is also about talking to peers who can give you help and advice because as managers they face similar problems to you. Without them, management can actually be quite lonely.

P OK, so once you're a manager are there any other tips?

D I suppose one of the biggest complaints I hear from new managers is that they say 'I've been in meetings all day and haven't got any real work done'. I always have to tell them 'that's your job'. Managers delegate, they coach, they build relationships and they monitor performance. Your new role is strategic. It isn't so hands-on. The other tip I always give is that when you take over from your previous boss, listen to his or her advice but remember that you can also do things differently. You don't have to be a clone. Develop a style based on your personal strengths.

P Dede McGee. That's all we have time for now. Thanks very much for talking to us. If you'd like more information on this topic or any others in today's programme just visit our website at www. …

Overview

11.1   Business topic: Ethical economics

READING   **Coffeenomics**

VOCABULARY   **Financial and trade terms**

SPEAKING   **The economics of your country**

GRAMMAR   **Articles**

LISTENING   **Fairtrade**

SPEAKING   **Giving reasons and benefits**

11.2   Business skills: Discussing trends

SPEAKING   **Alternative energy sources**

READING   **Good greed**

VOCABULARY   **Describing trends**

LISTENING   **Reasons for trends**

SPEAKING   **Discussing trends**

WRITING   **A proposal**

11.3   Learning strategies: Longer texts

Multiple-choice questions

PHOTOCOPIABLE

© 2009 Heinle, Cengage Learning

Useful language from Module 11

Wordlist

ascend/ascent	descend/descent	go down	middlemen
break-even total	disparity	go up	overheads
change hands	factor	gross domestic	peak
charities	fall	product	remain stable
crash	fluctuate/	increase	rise
decline	fluctuation	level out	soar
decrease	freight	mark-up	

Expressions

Another reason for

as

As a result of

because

due to the fact that

In response to your enquiry about …

At present the company seems to be performing well / badly

On the one hand... but on the other …

One advantage / disadvantage is that …

One other thing to consider is …

Despite … I would still suggest that …

Overall, I would strongly recommend that …

The fact that … makes this a good / poor investment opportunity.

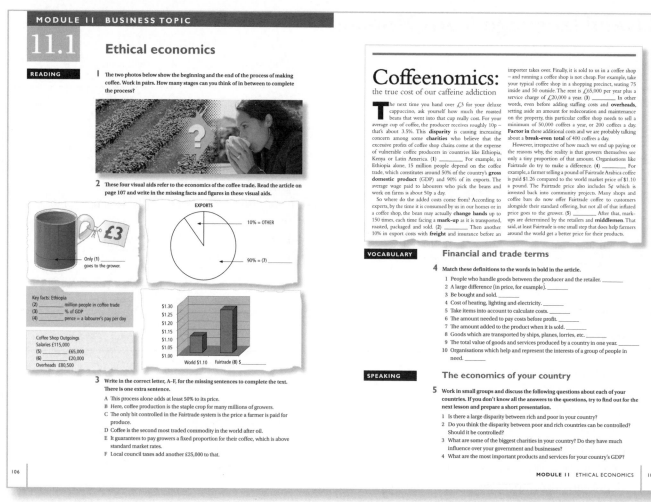

Student's Book pages 106 and 107

Coffeenomics

READING

1 First ask the class what they think the section title, *Ethical economics*, means or refers to. Students then work in pairs to brainstorm a list of stages in the process of making coffee. Take answers afterwards from the class and build up a complete list on the board.

Possible answers
- coffee grown
- coffee picked
- coffee transported
- coffee packed
- coffee sold and shipped
- coffee sold on to shops
- coffee bought and drunk

2 Before students start exercise 2, ask them to look at the title of the article on page 107, *Coffeenomics*, and say which two words have been combined to make this (unreal) word. The words are *coffee and economics*.

Students then study the four visual aids from a presentation and find the missing facts and figures in the article.

Answers
1 10p (pence)
2 15
3 50
4 50
5 rent
6 service charge
7 coffee
8 1.26

3 Students complete the text with sentences A–F.

Answers
1 B
2 A
3 F
4 E
5 C
D is the extra sentence.

Financial and trade terms

VOCABULARY

4 Students match the words in bold from the article to the definitions.

Answers
1 middlemen
2 disparity
3 change hands
4 overheads
5 factor in
6 break-even total
7 mark-up
8 freight
9 gross domestic product
10 charities

Extension
Ask in-work students to describe aspects of their business using as many of the words as possible, eg Do they have to deal with 'middlemen' or can they supply their customers directly?

The economics of your country

SPEAKING

5 The four questions require some level of knowledge about the economics of a country. Make sure at least one person in each group has a good knowledge of their country's economy. An alternative is to discuss the questions as a class and ask students who know a lot on the topic. With pre-work students, the questions make a useful research project which they could carry out online and then report back on in the next lesson.

Student's Book pages 108 and 109 (reproduced)

GRAMMAR Articles

I Write in the missing articles *the, a, an,* or 0 (the zero article) in this text about Fairtrade.

(1) _____ Fairtrade is (2) _____ international certification mark used in 21 countries as (3) _____ marketing initiative to help developing nations. Britain has (4) _____ largest Fairtrade market in (5) _____ world, which has seen (6) _____ amazing increase over the last five years. The organisation is also strong in (7) _____ Netherlands, where Fairtrade first started, and in Switzerland and Scandinavia. Originally started in 1989 as (8) _____ scheme to help poor producers, (9) _____ Fairtrade Foundation was established three years later. Now there are over (10) _____ 550 certified producers representing over one million farmers in 52 countries.

LISTENING Fairtrade

2 Can you buy these Fairtrade products in your country? Would you buy these products even if they were more expensive? Why? Why not?

3 11.1 Listen to an interview with Ian Bretman, the deputy director of the Fairtrade Foundation. Choose the best ending A, B or C for each sentence 1–8.

1 The Fairtrade Foundation began in
A 1989.
B 1990.
C 1992.

2 When the United States withdrew from the international coffee agreement, the price of coffee decreased by
A 50%.
B 0.5%.
C twenty million.

3 One way Fairtrade helps farmers is by giving advice on how to
A diversify by growing other crops.
B produce more coffee.
C be profitable in a global market.

4 One of Fairtrade's main messages to governments is that
A trade can be managed more effectively.
B economic growth is the best strategy.
C they must invest more in producers.

5 Ian believes that Fairtrade and free trade
A cannot both exist.
B can operate together.
C are basically the same thing.

6 Even though a country may increase its wealth through business, this does not guarantee
A it can compete internationally.
B everyone receives the benefits.
C social justice.

7 If producers are successful, they will also
A invest in the economy.
B become the people who buy products.
C be able to supply more coffee.

8 As well as improving its public image, a Fairtrade company will
A sell more.
B attract more talented staff.
C attract well-informed consumers.

SPEAKING Giving reasons and benefits

4 A coffee shop in your town is thinking of selling Fairtrade coffee. However, it is concerned that this may be more expensive.

Imagine you and your partner work for Fairtrade. You are going to try and convince the coffee shop to use coffee from your producers. Discuss and prepare:
• a list of reasons why the coffee shop should change.
• a list of benefits for the coffee shop, its staff and its customers.
Afterwards, present your ideas to the rest of the class.

Student's Book pages 108 and 109

Articles

GRAMMAR

I This grammar section should be a review of articles for students but if they have difficulties they should refer to the grammar summary on page 130. When checking the answers, ask students to give their reasons.

Answers
1 0 (*Fairtrade* is the name of the organisation)
2 an (singular noun)
3 a (singular noun mentioned for the first time)
4 the (before a superlative)
5 the (there is only one)
6 an (singular noun)
7 the (name of country)
8 a (singular noun)
9 the (refers to 'foundation' – there is only one)
10 0 (plural noun)

Photocopiable activity 11.1
See page 176.

Fairtrade

LISTENING Track 11 (CD2)

2 Students look at the products and discuss the questions as a class. Find out how well known Fairtrade is in the students' countries.

3 11.1 Ask students to read the questions before they listen. They then listen and choose the best endings for the eight sentences.

Answers
1 C   2 A   3 C   4 A   5 B   6 B   7 B   8 B

11.1 Listening script
I = Interviewer   **IB** = Ian Bretman

I So, Ian. I understand that the original idea for Fairtrade came in 1989. How did it happen?

IB Actually, the Fairtrade Foundation itself was finally set up in 1992, but yes, you're right, the catalyst for the spread of Fairtrade was three years earlier when the international coffee agreement that controlled prices collapsed with the withdrawal of the US. At that time coffee was the world's biggest agricultural commodity. In a few months the price fell by half. It was a huge disaster for the twenty million people growing and processing coffee around the world. Many of the producing countries were dependent on coffee for over half their exports.

I Can you give us some examples of how you help, exactly?

IB One way is that we encourage producers to learn how to compete effectively in international markets. We help farmers coming into the system to develop the capacity to cope with fulfilling demand and we set a minimum guaranteed price for their products.

I I see. But as well as helping farmers directly, you also have influence on governments, don't you? I mean, governments are talking more and more about fairer global trade …

IB Yes, we're finding that the issues we've been talking about for the past ten years are moving up the agenda. For example, we're having more of a debate on how we can achieve economic growth and social justice, as both are needed. As a result, leaders of larger Fairtrade organisations have been invited to high-level international meetings and economic forums. We can use our experience to illustrate to governments how trade can be better managed.

I But how do you convince people who say economic growth is the answer to everything? Don't these people argue that Fairtrade isn't good for free trade?

IB Well, I worked in business for a long time and so I understand the need for a free market, but it seems unlikely to me that when it comes to social problems, like global poverty, the answer is just an economic one, because social choices have to be made, too. Our point is really about priorities. Increasing flows of trade will help wealth but that does not necessarily guarantee that this wealth goes down to the people who need it most. That requires a little bit more management. Fairtrade has practical experience on the ground in how you can combine the best of both. How you can get people to operate effectively and competitively while trading in a way that producers can earn a decent living and improve their lives. In the long run, if they do improve their lives, they too will become consumers and purchasers.

I So is this the message you give businesses to make them change to Fairtrade products?

IB It's in the interest of any business to take the message on board, not only to improve their public image but also as a recruiting tool for the future. The younger generation is well informed and wants to be part of the solution. Companies find that having a social conscience has a positive effect on recruiting and retaining good staff. Staff get excited about persuading consumers to buy products that make a difference to people's lives.

I It sounds like that's what motivates you, too.

IB For my part – yes – meeting the producers and seeing what a difference Fairtrade can make to their lives is really quite inspiring.

Giving reasons and benefits

SPEAKING

4 Students need to work in pairs and discuss the two items. Allow about four minutes and then ask each pair to present their ideas. As you listen, monitor and give some feedback on how to improve the discussion and the types of expressions that will help.

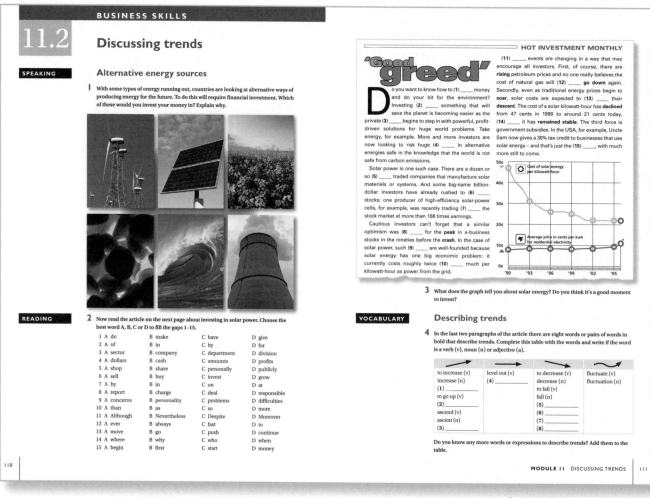

Student's Book pages 110 and 111

Alternative energy sources

SPEAKING

I Put students into groups of three of four to discuss which types of energies would be a good investment. Their responses may depend upon which part of the world they come from.

Possible answers

a) Wind power has already been implemented in many countries though some people say it can never provide enough energy on its own. The initial cost is also very high.

b) Solar power is being widely used either on people's own houses or in the form of huge areas of land with solar panels. The cost of technology is falling for this energy so it looks like a good investment.

c) Bio fuels which make use of residue from plants are already used in some cars. They look set to provide one solution to the lack of petrol fuels.

d) Coal is criticised for the pollution it creates and many countries are looking at alternatives which suggests it isn't a good investment. However, in some parts of the world such as China there are huge coal reserves which are only now being mined and used in power stations. In this case coal may still be a good investment but be bad for the environment.

e) Wave power has many of the same pros and cons as wind power.

f) Nuclear power has attracted bad publicity in the past but more recently many governments have returned to the idea of building nuclear power stations in the next century in order to solve the potential shortage of energy. Private investment may yet provide good returns.

Good greed

READING

2 Students complete the article.

Answers

1 B   2 B   3 A   4 C   5 D   6 B   7 C   8 D
9 A   10 B   11 B   12 A   13 D   14 A   15 C

3 Discuss the questions as a class.

Answer
The graph shows that while solar power costs twice as much per kilowatt-hour than traditional energy sources used on power grids at present, its costs have been falling continuously since the early nineties. The line showing the average price for power from the grid for residential energy is also climbing. If these trends continue, solar power may become very competitive, making it a good long-term investment.

Describing trends

VOCABULARY

4 Students find the trend words in the last two paragraphs of the article and complete the table. They may find it helpful to use a good dictionary to check whether the word is a verb, noun or adjective. If students know more trend words, these can be added to the table (see also the next Extension activity).

Answers
1 peak (n)
2 rising (v)
3 soar (v)
4 remained stable (v)
5 crash (n)
6 go down (v)
7 descent (n)
8 declined (v)

Extension
If students are using dictionaries, ask them to find out if the words have other forms, eg the verb *increase* can also be the noun *increase* and its adjective form is *increased*. You could draw this table on the board and ask students to complete it with more trend words in their different forms. Write in the first examples to help:

verb	adjective	noun
to increase	increased	increase
to fluctuate	fluctuating	fluctuation

Pronunciation
Students should mark the stressed syllable in the trend words. They can use their dictionaries to check. Pay special attention to stressed syllables which move in different word forms, eg *fluctuate / fluctuation*.

Photocopiable activity 11.2
See page 177.

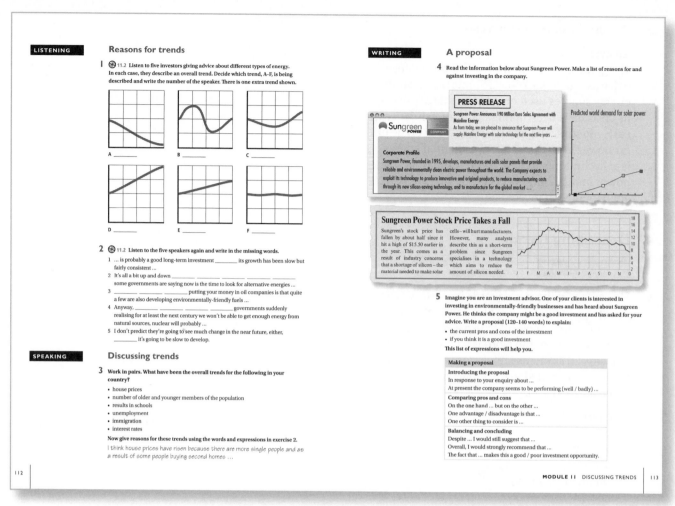

Reasons for trends

LISTENING Track 12 (CD2)

I 🔘 11.2 This listening continues the work on trend language on the previous page, but here students also focus on the language for explaining reasons for trends.

Answers
A no speaker
B 2
C 4
D 3
E 1
F 5

11.2 Listening script

S = Speaker

S1 I think wind power is probably a good long-term investment because its growth has been slow but fairly consistent over the last decade, and more and more wind farms seem to be appearing, so someone must be making money – unless it's all coming from government subsidies. So if you can spare some money for the next fifty years or so I'd say you're probably on to a good thing.

S2 The whole eco-investment craze is a bit risky at this stage. It's all a bit up and down due to the fact that some governments are saying now is the time to look for alternative energies and others are still using coal and oil. It's so political that you only need a change of government and the whole thing changes again. Certainly in the short term it's going to be difficult to predict …

S3 Actually, I'd say oil is still a good one – at least in the short term. It's really kept increasing very well and I don't know anyone who's lost. Another reason for putting your money in oil companies is that quite a few are also developing environmentally-friendly fuels …

S4 It's funny, because everyone was trying to get out of nuclear energy for a while. We all thought it would be replaced with wind power and solar energy. Anyway, as a result of governments suddenly realising for at least the next century we won't be able to get enough energy from natural sources, nuclear will probably have a bit of a revival. So I wouldn't move all your money out of that industry just yet …

S5 The one you hear about least is wave power but there are one or two companies that are investing heavily in the technology. I suppose with all the sea it's worth looking into, but overall I wouldn't expect it to do well for the small, short-term investor. Anyone with money here already won't have seen much return at all and I don't predict they're going to see much change in the near future, either, as it's going to be slow to develop.

2 11.2 Give students time to read extracts 1–5 before playing the recordings again. Students write in the missing words that are used to explain reasons for trends.

Answers
1 because
2 due to the fact that
3 Another reason for
4 as a result of
5 as

Discussing trends

SPEAKING

3 Students create sentences in pairs to describe recent real trends. Make sure they use trend words from exercise 4 on page 111, and linking expressions for explaining reasons from exercise 2 on page 112. At the end, ask different pairs to say some of their sentences. If students are from different countries it will be interesting to find out and compare the differences in trends and reasons from around the world.

A proposal

WRITING

4 Students can work alone or in pairs or small groups to read the information and then draw up a list of reasons for and against investing. Note that they can also add their own ideas, eg we know from the previous article on page 111 that solar energy is tipped to become a profitable investment.

Possible answers
(based on information given)

Reasons for:
– it has a new deal with Mainline Energy worth 190 million euros
– the company has over ten years' experience in a relatively new field
– it hit a high earlier in the year
– the recent fall is described by many analysts as a short-term problem.
– it has developed a new silicon-saving technology

Reasons against:
– its recent stock price fell by half
– there is a shortage of silicon.

5 Students use their list of reasons in exercise 4 to write a proposal. They will also find the list of expressions helpful. Advise students to make their proposal similar to a report, using sub-headings to help with organisation.

Possible answer

Dear Mr Keating

Proposed Investment
In response to your enquiry about Sungreen Power, the company seems to be performing well.

Findings
One thing to consider is their new sales agreement with Mainline Energy, worth 190 million euros. This should help their share price which recently halved. On the one hand this was caused by a shortage of silicon, but on the other hand Sungreen specialise in technology which requires less silicon.

Recommendations
So despite the fall, I would still suggest you consider investing. The fact that solar power costs have continuously fallen since the early nineties and look set to equal normal energy costs in the next few year makes this a good investment opportunity.

Feel free to call me to discuss any further queries you might have.

Best regards

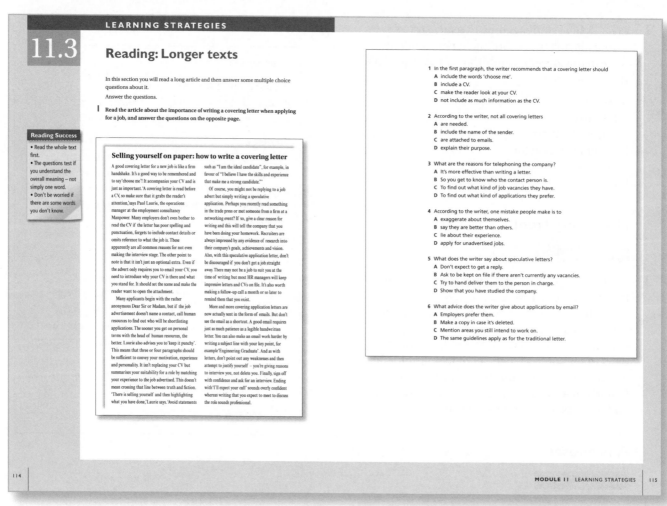

Refer students to the Reading Success tip before they read the text and answer the questions.

Answers

1 C   2 D   3 B   4 A   5 D   6 D

Overview

12.1   Business topic: Business Law

LISTENING   **A colour problem**

VOCABULARY   **Legal terms**

READING   **Colourful cases**

GRAMMAR   **Indirect questions and tags**

SPEAKING   **The BEC Vantage speaking game**

12.2   Business skills: Handling questions

LISTENING   **Difficult questions**

SPEAKING   **Responding to questions**

READING   **Press releases**

WRITING   **A press release**

12.3   Learning strategies: Discussions

Revising useful expressions

Good and bad advices

PHOTOCOPIABLE

© 2009 Heinle, Cengage Learning

Useful language from Module 12

Wordlist

case	litigation
court	prosecute
defence	rights
judge	sue
lawyer	trademark

Expressions

Can you explain what you mean?

Could you ... repeat that? / say that again?

Do you mind if I answer that at the end?

I can't really comment on ...

I'd like to come back to that point later on if that's OK.

I just need to check with someone first.

I'm afraid I'm unable to answer it at the moment ...

Let me get back to you on that.

Sorry, I didn't ... hear you. / catch that.

Sorry, I didn't understand the question.

Sorry I don't follow you ...

Thank you for asking that.

That's a good question

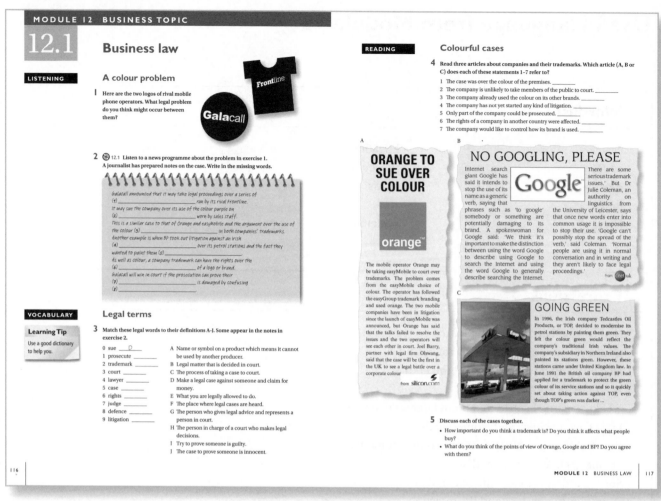

Student's Book pages 116 and 117

A colour problem

LISTENING Track 13 (CD2)

1 This first short discussion task leads into the topic of how trademarks can be too similar and cause legal proceedings between companies operating in the same area of business. Discuss the problem as a class.

Answer

In this case both phone operators are using logos which use the same colour. One operator could argue that customers will therefore confuse the brand and that their competitor is making use of their brand image.

Extension

🔊 **12.1** Before students do exercise 2, you could play the listening and students can compare their ideas in exercise 1 to those described in the interview. Find out which of the answers they gave are mentioned in the recording. This acts as a useful listening for general information before the next exercise.

2 🔊 **12.1** Students need to read the journalist's notes before they listen to the news programme and write in the missing words.

Answers

1 TV commercials
2 T-shirts
3 orange
4 petrol company
5 green
6 shape
7 business
8 colours

12.1 Listening script

P = Presenter   **R** = Rene

P Business news now, and the telecoms firm Galacall has announced it may be taking legal proceedings against the newcomer and potential rival in the telecoms market, Frontline. Frontline recently ran a series of TV commercials in which all its sales staff wore distinctive purple T-shirts. Galacall, whose trademark brand name appears in a similar shade of purple, hasn't said it will sue Frontline yet but is considering its position. Well, on the line to discuss this story is lawyer and legal expert in trademark law, Rene Mackersmann for the London-based firm Parkers and Mackersmann.

R Good morning.

P So Rene, I was wondering how serious Galacall is about all this? Surely they only have a case against a company which infringes the trademark by using a similar name, don't they?

R Well, no. In fact there are a number of examples where companies or brands have tried to prevent others from using what they consider as trademark colours. Take the case of the mobile phone company Orange trying to stop easyMobile using the colour orange. The easyGroup company had used orange on all its previous ventures, but when it launched a rival mobile phone brand, the operator Orange said easyMobile was breaking the law by using its colour in the same marketplace. Then there was the oil company BP, whose logo is green and yellow. They took out litigation against an Irish petrol company who tried to paint its petrol stations green.

P So do you think you can use the same colour as long as your product is different?

R Absolutely. For example, the food manufacturer Heinz uses turquoise on its cans but it couldn't stop someone from using the same colour on, say, bicycles.

P Can you tell me if there's anything else you can buy the rights on?

R Oh sure. Trademarks mean firms have rights over anything like colour or shape.

P Shape as well?

R Absolutely. Take Toblerone. They have the rights on triangular boxes for their chocolate.

P So back to Galacall and Frontline. I'd like to know what you think the outcome will be if it ever gets to court. Who'll win?

R Well, I'm not the judge, but if the prosecution can prove the colour will confuse customers and damage Galacall's business then they might just win it.

P Rene Mackersmann of Parkers and Mackersmann, thank you very much.

R You're welcome.

Legal terms

VOCABULARY

3 Students match the words to the definitions. They can refer to the notes and listening script as well as using a dictionary.

Answers
1 I 2 A 3 F 4 G 5 B
6 E 7 H 8 J 9 C

Colourful cases

READING

4 Two of the three articles provide students with more background on two of the cases mentioned in the listening. The other article is about quite a famous issue linked with the search engine, Google.

Students match the statements to the case. When checking answers, ask students to refer to the part of the text which gives the answer.

Answers
1 C (the 'premises' refers to the petrol station)
2 B (*Normal people ... aren't likely to face legal proceedings*)
3 A (*The operator has followed the easyGroup trademark branding and used orange.*)
4 B (*Google has said it intends to stop ...*)
5 A (*Orange may be taking easyMobile to court ... though easyMobile is part of a bigger company called easyGroup.*)
6 C (TOP is an Irish company but BP can only sue its stations in Northern Ireland which come under United Kingdom law.)
7 B (Google had said it intends to stop the use of its name ... / A spokeswoman said: *We think it's important to make the distinction between ...*)

5 Put students into pairs or small groups to discuss the questions. With the question about trademarks, students could comment how much they think a brand name affects what they buy, or if their own company's trademark is important for it. The second question is more open to different points of view with students saying if they think companies like Google have a fair case.

GRAMMAR

Indirect questions and tags

1 ⊙ 12.1 Listen to the news programme from exercise 2 on page 116 again. Re-write the direct questions below as indirect questions and tags.

0 How serious is Galacall about this?
I was wondering how serious _Galacall is about this_____?

1 Do they only have a case against a company which infringes the trademark by using a similar name?
They only have a case against a company which infringes the trademark by using a similar name, _____?

2 Can you use the same colour as long as your product is different?
Do you think _____ as long as your product is different?

3 Is there anything else you can buy the rights on?
Can you tell me if _____ you can buy the rights on?

4 What do you think the outcome will be if it ever gets to court?
I'd like to know what _____ if it ever gets to court.

2 Why do you think the speaker uses indirect questions and tags?

3 Read these questions and comments. Find the mistake in each one. Check for word order, an incorrect word or a missing word.

1 Do you think will business become more global in the future?
2 I was wondering you think the most important thing is when setting up a new business.
3 Good marketing is more important than a good product, is it?
4 In the future, people will reduce how much they travel by plane, won't it?
5 Do you think can employees work as well from home as from an office?
6 I'd like to ask you what are your plans for your future career?
7 What kinds of work experience you think would help students at business school?
8 You've studied English for three years, aren't you?

4 Work in pairs. Take turns to ask and answer the questions in exercise 3.

SPEAKING

The speaking game

5 Practise asking and answering questions by playing this game.

• Work in groups of three or four.
• You will each need two counters, for example a small coin.
• Place one counter on the START square on the outer track, and the second counter on any square on the inner track – it doesn't matter which one.
• Each player takes turns to roll the dice.
• Move both counters clockwise according to the number of squares on the dice.
• When you land on a square on the outer track you must ask any player of your choice a question about the topic written on that square. Your question must begin with the words shown on the square on the inner track.
• A FREE QUESTION square means you can choose any topic to ask about.
• If the rest of the players think a speaker made a mistake when asking a question, he or she misses a go.

websites	meeting skills	applying for a job	FREE QUESTION	ambitions
setting up a new business				dress code
recruitment	I'd like to know	Can you tell me	Why	holidays
team building	Where		Do you think	customers
FREE QUESTION	Who		Is	shopping / prices
giving presentations	How		What	emailing
forms of advertising	What		How	FREE QUESTION
food and drink	Do		Can	market research
training / education	Does		What do you think	management skills
ways of working	Could you tell me	I was wondering	Are	the latest news
home or country				hotels / travel
START FINISH	online business	FREE QUESTION	selling	qualifications

118

MODULE 12 BUSINESS LAW   119

Student's Book pages 118 and 119

Indirect questions and tags

GRAMMAR

1 ⊙ 12.1 Students at this level will still have problems with word order when using indirect questions and even greater difficulties using tag questions effectively. Give them time to read 0–4 before they listen to 12.1 again. With stronger groups ask them to try and predict the answers before listening.

Answers
1 don't they
2 you can use the same colour
3 there's anything else
4 you think the outcome will be

Extension
Ask students to try and summarise the rules based on what happens in 0–4. After some suggestions ask them to look at the grammar summary on page 130 and check if they are correct.

2 Elicit from students the fact that a speaker can sound more polite and less direct by using indirect questions and tags. They are especially useful if you want to encourage people to give their opinions and get them talking.

3 Students correct sentences 1–8. Note that sentence 7 is a direct question.

Answers
1 Do you think business **will** become ...
2 I was wondering **what** you think ....
3 ... a good product, **isn't** it?
4 ... by plane, **won't they**?
5 Do you think employees **can** work ...
6 ... what your plans for your future career **are**?
(or) ... what your plans **are** for your future career?
7 ... experience **do** you think would help ...
8 ... for three years, **haven't** you?

Pronunciation
With question tags, the intonation rises if we are very uncertain and falls if we are asking to check and confirm information we think we know. Write the following sentences on the board with the arrows and drill them.

Good marketing is more important than a good product, **isn't** it? ↘

You've studied English for three years, **haven't** you? ↗

4 Students take turns to ask and answer questions 1–8 in exercise 3.

Extension

Ask students to prepare five direct questions for a colleague about their work and life. Then tell them to swap these questions with their partner who must rewrite them as indirect questions or sentences ending in a question tag. Finally, students ask and answer their final versions of the questions with a partner.

Photocopiable activity 12.1

See page 178.

The speaking game

SPEAKING

5   You will need to have some dice for this lesson so that each group has one to roll. Put students into groups of three or four and let them study the instructions for the game. Students work their way round the board creating questions for other players.

The question does not have to include the exact words on the topic square. Here are some examples:

(home or country) *Could you tell me where you are from?*

(ways of working) *Does your company use flexitime?*

(training / education) *Do you think people should continue their education throughout their lives?*

(food and drink) *I was wondering what a favourite dish is in your country.*

(forms of advertising) *How effective do you think leaflets are compared to word-of-mouth advertising?*

Alternative

You may not want to follow the game format in some classes (such as one-to-one lessons). If that is the case, just ask your student or students to create questions at random using combinations from the board for practice.

BUSINESS SKILLS

12.2 Handling questions

LISTENING

Difficult questions

1 Discuss why people might ask questions in the following situations.

   A A customer wants to return an item.
   B An employee receives a pay cheque at the end of the month.
   C A student gets poor marks for a business exam.
   D A manager discovers an employee has been sending emails to friends.
   E A public relations manager is explaining a faulty product to journalists at a press conference.

2 12.2 Listen to five conversations. Match the situations A–E in exercise 1 to conversations 1–5.

   Conversation 1: _____
   Conversation 2: _____
   Conversation 3: _____
   Conversation 4: _____
   Conversation 5: _____

3 12.2 Listen again and match the questions 1–6 to the responses A–F.

1 What else was I supposed to write?
2 Do you have any ideas about what caused the problem?
3 How soon will these items be back on the shelves?
4 Why hasn't it been included?
5 Can I exchange it for another one?
6 You do know our policy with regard to this, don't you?

A I just need to check with someone first.
B Sorry, I don't follow you.
C I'm afraid I'm unable to answer that at the moment.
D Can you explain what you mean?
E Let me get back to you on that.
F That's a very good question.

4 Write the responses A–F from exercise 3 into this language summary.

Handling questions
Delaying your answer
Do you mind if I answer that at the end?
(1) _____
(2) _____
(3) _____
I'd like to come back to that point later on, if that's OK.
Commenting on the question
(4) _____
Thank you for asking that.
Asking for further explanation or repetition
Sorry, I didn't understand the question.
(5) _____
Sorry, I didn't hear you. / catch that.
(6) _____
Could you repeat that? / say that again?

SPEAKING

Responding to questions

5 How would you respond to a question in the following situations?

1 A job interviewer asks you a very complicated question. You need him to repeat it.
2 A journalist telephones you to ask about a possible new joint venture between you and another company. It is true but the final contract hasn't been agreed yet.
3 You're a politician and an angry member of the public asks you why you have increased the rate of tax for homeowners.
4 It's your first day at a banking call centre. A customer calls and asks about taking out a $5,000 loan but wants a different interest rate to the one advertised.
5 Someone interrupts you in the middle of trying to explain a complicated new system.
6 You are a PR representative for a pharmaceutical company. A new skincare product has given some customers red spots on their faces. You are answering questions at a press conference.

6 Think of a question for each of the situations in exercise 5. Then work in pairs and take turns to ask your question and give an appropriate response.

Student's Book pages 120 and 121

Difficult questions

LISTENING Track 14 (CD2)

1 Students could discuss the situations in pairs or as a class. Ask students to think of possible direct questions the people would ask. You may also want to give a few examples for the first situation to give them the idea.

Possible questions

A The customer might ask: *Can I have a refund? Can I exchange this for something else?* The shop assistant might ask: *When did you buy it? Do you have the receipt? Did you pay by credit card or cash?*

B The employee might ask: *Why wasn't I paid for that overtime I did? Why is the tax higher this month?*

C The student might ask: *What did I get wrong? Why was my mark so low?* The teacher might ask: *What went wrong? Did you revise?*

D The manager might ask: *Have you read our policy on sending emails? Why did you send so many?*

E The journalists might ask: *What is the company doing to solve the problem? Will you be giving customers a refund?*

Extension

Write students' suggestions for each situation on the board and if any of the questions contain mistakes use this opportunity to clarify any points of grammar. At the end, put students into pairs and ask them to roleplay each of the situations using the questions they have brainstormed.

2 12.2 Students listen to the conversations and match them to the five situations in exercise 1.

Answers
Conversation 1: C
Conversation 2: E
Conversation 3: B
Conversation 4: A
Conversation 5: D

12.2 Listening script
Conversation 1
S = Student   T = Teacher

S I'm sorry but I don't understand this mark. Why was it so low? I mean, I thought I'd answered everything. What else was I supposed to write?
T Look, I can't really comment on that until I've looked at it. Give me a day and let me get back to you on that. OK?

Conversation 2
PRM = PR Manager J = Journalist

PRM OK. Are there any questions? Yes?
J So you've announced that you'll be recalling all the items from supermarkets and stores, but do you have any ideas about what caused the problem?
PRM That's a very good question. We're looking into it at the moment, and we hope that we will know more very soon.
J How soon will these items be back on the shelves?
PRM I'm afraid I'm unable to answer that at the moment. I can assure you, however, that we're doing everything we can to sort this problem out as quickly as possible.

Conversation 3
E = Employee M = Manager

E Can I have a word?
M Sure.
E It's just that this doesn't seem to be right. I did some overtime the month before last. Why hasn't it been included?
M Sorry, I don't follow you. If it was for the month before last it would have been on your last cheque.
E But don't you remember? You forgot to add it and said you'd add it to this month's ...

Conversation 4
CS = Customer Service C = Customer

CS Hello. Customer Service.
C Hello, I bought a Barbie doll house set and I'm afraid it's the wrong one.
CS Sorry, I didn't catch that. A Barbie what?
C A Barbie doll house set. You know. It has kind of pink wallpaper.
CS But is there something actually wrong with it?
C I think it's the wrong colour or something. I don't know really. It was my daughter who said it was wrong.
CS Well, we can only take it back if it's faulty.
C Can I exchange it for another one though?
CS Sorry. Can you wait a moment? I just need to check with someone first.

Conversation 5
M = Manager E = Employee

M Sorry Peter, can I have a quick word before you go?
E Erm, well, I am in a bit of a rush.
M It won't take long. Let's use my office.
E OK.
M Take a seat. I'm aware that you've been using computers for personal use during your lunch breaks. You do know our policy with regard to this, don't you?
E Sorry, can you explain what you mean? Is there a problem?

3 🔘 12.2 Students listen out for the questions and match them to the responses.

Answers
1 E 2 F 3 C 4 B 5 A 6 D

4 Students categorise the questions to complete the language summary.

Answers
1, 2, 3: A, C, E
4 F.
5, 6: B, D

Responding to questions

SPEAKING

5 Students could work in pairs to decide on an appropriate response to each situation. There may be more than one possibility in some situations.

Possible answers
1 Sorry, I didn't understand the question.
2 I'm afraid I'm unable to answer that at the moment.
3 That's a very good question.
4 I just need to check with someone first.
5 I'd like to come back to that point later on if that's OK.
6 I'm afraid I'm unable to answer that at the moment.

6 Students in pairs roleplay each of the six situations in exercise 5. One student makes and asks the type of questions for a situation, and the other student gives an appropriate response.

Possible conversation (1)
A: If I was talking to your colleagues, what do you think they would say is your greatest strength but also your main weakness when it comes to dealing with other people?
B: Sorry, I don't follow you? Do you mean my colleagues in my current job?
A: Yes or any previous work colleagues?
B: Well, first of all, they'd say I was ...

Extension
For more practice with this language point, students could roleplay the situations in exercise 1 on page 120 (which they might have done earlier) and this time use some of the responses.

Reproduced Student's Book pages

READING

Press releases

1 Read the 'How to ...' article on writing press releases and answer the following questions.

1 Why do people write press releases?
2 When will newspapers or broadcasters use your news?
3 What is the advantage of a press release over normal advertising?

How to ... write a press release

You may think that writing press releases only works when you have important news to share or company announcements to make but that is wrong! You can write and submit press releases which will get published in newspapers or broadcast on TV or radio at any time if you give an interesting slant to what you are submitting. Here are some interesting ideas to help get your press release picked up by the media:

• Write a story about how your business helps your community or solves a problem for local people.
• Write a press release if your company has raised money for charity.
• Tell your personal story: maybe you set up your business from nothing or you are a local success story.
• Relate your story to what is happening today – watch the news, check out what the 'hot topics' are and find a way to 'spin' a story from that.
• Make sure the press release doesn't sound like an advertisement. The idea is that consumers will think they are reading a news story rather than being sold something.

2 A local newspaper has received four press releases this morning. According to the article above, which release (A–D) isn't a good one? Tell your partner why.

A As many of you are aware, environmental concerns are now at the front of everyone's minds. But while many companies say they are concerned, we at Beavis and Son are taking this very seriously, and we are therefore pleased to announce our new 'buy a bag for the Amazon' scheme. Unlike most stores, where you get a free plastic bag which you then throw away, at Beavis and Son we will sell you a strong reusable bag, with the cost going to a charity which saves the rainforests of the Amazon ...

B It is always good to hear of a local success story and we are delighted that Rainer's Furnishings are now going global with the opening of their first ever factory overseas. The company will be taking over a firm based in Poznan in Poland and re-equipping the factory there. Contrary to recent suggestions that the company may use this as an opportunity to reduce the size of its local factory, the company's managing director Malcolm Storey was able to confirm with staff at a recent meeting that this was not a step towards downsizing or cost-cutting but expansion ...

C I am writing to inform your readers of our spring sale starting next week. All clothing items will have discounts saving you as much as 20% ...

D While we are sad to see her go, we are celebrating the retirement of our founder Roselyn Cooper-Hennes. Roselyn is handing over the running of her company to her two sons, Richard and Mark, exactly thirty years after founding the company. As many local people will know, Roselyn was an active member of the local council. Perhaps they don't know, however, that Roselyn actually started the business from a small kitchen in a tiny house ...

3 Match the press release (A, B, C or D) to the statements below.

This press release ...
1 is more like an advertisement. _____
2 starts to tell a story. _____
3 is about raising money for charity. _____
4 refers to a 'hot topic'. _____
5 describes a recent achievement. _____
6 explains a benefit to the customer. _____
7 refers to some bad publicity. _____

4 Work in groups of three. You are the editors of the newspaper. This week there is only space for one of these press releases. Discuss which one to use.

5 Look at the underlined phrases in the four press releases and write them next to these functions.

Introduces the news _____

Refers to reader's knowledge _____

Announces good news _____

Handles bad news _____

WRITING

A press release

6 Write a press release using the information below.

You work in the press office for a local theatre called the Everyman. The manager has just sent you this email. He wants a press release to be sent to the editor of the local paper. Use the email and the handwritten notes you have already made. Try to use some of the expressions in exercise 5. Send your press release in the form of a letter to the editor.

Handwritten notes:
• Recent reports in the press that the theatre might be closing are totally untrue
• The next musical stars the TV actor Rene Travis
• Café will also be open during the day selling snacks and sandwich lunches – people shopping will be interested
• There will be cabaret nights in the café
• Money for the new café was raised by the organisation 'Friends of the Everyman' and a grant from the local council

Email:
Attachment: cafesketch.pdf

Hi
I've just had a date for the opening of the new café at the side of the theatre. It's May 1st so can you let the local press know? There will be an opening celebration at 7pm with local people invited. By the way, it will also have Internet access so that's probably worth a mention too.

Unfortunately there isn't a show on May 1st but our musical Guys and Dolls starts on May 3rd so try to fit that in somewhere.

Thanks a lot.
Richard.

PS There's a design of the café attached. Maybe they'll print that as well!

MODULE 12 HANDLING QUESTIONS 123

Student's Book pages 122 and 123

Press releases

READING

1 Begin by asking students if they know what a press release is and whether they ever use them where they work. Pre-work learners may also know that their college or place of study lets the local press know about its academic successes or notable events. Then ask students to read the 'How to...' text and answer the questions. Note that the answer to question 3 isn't in the text but students should be able to guess.

Answers
1 When they have important news, company announcements, or at any time when it's possible to to give an 'interesting slant'.*
2 When the story explains how your company has helped the local community or has raised money for charity. Also the story might be about success or relate to other hot topics. They won't use it if it seems like an advert.
3 One advantage is that a press release is free publicity and also that the public tend to take more notice of the company than they would from seeing an advertisement.

*You may need to explain the term, 'interesting slant'. This often refers to newspaper stories which take an ordinary or even potentially uninteresting event but manage to make it interesting in some way.

2 Give students one minute to read the four press releases quickly for general meaning, and then to say which one isn't good.

Answer
Text C isn't a good press release because it reads like an advertisement. It announces a sale with discounts and there is no suggestion that the company has done anything useful for the community.

3 Students now match the four texts to the statements. Allow about five minutes for this more detailed reading.

Answers
1 C 2 D 3 A 4 A 5 B 6 C 7 B

4 Students work in groups of three (or four) and discuss the releases. They can argue which one they think readers will be most interested in and also refer back to the 'How to ...' article and its suggestion for what makes a good release.

5 In this exercise, students focus on expressions to structure a press release.

Answers
- Introduces the news: *I am writing / It is always good to hear*
- Refers to reader's knowledge: *As many of you are aware / As many local people will know*
- Announces good news: *we are therefore pleased to announce / we are delighted / we are celebrating*
- Handles bad news: *Contrary to recent suggestions / we are taking this very seriously*

A press release

WRITING

6 Students write a press release in the form of a letter to the editor of a newspaper. Students could begin by underlining or highlighting any key information or words from the information in the email and the handwritten notes as well as think how they can use the expressions in exercise 5.

Possible answer

> Dear Editor
>
> Contrary to recent suggestions that the Everyman Theatre may be closing, we are pleased to announce the opening of our new café on May 1st. We are celebrating this event with a party for local people at 7pm. After that, the café will be open during the day for lunchtime shoppers as well as in the evenings for theatre audiences. We also intend to hold regular cabaret nights in the café.
>
> Money for the café was raised by 'Friends of the Everyman' and this also helped pay for the Internet access facilities. Two days after the café opening, the musical 'Guys and Dolls' will start on May 3rd in the main theatre, starring well-known TV actor Rene Travis.
>
> Please find enclosed designs for the new café.
>
> Yours sincerely

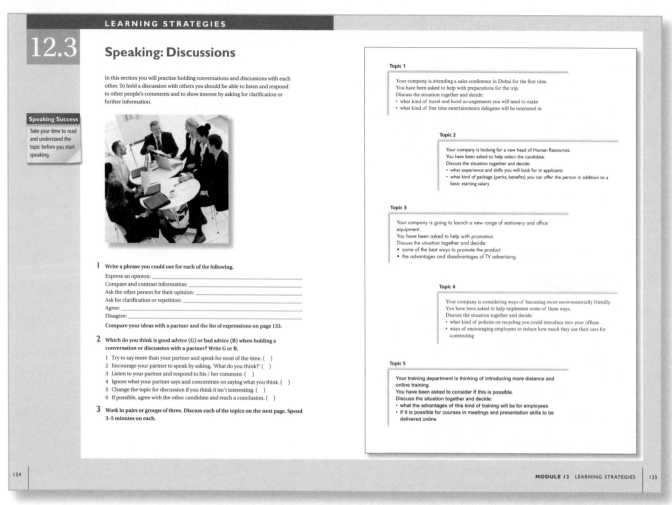

1 This exercise is a review of expressions that have come up during the student's book or that they might already know. Each student could write one expression for each category and then share their ideas with other students so that everyone has a good selection of expressions to draw on during the exam.

Possible answers

Express an opinion: *I think … / In my opinion … / I feel that … / It's important that …*

Compare and contrast information: *On the one hand … on the other hand … /*

Ask the other person for their opinion: *What do you think? / How do you feel about … ? / Do you agree?*

Ask for clarification or repetition: *Do you mean …? / Sorry, I don't quite follow you. / Can you repeat that?*

Agree: *That's right. / Yes, and … / I agree … / Sure.*

Disagree: *I know what you mean, but … / Yes, but … / Don't you also think, though, that …*

2 Students can discuss this exercise in pairs or groups, but make sure they are very clear on the correct answers at the end. To extend this, students could rewrite any statements marked B to make them give good advice (see these in brackets below).

Answers
1 B
2 G
3 G
4 B (Listen to what your partner says and respond appropriately.)
5 B
6 G

3 Students work in pairs and discuss the topics on page 125. You can set a time limit of about three minutes per discussion. When students finish the first topic, they move on to the next. After they have discussed two or three of the topics you could stop everyone to give some general feedback. Give praise for pairs who are collaborating well. Give feedback on any expressions or if necessary input any new phrases which you think might help their discussions.

Photocopiable activity 12.2
See page 179.

PHOTOCOPIABLE

© 2009 Heinle, Cengage Learning

1.1   Ways of working

Student A: temp

You are going to be interviewed by a journalist of a local newspaper for an article on different ways of working. Read and complete the information below with your own ideas. Write two more sentences about temping. Then answer the journalist's questions.

You're a qualified _____ but at the moment you're temping in different companies because you've only lived in this area for _____ months. You're temping while you look for a permanent job. You've been applying for jobs but in _____ months you've only had two interviews.

You've been qualified since _____ and you have worked as a _____ for _____ years.

You've had _____ temporary jobs since you moved here. You enjoy temping because _____, but you don't like _____ . The pay is _____ and the hours are _____ . Each company is different, but you haven't had any bad experiences yet.

Currently you're working at _____ as a _____ . You've been working there since _____. You hope that the position could become permanent.

Student B: journalist

You are a journalist on the business section of a local newspaper. You are going to interview people for a series of articles on different ways of working. Prepare questions using these prompts. Add two more questions. Then interview someone who is working

what / do?	why / enjoy / temping?
where / work ?	what / not like / about temping?
why / do / temporary work?	what / be / pay and hours / like?
how long / look for / a permanent job?	have / bad experiences as a temp?
how long / be / qualified?	which company / work / at the moment?
how long / work / in your profession?	what / be / your position there?
how many jobs / have?	how long / work / there?

1.2 Making contacts

Special events promoter

MusicWorld Entertainments

orchestras – bands – solo artists

Jasmine
the flower experts

Sales representative

Director

Formal dress hire
Ladies and gentlemen

SUITS AND MORE LTD

BEST CHOICE TRAVEL

SPECIALIST HOLIDAY OPERATORS
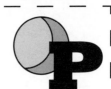

CUSTOMER SERVICES REPRESENTATIVE

Chocolate World

Assistant
product development

chocolate fountains & chocolate sculptures

Marketing manager

UK & Northern Europe
Premier Hotel Chain

Venus Beauty Salons

PROMOTIONS MANAGER
HAIR STYLISTS – MAKE UP SPECIALISTS

Sales representative
car hire, chauffer & self drive

Classic Cars Ltd

CLEAR PRINTERS LTD

ASSISTANT MANAGER

business stationery – promotional literature – events

Photographic assistant
Focus Photographic Agency
press - special occasions - PR events

PHOTOCOPIABLE

© 2009 Heinle, Cengage Learning

2.1 The past

Business Profile A

1 Complete the profile by adding the verbs in the correct past tense form.

work be hold create receive help spend be

Vivienne Cox, who _____ born in 1958, runs two of the largest divisions of the oil and gas giant BP. She _____ for BP since graduating from Cambridge University in 1981, and in her early career she _____ a variety of commercial posts. She was appointed as the CEO of Air BP in 1998. She _____ three years as vice president of BP Oil, where she _____ responsible for oil supply and trading. In 2005, she _____ BP Alternative Energy, which will invest $8bn in low carbon energy and in 2006 she _____ the Veuve Clicquot Business woman of the year award. Outside of work, she _____ the St Frances Hospice Charity in the UK for many years.

2 Using the prompts, write some questions for an interview to find out about Profile B.

date of birth?

education?

first job / company – when? what?

early career?

main career responsibilities?

important achievements?

recent career decisions / actions?

awards or recognition by industry / public?

interests outside of work?

- -

Business Profile B

1 Complete the profile by adding the verbs in the correct past tense form.

deal in share sell live drive give become start have

Ingvar Kamprad, who was born in 1926, is best known as the creator of IKEA, the most successful home furnishing company in the world. He _____ working as a young boy, selling matches to local villages. In his early career, Kamprad _____ a variety of goods such as pens and picture frames, but he _____ furniture since 1953. Kamprad _____ in Switzerland since 1976, where he _____ known as a man of contrasts: he _____ the same old Volvo for nearly twenty years, but he also _____ a Porsche for a number of years. In 2000, he _____ IKEA staff a millennium bonus: he _____ the value of one day's worldwide sales equally among all employees. He is the chairman of the INGKA Foundation, which is the wealthiest charity in the world.

2 Using the prompts, write some questions for an interview to find out about Profile A.

date of birth?

education?

first job / company – when? what?

early career?

main career responsibilities?

important achievements?

recent career decisions / actions?

awards or recognition by industry / public?

interests outside of work?

2.2 Presenting a company

Company Fact Sheet A

name of company	A	B	C
date founded	1849	_____	1907
main products	health care	media	_____
divisions	4	_____	5
employees	106,000	_____	112,000
turnover	$48.371 billion	_____	_____
net income	$19.337 billion	_____	$26.311 billion

Company Fact Sheet B

name of company	A	B	C
date founded	1849	1990	_____
main products	_____	media	oil and gas
divisions	_____	7	5
employees	_____	96,000	_____
turnover	_____	$44.70 billion	_____
net income	$19.337 billion	$7.4 billion	_____

Company Fact Sheet C

name of company	A	B	C
date founded	_____	1990	1907
main products	health care	_____	oil and gas
divisions	4	_____	5
employees	_____	96,000	112,000
turnover	$48.371 billion	_____	$318.845 billion
net income	_____	_____	$26.311 billion

PHOTOCOPIABLE

© 2009 Heinle, Cengage Learning

3.1 Starting a business

Work in groups of four. You are going to start your own business and persuade people to invest in your company. Choose a business from the list below or use your own ideas, then prepare a brief business plan to present to potential investors.

bar	sandwich shop
coffee shop	courier service
internet café	estate agent's
beauty salon	bed and breakfast
gardening services	dating agency

Business plan

brief description of business:

product / service:

name of business:

market trends / estimates:

location:

objectives (first 12 months):

target customers / market:

promotion / advertising:

management team:

prices:

start-up costs:

PHOTOCOPIABLE

© 2009 Heinle, Cengage Learning

3.2   Leaving and taking messages

C Ms / Mr Butler County Hotel   794 88 22

Telephone Christine Ross to tell her that the seminar room for her training day has been double-booked in the morning. You need to know if she can change the date of the seminar or use a smaller room.

C Ms / Mr Coutt Open University 0221 837 243

Telephone Carl de Boor to confirm that he can take his Accountancy exam while he is in Berlin. You have made arrangements with the university there to provide a room and an invigilator. This will mean an additional cost of €275 to the fees, so you'd like him to confirm his agreement in writing.

C Ms / Mr Ritchie Training Ways 619 552 994

Telephone Fiona Paterson. There's been a problem with the seminar timetable. You need to change the time of her workshop from 11 a.m. to 9 a.m. Apologise for the mistake but make sure she agrees to the change.

C Ms / Mr Devereux Routledge Finance 078 447 221

Telephone Sue Watts about some training materials her company has sent you. They have sent the Spreadsheet Training Pack instead of the Database Pack. Ask her to send the correct materials by courier because the course starts tomorrow

C Ms / Mr Wilson   Chamber of Commerce
0521 883 962

You organise training courses and one of your trainers has dropped out at the last minute. The course is five two-hour sessions on Computer-aided Design. Telephone Bill Garnier, who has led similar courses, and ask him if he can lead the course.

C   Ms / Mr Lowe 798 476 877

You are scheduled to start teaching a ten-week course on Basic Accounting, but family problems mean you can't do the course. Phone the course organiser, Douglas Simm, to tell him. Be very apologetic because the course starts next week.

Christine Ross

Carl de Boor

Fiona Paterson

Sue Watts

Bill Garnier

Douglas Simm

PHOTOCOPIABLE

© 2009 Heinle, Cengage Learning

4.1   Modals

1   Work in pairs. Decide if the modal verbs in sentences 1–12 are correct or incorrect, and write ✓ or ✗ next to them. For the incorrect sentences, write the correct modal verb(s).

2   Work with the rest of the class. In your pairs, you have €50 to bet on your decisions about the sentences. You can bet in multiples of €10. If you win the bet, you double your money. If you lose the bet, you lose the amount you bet. The pair that has the most euros at the end wins. Follow the example your teacher gives.

1   Their marketing campaign **needn't have been** very successful, because they've just sacked their marketing manager. ☐

2   The television channel **couldn't** show the advert before nine o'clock because of its adult content, so the company withdrew it and made a new one. ☐

3   Food packages **don't have to** carry a warning to consumers if the product contains nuts since the introduction of strict new laws. ☐

4   The Advertising Standards Authority says companies **couldn't** say things about products that are untrue. ☐

5   We **don't have to** use marketing emails everywhere; some countries don't allow it. ☐

6   There are strict rules about advertising tobacco and we **must** break them. ☐

7   A: I've brought you some brochures for the new office furniture you want.
B: Thanks, but you **needn't have**. I've decided not to change anything. ☐

8   We got so many customers through word of mouth that we **didn't need to** pay for any advertising. ☐

9   These ideas from our new advertising agency are fantastic. We **ought to have** changed agencies earlier. ☐

10   A: I've got 33 spam messages in my inbox.
B: You **needn't** update your anti-spam software, it's obviously not very good! ☐

11   The prices in this brochure **can** be right – it says here €34 for a laptop computer! ☐

12   Apparently we **can** reach more than three million customers by advertising on these websites. ☐

PHOTOCOPIABLE

©2009 Heinle, Cengage Learning

4.2   Delegating

Check the department's stationery supplies and order anything that is needed.

Go to the airport to meet the new Division Head and take her to her hotel. She is arriving tomorrow at 7 a.m.

Prepare a confidential one-page report on bad time-keepers in the department.

Represent the company at the local council's presentation of Business Awards on Friday evening.

Organise the new rota for security staff following last month's job cuts

Collect suitable images for the company's new website and send to the designer by tomorrow afternoon.

Set up and maintain a notice board where staff can post non-work related information.

Draft a questionnaire to evaluate customer satisfaction with your company's services.

Handle the monthly visit from the catering supplies representative.

Get quotes for new office cleaning services and make a recommendation.

Talk to the younger staff about dress code and inappropriate dress.

Take over the organisation of the company stand at next month's trade fair.

PHOTOCOPIABLE

© 2009 Heinle, Cengage Learning

5.1 Reporting

agree	'You're right, it's too late to change the order now.'
apologise	'I'm so sorry I missed the meeting.'
argue	'I'm not really sure about that. People just aren't interested in abstract art.'
ask	'Are the pictures originals or prints?'
call	'I'm just phoning to say that tomorrow's board meeting has been cancelled.'
comment	'Well, people often resist change at first, you know.'
conclude	'To sum up, then, nobody is in favour of this move.'
disagree	'No, I don't agree with changing to hot-desking.'
explain	'First, you select the product you want, then you put your money in.'
suggest	'How about taking a break for a few minutes?'
tell	'Don't worry, it's not serious.'
think	'I think they need to reconsider their offer.'

PHOTOCOPIABLE

© 2009 Heinle, Cengage Learning

5.2   Expressions for meetings

Case study: Paper products plc

Your factory is located one kilometre away from the nearest town, and is a major employer in the area. However, an environmental pressure group is campaigning for the factory to close because of pollution. The factory manager has called a meeting to decide on a public relations strategy for the company. Discuss these ideas. There is only enough money to spend on one idea.

1   Improve the area around the factory by planting gardens and re-painting the factory.
2   Help local schools and schoolchildren.
3   Run a series of articles in the local press and have an exhibition at the local library.
4   Hold an open day for local people.
5   Invite the environmental group to be part of a joint company and community committee.
6   Sponsor local sports clubs and events in the community.

Factory manager

You think that it is impossible to talk to environmentalists. You want to convince the local community that the factory is 'clean'. You like the idea of an open day with free food, entertainment and a guided tour of the factory. You also think that sponsoring local sports will be excellent PR. Think of two more reasons which support your ideas before you start the meeting.

Production manager

You don't believe the environmental group has any real power. You think that it's a good long-term investment for the company to help local schools buy computers and give funding to school projects. You also think the community will feel more positive about the factory if it looks better and 'greener'. Think of two more reasons which support your ideas before you start the meeting.

Quality manager

You know that the environmental campaign is based on incorrect information and ideas. Involving the campaigners in a joint committee could change that. You also think you will reach a big audience by using the local press to explain how the factory works and complies with the regulations. Think of two more reasons which support your ideas before you start the meeting.

I see your point, but …	I'd go along with you there.	I disagree. I think …
I think that …	I agree that …	Do we all agree?
Sorry, I don't quite follow you.	Let's move on.	I'd like to know more about …
What do you think?	I'd like to suggest that …	Can I just come in here?

PHOTOCOPIABLE

© 2009 Heinle, Cengage Learning

6.1 Passives

Student A

1 We **give** / **are given** a verbal warning to employees who break safety regulations.
2 The project **should approve** / **should be approved** on time.
3 What's the name of the other person who **founded** / **was founded** Microsoft with Bill Gates?
4 It **rumours** / **is rumoured** that Goldstar is bankrupt.
5 The recommendations **are looking** / **are being looked** at this week. We hope for a decision soon.
6 Following restructuring, your staff **will send** / **will be sent** to the main plant.
7 In the last six months, 30 people **have taken on** / **have been taken on** in the retail section.
8 I heard that their overseas offices **are closed** / **will be closed** next month.
9 The report concluded that Ms Stone **dismissed** / **was dismissed** unfairly.

1	2	3
4	5	6
7	8	9

Student B

1 The new CEO **is announced** / **will be announced** at the meeting.
2 We believe staff **must give** / **must be given** proper training.
3 New investment **will need** / **will be needed** to finance the expansion.
4 The franchise **sold** / **was sold** after poor financial results.
5 The improvements they **are making** / **are being made** to the service are excellent.
6 The clothing chain **has opened** / **has been opened** 23 new stores this year.
7 It **thinks** / **is thought** that they intend to make 200 people redundant.
8 We **pay** / **are paid** a bonus three times a year to all production staff.
9 The committee **decided** / **was decided** to accept the proposal

1	2	3
4	5	6
7	8	9

6.2   Emailing

Student A: tourist

You have booked a cruise with Global Oceans in May followed by a visit to see friends in June. For this visit you have booked four nights, 1–4 June, at the Baltic Villa Hotel via an Internet booking site, but you haven't received any confirmation of the booking.

1   Write an email direct to the hotel to ask if they have a room reserved for you. Remember to give your name, the dates and the name of the online booking site you used. Give the email to Student B.

2   Read the email from Global Oceans Ltd and decide what you want to do. Write an email to Global Oceans Ltd to tell them your decision. Give the email to Student C.

3   Read the email from the Baltic Villa Hotel. Decide if you need to change any of your plans for the first week in June and write a reply to the hotel.

Student B: hotel manager, Baltic Villa Hotel

You received a provisional booking from Global Oceans, a tour operator, for a coach party on the weekend of 2–4 June, which will give you 100% occupancy that weekend.

1   Write to Global Oceans asking them to confirm the bookings. Ask them for exact numbers and remind them of the discount you can offer them. Give the email to Student C.

2   Read the email from a customer and decide what to reply. Write an email to the customer and give it to Student A.

3   Read the email from Global Oceans. Think about your occupancy rate for the first week in June and write an email to Global Oceans OR to your individual customer.

Student C: bookings manager, Global Oceans Ltd

You organise coach tours and cruises in the Mediterranean and Scandinavia. One of the ships has technical problems and the Mediterranean cruise scheduled for May will now take place in the first week of June. You also have problems because a coach tour for the week 1–7 June is only 50% booked and you have to decide whether to cancel it or not.

1   Write to your cruise customers to ask them if the new dates are acceptable and offer them an alternative Scandinavian cruise for the original dates. Give the email to Student A.

2   Read the email from the Baltic Villa Hotel and decide what to reply. Write your reply and give the email to Student B.

3   Read the email from your cruise customer. Decide on a response and write a reply to the email.

PHOTOCOPIABLE

© 2009 Heinle, Cengage Learning

7.1   Comparatives and superlatives

Write the job title of someone who ...

1 has to balance the books: a_____
2 assists in the day-to-day administration of a department: a_____ a_____
3 takes decisions on ideas for adverts: a_____ e_____
4 designs buildings: a_____
5 is responsible for all aspects of a product: b_____ m_____
6 deals with client complaints and quality of service: c_____ s_____ assistant
7 checks that your workplace is safe: h_____ and s_____ inspector
8 is in charge of running a hotel: h_____ m_____
9 hires and fires people: h_____ r_____ officer
10 gives legal advice: l_____
11 oversees the publication of a magazine: e_____
12 is responsible for the promotion of a company's products: m_____ m_____
13 handles the administrative tasks of an individual manager: p_____ a_____
14 is responsible for a company's public image: p_____ r_____ officer
15 is in charge of selling products: s_____ d_____
16 writes computer programs: s_____ developer
17 makes travel arrangements and sells holidays: t_____ a_____

Name two jobs that are **more challenging than** working in Human Resources and say why.	Name two jobs that **aren't as rewarding** as running your own business and say why.	Name three jobs that are **more boring than** working as a magazine editor and say why.

Use the words below and give three differences (with the reasons) between working as a lawyer and an advertising executive.
 	
glamorous   varied
         responsible
	Use the words below and give three differences (with the reasons) between working in customer services and in marketing.
	
	frustrating repetitive
	         enjoyable
		Give three reasons why working as an accountant is **better than** working as a software developer.

Give three reasons why you would prefer to work as a travel agent rather than a personal assistant.	Talk for one minute about the **most boring** job you could imagine doing.	Talk for one minute about the **most frustrating** job you could imagine doing.
Talk for one minute about **the most challenging** job you could imagine doing.	Talk for one minute about **the least rewarding** job you could imagine doing.	What is your ideal job? Talk for one minute about why it would be **the best** job for you.

PHOTOCOPIABLE

© 2009 Heinle, Cengage Learning

7.2   Selling

A set of golf clubs €...........

You've just been made a director of your company.

A set of encyclopaedias on CD €...........

You've just started an on-line course of study.

A set of kitchen knives €...........

You've just moved into a new house.

A leather briefcase €...........

You're looking for a new job.

An automatic translator in six languages €...........

You're going on holiday next week.

A portable DVD player €...........

You have a long daily train journey to your new job.

Ear plugs €...........

Your desk at work is next to a room full of noisy machinery.

A book called Wedding planning and etiquette €...........

You're getting married next year.

A GPS navigation system for a car €...........

You've got a temporary job as a delivery driver.

A Rolex watch €...........

You're responsible for buying the Managing Director's retirement gift.

PHOTOCOPIABLE

© 2009 Heinle, Cengage Learning

8.1   -ing form and infinitive

to fix the broken door yesterday.	While Sue is ill, we've arranged
to take on a temporary receptionist.	With their reputation, they can't afford
to treat their customers badly.	Have you considered
advertising in the local paper?	The company decided
to advertise on the Internet.	They've delayed
taking on new staff until next year.	On Friday nights, we enjoy
socialising after work.	Ask the technician – she's good at
fixing printers.	As a trainer, I'm interested in
helping people improve their skills.	His job as global director involves
travelling abroad every month.	I don't think we'll manage

to finish today, I'm sorry.	Andrew, would you mind
meeting this client on my behalf?	Next year, I'd prefer
to travel less often.	In general, staff don't want
to socialise with management.	Would you like
to help me run this project?	Before going to Rome, she practised
speaking Italian every day.	It was a great course, we learned
to speak Italian and laughed a lot.	If you want loyal clients, I recommend
treating them more politely.	What do you suggest
doing about this problem?	What time did we agree
to meet? I've forgotten.	The contractor promised

8.2   Linking phrases

A	B
A 1 the meal was satisfactory	**B** 1 business is not good
A ...we've decided not to eat there again	**B** ... not listening to our customers
A 2 she does a fantastic job	**B** 2 we need a new warehouse building
A ... recent personal problems	**B** ... it has to be available now
A 3 he gives the impression of listening to you	**B** 3 the increase in prices
A ... he never remembers what you say	**B** ... sales did not fall
A 4 complaining several times	**B** 4 we were satisfied with your service
A ... he got a refund	**B** ... we've decided not to use you again
A 5 the course was cancelled	**B** 5 he had no experience
A ... lack of interest	**B** ... having no qualifications
A 6 the office block was brand new	**B** 6 the marketing campaign was redesigned
A ... it had no parking area	**B** ... a disastrous launch
A 7 the legal action	**B** 7 he wrote a letter to the CEO
A ... we can't make any comment	**B** ... he sent a copy to the press

even so	moreover
despite	but
however	in spite of
because of	nevertheless
after	as a result of
furthermore	in addition to
due to	following

PHOTOCOPIABLE

© 2009 Heinle, Cengage Learning

9.1   Branding

Case study: *SwiftFly Airlines*

Your airline company, SwiftFly, is a budget airline operating in Europe. In recent months, bookings have slowed down. There have been news stories about 'low-quality' tourism in which budget airlines have been criticised. In addition to this, the airline industry in general has an increasingly bad environmental image. Hold a meeting to:

- discuss what you can do to improve your brand image
- discuss the advantages and disadvantages of each person's ideas
- take a decision on one idea that you are going to carry forward

---

Chief Executive

Here are some ideas you have considered before the meeting. Think about the positive effect each one could have on your brand image. Add two more ideas of your own.

- Attract more business travellers
- Introduce on-line check-in for travellers with hand luggage only
- Create executive departure lounges at airports, with an access fee of €10
- Create partnerships with car hire firms and hotels, with discounts for SwiftFly customers
-
-

Commercial Director

Here are some ideas you have considered before the meeting. Think about the positive effect each one could have on your brand image. Add two more ideas of your own.

- Start an air miles or loyalty cards scheme
- Make tickets available through selected agencies as well as via the internet
- Change your advertising strategy – place advertisements in the business press
- Create partnerships with package holiday companies
-
-

Communications Director

Here are some ideas you have considered before the meeting. Think about the positive effect each one could have on your brand image. Add two more ideas of your own.

- Attract more family travellers
- Introduce priority boarding for a fee of €15
- Sponsor 'quality' events, such as golf tournaments
- Re-introduce complementary on-board snacks and drinks
-
-

PHOTOCOPIABLE

© 2009 Heinle, Cengage Learning

9.2   Telephone words

Call C1

You are Ms / Mr Helmsley. Telephone your car insurance company. Your new premium is €873.98 but last year it was €305.19. Your policy number is 58091782. You don't have a mobile phone but your office number is 0771 2478.

Call C2

You are Ms / Mr Wainwright. Telephone the small business advisor, Jason Donnella at your bank. He authorised a loan for €27,500 but it has not appeared in your bank account. In fact, your statement says you are €805.60 overdrawn. You have urgent payments of €25,000 to make. Your account number is 799 101 833. Your phone number is 798 205 1776.

Call C3

You are Ms / Mr Ménard. Telephone your Internet Service Provider. You have been billed for €499.90 for the last three months, but you have a flat-rate contract of €49.99 per month. Your contract ID number is X9833370. The phone you're connected to the internet with is 91 652 654.

Call R1

You work at Direct Car Insurance. Deal with the customer's call and take details of their policy number and any other relevant information. Ask for a mobile number so you can return the call when you have information for them.

Call R2

You work at a bank. Take a call for Mr Donnella, who has just been sacked. Take the details of the caller (including the account number) to pass on to the manager, and arrange a time to return the call.

Call R3

You work on the technical support desk of Purple telecommunications. Take the customer's call. Find out the customer's contract ID number and internet phone number first. You only deal with technical problems. The Customer Care number is 920 902 290.

call back	put down	tied up
get back	put on hold	write down
hold on	put through	
look up	read back	

PHOTOCOPIABLE

© 2009 Heinle, Cengage Learning

10.1   Verb + noun combinations

this business.	a great deal from failure.	a brand, not just a product.
It helps to **plan** a	It's essential to **develop**	People try harder if you **offer**
strategy before you start.	an understanding of your area..	them incentives.
Only the best **achieve**	Nobody **knows** all	The secret is to **fill**
success.	the answers.	the gap in the market..
You should **set**	You have to **take**	You need your staff to **understand**
clear targets to aim for.	risks to be successful.	your values.
Try not to **miss**	Good managers can **give**	All managers **experience**
any good opportunities.	clear orders.	difficulties at some point.
Recognise your	Choose the best candidate when you **recruit**	A key part of a manager's role is **overseeing**
weaknesses.	staff.	the work of others.
You can **learn**	They **developed**	It's not easy to **succeed** in

PHOTOCOPIABLE

© 2009 Heinle, Cengage Learning

10.2 Planning

Work in groups of four. You work for a film production company which is going to film a pop star, Matt, on his solo motorbike trip across Asia. In your group, assign the following roles: marketing director, PR director, head of logistics, executive producer.

1 Read all of the documentation and decide which tasks are your responsibility.

2 Hold a planning meeting and draw up a Gantt chart to show who is doing what, and when. The chart should run from March until September.

To: **Production team**
Subject: **Lone Biker Film Project**

Dear all,

I met with Matt and the film's backers yesterday to go over some of the details of his trip and I think we're now in a position to go ahead with the project. Matt will set off from London on April 15th and will arrive (hopefully!) in Beijing on June 30th. The route takes in all the countries in the list I sent last week, with the addition now of Mongolia. We need to get visas and travel authorisation as soon as possible for Matt and everyone on the support team that will travel with him. This needs to be done before April – we don't want any last minute panics. We'll need the names of the cameraman and of the support team (which includes the executive producer) for the travel documents, but we can start contacting the embassies while we're finalising them. I also want all of the in-country support contacts under contract before the trip starts. Suzanne: we need to meet to talk about the editing schedule. Can you call me?

That's all for the moment.

From: *Suzanne*

Taken by: *Liza*

Message:

Suzanne is on her way to Hong Kong – she'll call you on arrival. She says if the film is shipped to her while Matt is travelling instead of waiting until the end of the trip, she could work on it through the summer and have it ready for a final edit by late August.

I love these ideas to promote both Matt's departure from London and his arrival in Beijing! Can you work on getting more press and celebrities to commit to each date and let me know your deadlines for each event. Also, when are the press releases to announce the film going out?

Thanks

Subject: Lone Biker Film Marketing & Distribution
Hi,
Further to my memo on this project, I need you to give me some dates for the marketing campaign for the film (it should be edited by the end of August). How are the distribution talks going? When will we finalise contracts with the distributors?
I also think we should look into merchandising – T-shirts and hats would be good. Can you let me have a schedule for that?
Thanks

PHOTOCOPIABLE

© 2009 Heinle, Cengage Learning

11.1 Articles

Student A:

1 Work on your own. Match the use of the articles *the*, *a* or 0 article (no article) in sentences 1–10 to the rules below.
2 Compare your answers with Student B. Does he / she agree?
3 Decide if sentences 1–10 are true or false. Correct the false sentences.

How much do you know about Fairtrade coffee?

the **is used before**
- some countries
- superlative forms
- when there is only one of something
- to refer to something already mentioned

a / an **is used before**
- jobs
- singular nouns
- some numbers

0 article is used before
- cities / towns / most countries
- plural nouns

1 Coffee is **the** most traded commodity in the world.
2 Coffee makes up 50% of **Ethiopia's** exports.
3 **A** farm labourer in Africa earns about €5 a day picking coffee.
4 **Fairtrade** is an international organisation which represents consumers.
5 An average cup of coffee costs €3. 10% of **the** price goes to the farmer.
6 Fairtrade started in **the** Netherlands.
7 Fairtrade pays better prices to **farmers** than the world market price.
8 Fairtrade represents about **a** million coffee growers.
9 Fairtrade's initiative is **a** success in over forty countries.
10 **Consumers** will pay more for ethically-traded goods.

- -

Student B:

1 Work on your own. Complete the sentences 1–10 with *the*, *a* or 0 article (no article).
2 Compare your answers with Student A's sentences. How many did you get right?
3 Decide if sentences 1–10 are true or false. Correct the false sentences.

How much do you know about Fairtrade coffee?

1 Coffee is _____ most traded commodity in the world.
2 Coffee makes up 50% of _____ Ethiopia' exports.
3 _____ farm labourer in Africa earns about €5 a day picking coffee.
4 _____ Fairtrade is an international organisation which represents consumers.
5 An average cup of coffee costs €3. 10% of _____ price goes to the farmer.
6 Fairtrade started in _____ Netherlands.
7 Fairtrade pays better prices to _____ farmers than the world market price.
8 Fairtrade represents about _____ million coffee growers.
9 Fairtrade's initiative is_____ success in over forty countries.
10 _____ consumers will pay more for ethically-traded goods.

11.2 Trends

Student A:

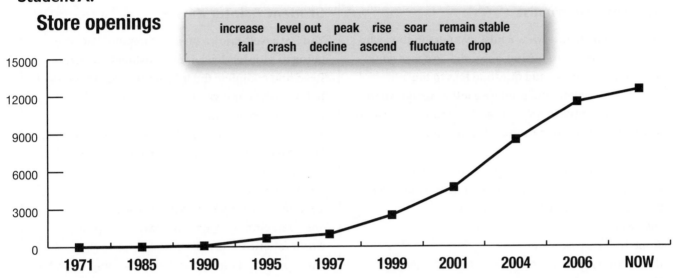

Student B:

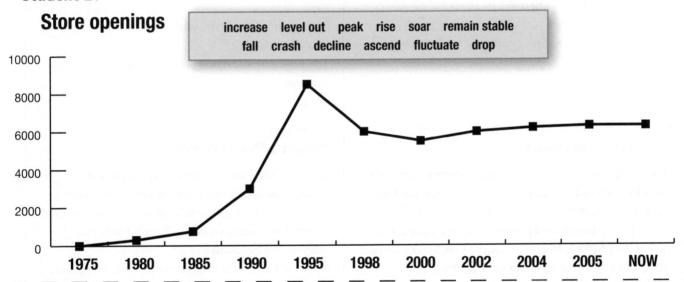

Student C:

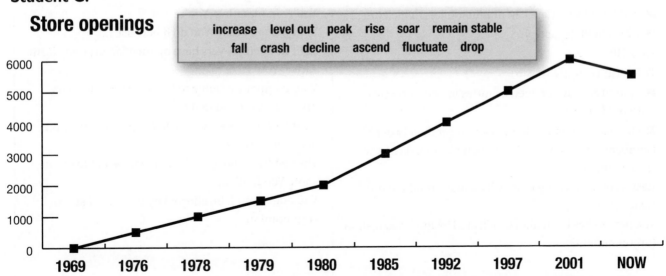

PHOTOCOPIABLE

© 2009 Heinle, Cengage Learning

12.1 Indirect questions

Student A: journalist

You are going to interview a business personality, who may be involved in a business scandal. Prepare your interview questions: add question tags to the information below, and prepare a follow up question using the prompts in brackets and an indirect question form. Add one more question of your own.

The person
- used to work for Broadleaf plc (why / leave?)
- has lots of experience in multinationals (which ones?)
- works in corporate law (exact job?)

His / Her
- job isn't easy (why / do)
- employers have offices in China (would / like to?)
- company is about to be taken over (when?)
- CEO was investigated last year (any comment?)

Results of the investigation will be made public soon (when?)

The person has been directly affected by the investigation (any comment?)

Student B: interviewee

You are a well-known business person. You are going to be interviewed for a business magazine. Read and complete the information about yourself below with your own ideas. Then answer the journalist's questions.

You used to work for Broadleaf plc. You left because …

You've had experience in multinational companies
    For example …

You're in finance. You're a …

Your job isn't easy. You do it because …

Your new employers have offices in Europe and North America. You'd like to …

Your company is going to take over a competitor. It's scheduled for …

Your CEO was under investigation last year. You can't ….

The results of the investigation will be made public soon. You don't …

You might be affected by the investigation. In your opinion, …

Student C: journalist

You are going to interview a business personality, who may be involved in a business scandal. Prepare your interview questions: add question tags to the information below, and prepare a follow-up question using the prompts in brackets and an indirect question form. Add one more question of your own.

The person
- was made redundant by Evergreen plc (why ?)
- had lots of experience in multinationals (which ones?)
- works in PR (exact job?)

His / Her
- job isn't easy (why / do)
- employers have opened factories in Latin America (would like to?)
- company is going to launch a new product (when?)

Company was accused of copyright violation last year (any comment?)

Results of the investigation will be made public soon (when?)

The person has been directly affected by the investigation (any comment?)

Student D: interviewee

You are a well-known business person. You are going to be interviewed for a business magazine. Read and complete the information about yourself below with your own ideas. Then answer the journalist's questions.

You used to work for Evergreen plc. You left because …

You've had experience in manufacturing companies.
    For example …

You're in planning. You're a …

Your job isn't easy. You do it because …

Your new employers have opened factories in North Africa. You'd like to …

Your company is going to launch a revolutionary product. It's scheduled for …

Your company was accused of copyright violations last year. You can't …

The results of the investigation will be made public soon. You don't …

You doubt you'll be affected by the investigation. In your opinion, …

PHOTOCOPIABLE

© 2009 Heinle, Cengage Learning

12.2 Thinking on your feet

Ways of saving money spent on energy use in our offices	Ways of reducing time spent by staff on cigarette breaks	Ways of boosting sales of a shampoo that has been on the market for five years
Ways of thanking an employee who has been with the company for 25 years	Ways of reducing the number of days lost through sickness	Ways of improving busy senior managers' level of English
Ways of improving the concentration of people who sit in front of computers all day	Ways of recruiting younger people to join the company	Ways of reaching a younger target audience through advertising
Ways of improving team spirit in the company	Ways of rewarding sales performance other than with money	Ways of improving the company's environmental image

1.1 Ways of working

Summary of activity: Pair work activity; role play information gap

Language practice: Present simple, present continuous, present perfect simple, present perfect continuous.

When to use: Any time after the grammar section in 1.1.

Procedure: Photocopy and cut up enough worksheets to make one role card per student.

Give one role card to each student, explaining that they are going to be either a temp or a journalist. Tell them to find a partner who has the same role card. If you have an extra student, assign an extra Student B card. Alternatively, you may wish to match weak students with stronger students rather than let the students find their own partners. The students work together to prepare their roles as temps and journalists.

Tell the students to form new pairs so that each temp, Student A, is working with a journalist, Student B. Again, you may wish to designate the pairs according to your students' abilities. If you have an extra student, there will be one group with two journalists.

The journalists should take notes of the answers given during the interview.

Students who finish quickly can reverse roles, with Student A asking questions about Student B's job as a journalist.

Feedback: Ask some of the journalists to tell the class one or two things about the people they interviewed. Find out which temp has had the most (or most unusual) jobs.

Follow-up: Student B's notes can be used to write up a short article for the newspaper. Student A can rewrite their own information in the 3rd person, or can use the notes from a different pair of students.

Teacher role: Monitor and give help with ideas (for A students) and accuracy (for B students) during the preparation stage.

1.2 Making contacts

Summary of activity: Mingle activity; exchanging personal and professional information

Language practice: Personal information, expressions for job responsibilities

When to use: For pre-work students, the business cards can be used after exercise 1 on page 10 and exercise 11 on page 11. For in-work students, use any time after exercise 11.

Procedure: Photocopy and cut up enough worksheets to make one business card per student. Arrange the students in groups of ten or less, and distribute a set of cards in each group. Arrange the groups as evenly as possible. For example, if you have 16 students, have two groups of eight, rather than one of ten and one of six.

Tell students to write their own name in the space on the business card. Tell them not to show their card to anyone else. Explain that the students are at a networking event, and that they have to talk to as many people as they can. The objective is to find out about the other students' jobs and to guess the theme of the networking event.

Before the students begin the activity, with the whole class, review the expressions in exercise 1 page 10. Give students a couple of minutes to prepare their roles and to check any necessary vocabulary with you before starting the activity.

Remind students that the objective is to talk to as many people as they can to find out the theme of the event. You may wish to set a time limit and/or make the activity competitive between the groups.

If possible, divide the classroom space so that the groups will not get mixed up during the activity. Encourage students to move around within their groups and find out about as many people as possible.

Feedback: Ask students if they know what the theme of the event is. (A wedding trade fair)

Follow-up: Students can write an email to one of the contacts they made, arranging a meeting or asking for further information about that person's business.

Teacher role: Monitor and give help during the preparation stage.

2.1 The past

Summary of activity: Completing a profile of a famous business person, followed by an information gap pairwork activity

Language practice: Past simple, present perfect, present perfect continuous

When to use: Any time after exercise 4 on page 18

Procedure: Photocopy and cut up enough worksheets to make one profile card per student.

Ask students to work in pairs with someone who has the **same** profile. You may wish to match weak students with stronger students, rather than let the students find their own partners. (If you have an odd number of students, have one group of three with a profile B card.)

Tell the students there are two stages to the activity. In stage one, they should do exercise 1. When they have completed the text correctly, they should go on to exercise 2.

For stage two, explain to students that they are going to change partners so that a profile A student is now working with a profile B student. Again, you may wish to match the pairs according to your students' abilities. The pairs take turns to ask and answer the interview questions.

Students who finish quickly can compare the information they found out with their original partner, or with other students who had the same original profile. Ask them to name other powerful business people and discuss the possible reasons why it's easier to name men than women, and why there are more men entrepreneurs.

Feedback: Ask what information students have found out that they didn't know before the class. Go over the answers to the exercises.

Follow-up: Students can write up the answers to their questions in a paragraph.

Answers:
Profile A: was, has been working, held, spent, was, created, received, has been helping / has helped

Profile B: started, sold, has dealt in, has lived, became, has driven, has had, gave, shared

Teacher role: Circulate and give help as necessary during the worksheet stage. Monitor how well students do the worksheet tasks, and make a note of any common mistakes to feed back to the students.

2.2 Presenting a company

Summary of activity: Information gap, exchanging facts and figures

Language practice: Asking questions about a company, saying numbers

When to use: Use any time after exercise 4 on page 20.

Procedure: Photocopy and cut up enough worksheets to make one company fact sheet per student. Arrange the students in groups of three and give each student a different company fact sheet. If you have extra students, create a group where two students have the same fact sheet.

Ask students to read the information on their company fact sheet. Explain that they are going to give information about their own company and they must complete the information about the other companies by asking questions. The aim is for each group to guess what companies A, B and C are.

Give students a few minutes to work alone and prepare their questions. Then, working in their groups, students ask questions in turn to complete the missing information. When their fact sheets are complete they can check that they all have the same information. They should then speculate as to the names of the companies.

If students are not sure, you can write the following companies on the board for them to choose from:

Exxon Mobil   Fox Cable   CNN   Pfizer   Texaco
Time Warner   Merck   Bayer   Shell

Answer key: Company A Pfizer, Company B Time Warner, Company C Shell

Feedback: Before giving the identities of the companies, ask each group to give their suggestions.

Follow-up: The completed fact sheets can be used to prepare spoken presentations or written paragraphs.

Teacher role: Monitor and help students prepare questions during the first stage.

3.1 Starting a business

Summary of activity: Role play of a business scenario, group discussion and presentation

Language practice: Talking about the future (*will*, *going to*, the present simple and present continuous): vocabulary of business plans and new businesses

Part Three: Conversation between candidates

When to use: Any time after exercise 6 on page 27

Procedure: Photocopy one worksheet per student.

Divide the class into groups of four. Give a worksheet to each student. Tell students to read the instruction and give them twenty minutes to work together to prepare their business plan. All students should write notes on their sheets, as they will need them in the next stage of the activity. After twenty minutes, give the groups two minutes to finalise their business plans.

Divide each group into two pairs, pair A and pair B. All pair A students should now move groups so that they are working with different pair B students. Tell pair B students that they have £5,000 to invest. Pair A students present their business plan to pair B students, who have to decide how much to invest in the new business.

Then students change roles. Reorganise the pairs so they are working in new groups. If you have only two groups of four, the students can stay in their group and change roles. Now pair A students have £5,000. They listen to the business plan of pair B students and decide how much to invest.

Tell the students to go back to their original groups and add up how much money they have raised from the investors.

Feedback: Ask the groups how much investment they have raised. Who was the most successful? Why? Ask the investors to comment on the strengths and weaknesses of the business ideas they heard about.

Teacher role: Monitor and give help with ideas as necessary during the first stage.

3.2 Leaving and taking messages

Summary of activity: Pairwork, leaving and taking telephone messages

Language practice: Expressions for leaving and taking messages, and checking information

When to use: Any time after exercise 5 on page 33

Procedure: Photocopy and cut up one worksheet so that each pair of students has a set of caller role cards. Then cut up enough name cards for one per student and keep these for the second stage of the activity.

With the whole class, review the expressions in section 3.2, paying attention to the expressions in exercise 3, page 31 and in exercise 3, page 33.

Put the students into pairs and ask them to sit back to back, pretending to be talking on the telephone. Give one set of caller role cards to each pair of students and ask them to take it in turns to be the caller and receiver. (Place the cards upside down so that only the caller can read them.) Explain that the receiver should always say that the person the caller wants to speak to is **not** available and should take a message. Students will also need their notebooks to write the messages in. When a pair has used all the cards, they should check the details of the messages written down against the role cards.

Put the whole class together (or make two large groups if you have a very large class). Students will need the messages they have written down. Give a name card to each student. Tell students to mingle and to find someone in the class who has a message for them, and then to exchange the message information.

Feedback: Find out which information was most difficult to transmit and why.

Follow-up: Note any remedial work that needs to be done, for example on problem sounds, letters or numbers.

Teacher role: Monitor students during the phone calls to make a note of any areas for remedial work. If you have a monolingual group, you could focus on words or sounds that they can communicate to each other, but which could cause problems in communication with speakers of other languages.

4.1 Modals

Summary of activity: Grammar worksheet followed by class game

Language practice: Modals

When to use: Any time after exercise 8 on page 39

Procedure: Photocopy one worksheet for each pair of students. Revise the modal verb functions in exercise 4 on page 39 with the whole class.

Put the students into pairs and give one worksheet to each pair. Ask students to read instruction 1 and give them five minutes to complete the worksheet.

Then ask students to read instruction 2, and demonstrate the activity by writing this sentence on the board:

All our advertisements **must** *have final approval from the Managing Director before they are printed.*

Ask the students, in their pairs, to decide if the sentence is correct or not. Tell each pair to write down how much money (from €10 to €50) they want to bet, and then ask each pair to tell the rest of the class the amount of their bet and if they bet correct or incorrect. The pairs who said 'correct' win double the amount they bet. The pairs who said 'incorrect' lose the amount they bet.

Repeat with sentences 1–12. Pairs who correctly say a sentence is wrong must also give a correct alternative in order to win. With small classes, you can keep a record on the board, otherwise each pair should keep a record of their bets.

Answers:
1 can't have been, couldn't have been
2 ✓
3 have to, must
4 shouldn't, mustn't, can't
5 can't
6 mustn't
7 ✓
8 ✓
9 ✓
10 should, ought to
11 can't be
12 ✓ (*could* also possible)

Teacher role: Make a note of the sentences that cause most difficulty for any remedial work.

4.2 Delegating

Summary of activity: Card game

Language practice: Functional language for delegating

When to use: Any time after exercise 6 on page 41

Procedure: Photocopy and cut up enough worksheets to make a set of task cards for a group of three students.

Revise the expressions for delegating in exercise 4 on page 41 with the whole class.

Put the students into groups of three. If you have extra students, have groups of four rather than pairs. Give each group a set of task cards.

Tell students to shuffle the cards and deal them out, so that each student has four cards. Explain that each card has a task that they must delegate to someone else in their group. Give the students a few minutes to read through their cards, and then they take it in turns to delegate a task. If the other person accepts the task then they take the card. If they refuse then the delegating student must keep the card. The aim of the game is to give away all of the task cards, and the first person to do this is the winner.

Students who finish quickly can think of their own tasks (from their own jobs if they are in-work students) and delegate them.

Feedback: Find out which were the hardest / easiest tasks to delegate, and who was the most persuasive person delegating.

Teacher role: Circulate and give any help with vocabulary or pronunciation as needed.

5.1 Reporting

Summary of activity: Card matching (pelmanism) game

Language practice: Reported speech, reporting verbs

When to use: Any time after exercise 3 on page 48

Procedure: Photocopy and cut up enough worksheets to make one set of cards for each pair or group of three students. Arrange each set of cards into two piles, verb cards and direct speech cards.

Give one set of cards to each pair or group and ask them to spread out the cards face down. Explain that the smaller cards are verb cards and the larger ones are direct speech cards.

Students take it in turns to turn over a verb card and a direct speech card and decide if the verb matches the direct speech. If there is not a match, the cards are replaced. If the cards match, the student must make a reported speech sentence using the verb. The other student(s) must decide if the match and the reported speech sentence is correct. If it is correct, the first student keeps both cards, if it is not correct the cards are replaced. The game continues until all the cards are matched and the student with the most cards is the winner.

You may wish to demonstrate if the students are not familiar with the game.

The items are arranged on the worksheet showing the suggested matches, however there is some overlap in the sentences students can make. Tell students that they should be sure the match is correct before they make a sentence in reported speech, or they will have cards that they can't match at the end.

Students can check disputed sentences in the grammar reference on page 129, or ask for your judgement.

Groups that finish quickly can look at the cards again and decide which verb(s) matches most types of sentence (*tell*) and write down other reporting verbs they can think of (*say* is the obvious omission from the cards).

Feedback: Find out any disputed matches and discuss with the whole class. Go over any problem areas you noted as you monitored the activity.

Answers:

He / She agreed that it was too late to change the order.

He / She apologised that he / she had missed the meeting. (… for missing the meeting)

He / She argued that people weren't interested in abstract art.

He / She asked if the pictures were originals or prints.

He / She called to say that tomorrow's meeting was cancelled.

He / She commented that people often resisted change at first.

He / She concluded that nobody was in favour of the move.

He / She disagreed with changing to hot-desking.

He / She explained that first you selected the product and then put your money in.

He / She suggested that they should take a break for a few minutes. (… taking a break for a few minutes)

He / She told them not to worry and that it wasn't serious.

He / She thought that they needed to reconsider the offer.

Teacher role: Monitor to solve any disputes and note any areas that students repeatedly make mistakes with.

5.2 Expressions for meetings

Summary of activity: Case study discussion

Language practice: Functional language for participating in meetings

When to use: Any time after exercise 2 on page 52

Procedure: Photocopy enough worksheets to make one for each group of three students. Cut up the case study and the role cards, but keep the expression cards together.
Revise the expressions for meetings in exercise 5, on page 51 with the whole class.

Arrange the students into groups of three (or four with an extra production manager role card) and give the case study notes and three role cards to each group. Give each group the expression sheet (and some scissors) and ask them to cut up the sheet into separate expression cards. The cards should be placed face up on the table.

Ask the students to read the case study notes together and explain that they are going to role play a meeting to decide which public relations strategy to use. Each student should take a role card each and spend two minutes preparing for the meeting.

Tell the groups they have five minutes to decide which strategy to use, but that they must also use as many of the expression cards as possible. Each time they use one of the expressions, they take the relevant card. Tell students the objective is to persuade the others to adopt your PR idea, and to collect the most expression cards. Groups that finish quickly can work on developing their chosen PR strategy in more detail.

An alternative is to prepare a set of expression cards for each student and have them place the cards in the middle of the table as they use them, the objective being to get rid of all their cards first.

Stop the activity when the time is up or when most groups have reached or are reaching a decision.

Feedback: Find out which strategies were chosen and why. Remind students that completing an activity within a time limit activity is an important exam skill.

Follow-up: Students can write a report of the meeting following the instructions in exercise 4, page 53.

Teacher role: Monitor and note any problem areas that need remedial work.

6.1 Passives

Summary of activity: Grammar worksheet followed by noughts and crosses game

Language practice: Passives

When to use: Any time after exercise 6 on page 59

Procedure: Photocopy and cut up enough worksheets so that each group of four students has one Student A and one Student B sheet.

Revise the passive forms in exercise 1, on page 58.

Put the students into groups of four, split into pairs of two. Give each pair a Student A or Student B worksheet and ask them to read their sentences 1–9.

Students work together in pairs to decide which verb form is correct. As the pairs finish their sentences, check their answers before the next stage.

When both pairs in the group have corrected their sentences, then they can play the game of noughts and crosses. Check that the students are familiar with the game and if not, demonstrate quickly on the board.

Pair A students should read out the two options as full sentences to their opponents. Pair B students decide which option is correct, and if they choose correctly they can mark a 0 in the box in the grid with the same number as the sentence. If their option is incorrect, then Pair A mark an X in the box. The first pair to make a line of three 0s or three Xs wins.

The teams change over so that Pair B students read out their sentences.

Students can play more than once if they have sentences left after the first game. Ask them to draw a grid in their notebooks.

Answers:

A
1 give	6 will be sent
2 should be approved	7 have been taken on
3 founded	8 will be closed
4 is rumoured	9 was dismissed
5 are being looked	

B
1 will be announced	6 has opened
2 must be given	7 is thought
3 will be needed	8 pay
4 was sold	9 decided
5 are making	

Teacher role: Make a note of the sentences that cause most difficulty for any remedial work.

6.2 Emailing

Summary of activity: Role play, writing emails

Language practice: Functional language in emails, register

When to use: Any time after exercise 4 on page 63

Procedure: Photocopy and cut up one worksheet for each group of three students.

Arrange the students into groups of three and give each one a role card. Explain that the activity will have three stages and they should follow the instructions on their role card for each stage. Tell them that they will need some paper to write emails on.

Ask students to read their instructions and make sure everyone understands. Give students five minutes to write their first email. The students then pass the email to the relevant student in their group. Students read their emails and go onto the next stage. Students write a second and third email and pass it to the correct person. The contents of their emails will determine how they reply.

Feedback: Ask each group for the outcome of the email exchanges.

Teacher role: Circulate and try to keep the groups working at the same pace. Give help where necessary.

7.1 Comparatives and superlatives

Summary of activity: Optional worksheet, speaking game

Language practice: Comparative and superlative forms

When to use: Any time after exercise 7 on page 69

Procedure: Photocopy and prepare a worksheet and a set of prompt cards for each group of three students.

The worksheet activity is designed to review the names of different job titles in a company. This activity is optional. If you feel that your students are familiar enough with all the job titles, then you may decide to skip this activity.

Put the students in groups of three and give each group a worksheet and a set of prompt cards, with the cards faced down in a pile.

Students complete the worksheet and check their answers.

Next, explain the mini-presentation game using the prompt cards. Students take it in turns to turn over the top prompt card. They have to give their opinion and convince the other people in the group. If the other students agree that the presentation is convincing then the student keeps the card. If not, the card is replaced at the bottom of the pile. The winner is the student who has the most cards. Remind them that the object of the game is to be as convincing as possible in order to collect the cards.

Groups that finish quickly can further discuss the card: *What is your ideal job? Talk for one minute about why it would be the best job for you.*

Feedback: Ask students to report what some of their group said for one or two of the cards. Take a class poll of the most boring / most challenging jobs that were suggested.

Follow-up: As a written follow-up, students can write a paragraph on their ideal job.

Teacher role: Circulate and help with vocabulary if necessary.

Answers:

1 accountant	10 lawyer
2 administrative assistant	11 editor
3 advertising executive	12 marketing manager
4 architect	13 personal assistant
5 brand manager	14 public relations officer
6 customer services assistant	15 sales director
7 health and safety inspector	16 software developer
8 hotel manager	17 travel agent
9 human resources officer	

7.2 Selling

Summary of activity: Mingle activity, selling items to potential purchasers

Language practice: Comparatives and superlatives, functional language for selling

When to use: Any time after exercise 7 on page 71

Procedure: Photocopy and cut up enough cards so that you have two seller cards and one buyer role card for each student in the class, plus an extra set. Arrange the buyer role cards and seller cards into separate sets.

Do as a whole class activity. If you have fewer than ten students, remove items from each of the sets. For small classes where a mingle activity would not work well, do as a pair work activity. (See below)

Review the steps for making a sale in exercise 5, on page 71.

Give half of the students one buyer role card. Give the other half of the students (the sellers) two cards each. The sellers should first decide what price they are going to sell their items for.

Then students get up and mingle. The sellers want to find a buyer for their items. The buyers should make purchases according to their circumstances on the role card. The sellers should compare their items to help the buyer make the best purchase. When the buyer purchases an item, he / she keeps the card.

Encourage the students to move around and talk to as many people as possible.

When a purchase has been made, give the buyers another role card and the sellers a new card.

Stop the activity when most of the students have made a purchase.

Repeat the activity, reversing the roles of buyers and sellers.

Pair work alternative: Give each pair a set of buyer cards and two sets of sales cards. They should place the buyer cards face down between them and take a set of sales cards each. The students take turns in taking a buyer card and telling their partner about their situation. The partner can then choose a card he / she thinks appropriate and try to sell the item to the other student.

Feedback: Ask some of the buyers what they bought and why. Ask them to explain or justify their purchases.

Teacher role: Circulate and intervene if you wish if buyers are about to make the 'wrong' purchase. The roles and items allow for overlap, but you might prefer to encourage students to 'keep looking'.

8.1 -*ing* form and infinitive

Summary of activity: Dominoes game

Language practice: Verbs followed by -*ing* form and infinitive

When to use: Any time after exercise 4 on page 78

Procedure: Photocopy and cut up enough worksheets to make a set of dominoes for each pair of students. Shuffle up the domino cards well.

Put the students into pairs and give one set of dominoes to each pair. If you have an extra student, make a group of three. Students distribute the dominoes equally between them, without letting the others see their cards.

Explain that the aim of the game is to place the cards into a chain so that the sentence halves match to make a correct sentence. The first student places a card, and the other student adds a card if it fits to either side of the first domino. If the second student doesn't have a card that fits, then the first student continues. The game continues until one of the students has placed all his / her cards.

Students who finish quickly can ask you to check their domino chain and then match the sentences to the rules on page 130 of the Student's book.

Teacher role: Monitor and check that students are putting the correct dominoes down, and help with any disputes.

8.2 Linking phrases

Summary of activity: Grammar game

Language practice: Linking phrases of cause and effect, contrast and additional information

When to use: Any time after exercise 3 on page 82

Procedure: Photocopy one worksheet for each group of four students. Cut up two sets of sentence half cards and arrange them into piles of A and B cards. Cut up the linking phrases and keep separately.

Put the students into groups of four, and split them into Pair A and Pair B. Explain that the pairs are going to be opponents in a game. Give a set of A cards to Pair A, and B cards to Pair B. Give the group a set of linking phrase cards which they will use later.

In the first stage of the activity, tell each pair to match their sentence halves, so that they have seven sentences. Explain that the sentences need a linking word to connect them. When they have matched their cards, they should keep them face down in front of them.

In the next stage, both pairs of students place the linking cards face up in front of them. Pair A begin by turning over their first pair of sentence halves, and choose a linking word to join them. Pair A read out their completed sentence and if Pair B agree that the sentence is correct Pair A keep all three cards. However, if the linking word has been used incorrectly, then Pair B have the chance to make a correct sentence, and keep the cards. Then Pair B turn over their first pair of sentence halves and choose the correct linking word. The game continues until all the sentences have been completed. Note that once a linking word has been used, it cannot be used again. The winners are the pair with the most number of cards.

The game is a race to find an appropriate linking word and successfully make a sentence. There is some overlap which should allow for discussion of appropriacy and the logical relationship between the sentence halves. If students are left with a linking word that doesn't match their last pair of sentence halves, they have used the wrong word(s) in a previous sentence.

Teacher role: Monitor to see how accurate the students' sentences are, and to resolve any disputes.

Answers:

A 1 The meal was satisfactory. However, / Even so, we've decided not to eat there again.

A 2 She does a fantastic job despite / in spite of recent personal problems.

A 3 He gives the impression of listening to you but he never remembers what you say.

A 4 As a result of / After complaining several times, he got a refund.

A 5 The course was cancelled due to / because of lack of interest.

A 6 The office block was brand new. Nevertheless, it had no parking area.

A 7 Following the legal action, we can't make any comment.

B 1 Business is not good as a result of not listening to our customers.

B 2 We need a new warehouse building. Furthermore, / Moreover, it has to be available now.

B 3 Despite / In spite of the increase in prices, sales did not fall.

B 4 We were satisfied with your service. However, / Even so, we've decided not to use you again.

B 5 He had no experience in addition to having no qualifications.

B 6 The marketing campaign was redesigned as a result of / after a disastrous launch   .

B 7 He wrote a letter to the CEO. Moreover, / Furthermore, he sent a copy to the press.

9.1 Branding

Summary of activity: Case study discussion

Language practice: Functional language for participating in meetings

When to use: Any time after exercise 4 on page 87

Procedure: Photocopy and cut up one worksheet for each group of three students.

Give the case study notes and three role cards to each group. Tell the students to read the case study notes together. Then ask them to take a role card each and to spend three minutes preparing for a meeting to discuss ways to improve their brand image. Students should add two more ideas of their own to their role card.

Tell the groups that they have fifteen minutes to discuss their ideas. The objective of the meeting is to choose and agree on one idea that the company will take forward.

Stop the meetings when the time is up, or when most groups have reached or are reaching a decision.

Ask one member from each group to present their decision to the rest of the class.

Feedback: Have a short discussion on the similarity or differences between the decisions.

Teacher role: Monitor and note any problem areas that need remedial work.

9.2 Telephone words

Summary of activity: Pairwork game, short role plays making telephone calls and using phrasal verbs

Language practice: Telephone expressions including phrasal verbs

When to use: Any time after exercise 6 on page 91

Procedure: Photocopy and cut up one worksheet for each pair of students. Cut up the caller cards C1–C3 to make individual cards. Leave the receiver cards R1–R3 together, with the phrasal verb list. A whistle or something similar for calling the time limit would also be useful.

Arrange the seating of the students back-to-back (as if on the telephone) in an inner and outer circle, or in two lines.

Give out one receiver worksheet to each of the students on the inner circle. Distribute the caller cards so that each student on the outer circle has one role card each.

Explain that the students are going to make phone calls, and that the receivers respond appropriately, using the information on their worksheet, and will need to take notes. Explain that there is a time limit of three minutes on each call (because the caller's battery is running out or because the receivers have to meet targets) and when you blow the whistle, the call must finish. Callers move one seat to the left, and the receivers stay seated.

The receivers have a list of phrasal verbs on their worksheet and the aim is to use as many of them as possible. Receivers should tick off the phrasal verbs as they use them.
After the three calls, tell the students to swap their role cards and repeat.

Feedback: Find out how many times students used the phrasal verbs and who used them the most. Find out from the callers who was the most helpful receiver. Find out if anyone revealed that Mr Donnella had been sacked and discuss if that is appropriate or not.

Follow-up: Note any remedial work that needs to be done, for example on problem sounds, letters or numbers.

Teacher role: Monitor students during the phone calls to make a note of any areas for remedial work. If you have a monolingual group, you could focus on words or sounds that they can communicate to each other but could cause problems in communication with speakers of other languages.

10.1 Verb + noun combinations

Summary of activity: Card matching (pelmanism) game

Language practice: Verb + noun combinations

When to use: Any time after exercise 6 on page 97

Procedure: Photocopy and cut up one worksheet for each pair or group of three students. Shuffle the cards.

Give one set of 36 cards to each pair or group of students. Tell the students to lay the cards out in front of them face down. Explain that the aim of the game is to match sentence halves. Remind students that the sentences are examples of verb + noun combinations.

Students take it in turns to turn over two cards at a time. If the cards make a sentence, then the student can keep the cards and have another go. If the student can't make a sentence they replace the cards in the same place. Each student takes it in turns to find the matching sentence halves until all the cards are matched. The other students can agree or disagree with the matches. The student with the most cards wins.

Groups that finish quickly can choose three or more of the sentences to discuss or to give examples of.

Feedback: Find out any disputed matches and check with the whole class. Take up some points from the discussions that early finishers had.

Teacher role: Circulate to solve any disputes or problems.

Answers:
It helps to *plan a strategy* before you start.
Only the best *achieve success*.
You should *set* clear *targets* to aim for.
Try to not *miss* any good *opportunities*.
Recognise your *weaknesses*.
You can *learn a great deal* from failure.
It's essential to *develop an understanding* of your area.
Nobody *knows all the answers*.
You have to *take* risks to be successful.
Good managers can *give* clear *orders*.
Choose the best candidate when you *recruit staff*.
They *developed a brand*, not just a product.
People try harder if you *offer* them *incentives*.
The secret is to *fill the gap* in the market.
You need your staff to *understand* your *values*.
All managers *experience difficulties* at some point.
A key part of a manager's role is *overseeing* the *work* of others.
It's not easy to *succeed in* this *business*.

10.2 Planning

Summary of activity: Group discussion and planning task

Language practice: Functional language for participating in meetings, prepositions of time

When to use: Any time after exercise 6 on page 103

Procedure: Photocopy one worksheet for each group of four students. Blank sheets of A4 or A3 paper will be useful for the students to draw their Gantt charts on. (Make sure that students are familiar with a Gantt chart and bring one in as an example for them to refer to during the activity.)

Arrange the students into groups of four, and explain that they are going to role play a planning meeting. Ask them to read the instructions and the four pieces of information. Students decide which roles they want to play and what tasks they are responsible for. The students then play out the planning meeting and prepare a Gantt chart for the project.

Note that there are no 'correct' answers.

Feedback: Put each chart on the wall and have a class discussion of the similarities or differences, and / or evaluate the effectiveness of the planning.

Teacher role: Circulate to check that students identity their tasks in the first stage. Make a note of any areas that it would be useful to work on for Part Three of the Speaking Test.

11.1 Articles

Summary of activity: Grammar worksheet followed by True / False questions in pairs

Language practice: Articles

When to use: Any time after exercise 1 on page 108

Procedure: Photocopy and cut up one worksheet for each pair of students.

Arrange the students into pairs and give out the student A and B worksheets. Explain that for the first stage they should work on their own without looking at each other's worksheet. Then they work with their partner and check the answers to stage one.

In stage three, students can refer back to page 107 of the Student's book to check the information on Fairtrade.

Answers:
1 False – coffee is the second most traded
2 False – 90%
3 False – €0.75
4 False – Fairtrade represents producers
5 True
6 True
7 True
8 True
9 False – twenty countries
10 True, hence the success of Fairtrade

Teacher role: Circulate and give help as needed.

11.2 Trends

Summary of activity: Information gap

Language practice: Describing trends and graphs

When to use: Any time after exercise 4 on page 111

Procedure: Photocopy and cut up one worksheet for each group of three students.

Arrange the students into groups of three and give a different graph to each student. Tell the students not to show their graphs to the other students. Explain that they are going to take it in turns to describe their graph using the words on their worksheet, while the other two students draw the graph. When all the graphs have been described and drawn, students then compare what they have drawn with the original.

Write the names of the following shops on the board:
*Wendy's burger bars   Starbucks coffee shops
Bec's Ice Cream parlours*

Students discuss in their groups and match the shop names with the graphs. One of the shop names has been invented.

Answers: Starbucks: A, Wendy's: C, 'Becs' is invented.

Follow-up: Students can write a paragraph to describe their graphs, using the text on page 111 of the Student's book as a model.

Teacher role: Circulate and give help as needed.

12.1 Indirect questions

Summary of activity: Pair work: role play information gap

Language practice: Question tags and indirect questions

When to use: Any time after exercise 4 on page 118

Procedure: Photocopy enough worksheets for two role cards per student.

Before you begin the role plays, review question tags and different ways of starting indirect questions with the whole class. Remind students why we use question tags and indirect questions: to make questions more polite, or if you are not sure that something is correct.

Arrange the students in pairs and give out role cards A and B. If you have an extra student, have two Student As. Tell the students that first they are going to work alone; Student A prepares his / her questions and Student B prepares his / her answers. When everyone is ready, the interviews can begin.

When the interviews have finished, give out role cards C and D, making sure that students swap roles. Repeat the preparation and the interviews.

Feedback: Ask some of the journalists to tell the class one or two things about the people they interviewed.

Follow-up: Discuss any problems in using question tags or indirect questions.

Teacher role: Monitor and give help with ideas and accuracy during the preparation stage.

12.2 Thinking on your feet

Summary of activity: Group game where students have to come up with solutions for typical business problems quickly

Language practice: Language of suggestions, giving opinions

When to use: Any time after exercise 3 on page 124

Procedure: Photocopy one set of cards for each group of four to five students. Cut up the cards and hand one set to each group in a pile, face down. Explain that one student in each group will turn over the first card, read it aloud and ask for opinions. Each student then has 15 seconds in turn to make a suggestion. The student who is reading the card writes in note form the suggestion of each of the others. If they cannot think of anything to say within 15 seconds, the turn passes to the next player.

When all have had a turn, a vote is taken (students cannot vote for their own suggestion). The winner gets one point (if there is a tie, they get one point each).

The next student in the group then turns over the second card and asks for opinions. Repeat this until they have used all the cards or completed a round.

Follow-up: Ask the students to write an internal proposal for their boss based on the suggestion that they liked most in the game.

Teacher role: Model the target language before the activity and then monitor and check that students are using it properly during the activity. Get feedback at the end on what the ideas were that they liked most.

Workbook answer key

MODULE 1

1.1

Ways of working

1 1 flexible   2 permanent   3 full-time
      4 employee   5 freelance

2 1 for / at   2 on   3 in   4 round / over   5 to   6 on
      7 by   8 from   9 to   10 off   11 with   12 at

3 1 a five-days week
      2 since **for** a couple of months
      3 few **a few** extra hours
      4 I am not every day in the office **every day**.
      5 I miss to chat **chatting** to my colleagues.

4 1 /wɜːk/ as in *were* and /wɔːk / as in *fork*
      2 /tiːm/ as in *seem* and /taɪm/ as in *I'm*
      3 /liːv/ as in *see* and /lɪv/ as in *sit*
      4 /tʃaɪld/ as in *cry* and /tʃɪldrən/ as in *fill*
      5 /ʃeə/ as in *she* and /tʃeə/ as in *child*

5 1 have been doing
      2 have had
      3 have known
      4 have not been listening
      5 have been worrying
      6 has been
      7 have been thinking
      8 has been

6 **Suggested answer:**
      You have been working long hours. But have you been
      spending the extra time productively? Working longer
      hours doesn't necessarily mean that you are being more
      productive.

7 **Suggested answers:**
      1 check my emails. (present simple)
      2 leave work (present simple)
      3 am cycling. (present continuous)
      4 have a sandwich and a short walk. (present simple)
      5 is doing a training course (present continuous)
      6 go for a drink with a few colleagues. (present simple)
      7 am trying to work. (present continuous)
      8 make mistakes with my tenses. (present simple)

8 **Suggested answers:**
      1 I've been studying English since I was nine years old.
      2 I've been working for Bayer for eighteen months.
      3 I've only had my new mobile phone for three weeks.
      4 I've known that I want to have my own business since I
        was sixteen.
      5 I've been doing these exercises for about half an hour.

1.2

Making contacts

1 1 specialise   2 of   3 deal   4 report, in   5 for

2 A Legal advisor   1
      B Head of Sustainable Development   4
      C Personal assistant   0
      D Production foreman   2
      E Press officer   3
      F Car mechanic   5

3 1 Recruitment of staff at all levels
      2 Training, career development
      3 The HR manager
      4 Conferences and job fairs
      5 Knowledge of the advertising industry

4 Barney: Hello, Sara, good to see you again. Can I
      introduce you to Su Li?
      Sara: **How do you do,** Su Li? I'm Sara.
      Su Li: It's a pleasure. Please call me Su.
      Sara: **I am pleased to meet you**, too. Barney has told me
      about you. **How long have been here?**
      Su Li: I arrived in London two days ago.
      Sara: **And is this your first time** in England?
      Su Li: Yes, it is.
      Sara: **How do you like it**?
      Su Li: London is great, but rather expensive.
      Sara: Well, **can I join you** two for a coffee?
      Su Li: Yes, sure. Are you enjoying the conference?
      Sara: Yes, it has been very useful. I **have made** a lot of new
      contacts. And you?
      Su Li: Yes, it's new for me, but I have learned a lot.
      Sara: You work for Taylor Associates, **don't you**?
      Su Li: Yes, I am their Chinese agent. And you are with
      Featherstone, I think.
      Sara: Yes, **that's right**.

5 A David should write back or call suggesting a time to meet for a drink

B Ms Kowlowski doesn't need to reply (unless the item doesn't arrive!)

Suggested answer:

Hi Kate

Thanks for your message. I wasn't too surprised about the job either. I'd love to go for a drink. How about 6 o'clock next Wednesday at the Red Lion?

David

6 1 I am writing to inform you that we have received your order and it should arrive shortly.

2 I apologise for sending an incorrect invoice. I am now attaching the correct version.

3 Further to our meeting last week, please find attached the information you requested.

7 1 I'm sorry but I can't come to the meeting this afternoon. Please let me know what happens.

2 How about meeting at the restaurant? The bad news is that I only have an hour.

3 Good to see you last week and I hope to see you again soon.

8 **Suggested answer**:

Dear Mr Johnstone

I represent Luca Lighting, a company which specialises in high-quality lighting products.

I will be visiting your area next month and would be pleased to have the opportunity to demonstrate our range to you.

Please suggest a time that is convenient to you.

I look forward to hearing from you.

Yours sincerely,

1.3
Speaking: Talking about yourself

1 1 And **what** do you do?

2 **How long** have you been studying?

3 **Do** you have a job lined up afterwards?

4 **What kind of** company is it?

5 And **what** will your job **involve**?

6 And **how** do you feel **about** working for your father?

2 1 hobbies   2 ambitions   3 company's activity

4 job prospects   5 your opinion

3 **Students' own answers.**

4 **Suggested answers:**

1 Yes, I've been working for a company called Lacreal for the last six months.

2 At the moment I'm just working as a trainee in the sales department.

3 Yes, we manufacture and sell a range of cosmetic products.

4 We mainly sell to big department stores and pharmacies.

5 Not at the moment, but I hope to in the future.

6 Sorry, could you repeat the question?

7 I know a lot of people disagree with it, but I don't have a problem with it, actually.

8 My ambition is to be an international sales manager and to work abroad.

MODULE 2
2.1
Company benefits

1 1 company 2 flexible   3 promotion   4 pension
5 unpaid   6 holiday   7 off

2 1 care   2 on   3 break   4 pinch   5 place

3 1 E   2 A   3 D   4 C   5 G   6 F

4 1 joined
2 (correct)
3 have been working
4 have you been doing
5 (correct)
6 have taken
7 have developed
8 (correct)
9 moved
10 have been looking

5 **Suggested answer:**

Reynard Inc is based in Birmingham in the UK. The company was first set up in 1906 to make bicycles and motorcycles. It has over 50 years' experience in the manufacture of motorcycles. Today its main products are bicycles and motorcycles. The company has a subsidiary in the United States, and one in Hungary which opened last year. Recently it has agreed a new partnership with a Chinese factory.

6 I think we all recognise that incentives are important, // but why? // And what kind of incentives work best? // Should they be financial // or should we concentrate on praising employees for good work // or for achieving their targets? // The answer is not simple // because not every individual responds in the same way.

7

Long 'i' /aɪ/	Short 'i' /ɪ/
recognise	incentive
finance	promise
outline	individual
final	policy
behind	flexible
describe	benefit
	article
	division

2.2
Presenting your company

1 1 C   2 A   3 D   4 B   5 A   6 D

2
1 sixty percent
2 nineteen-oh-five
3 two thousand and eight
4 five million
5 three thousand two hundred and ten
6 (a) half
7 eleven over four
8 thirty-three point three percent

3 1 tell   2 brief   3 happy   4 all   5 out   6 show
7 gives   8 coming / listening

4 **Suggested answers:**
1 I'd like to begin by **telling you something about our product.**
2 At this point I will quote our CEO: **having a great product is not enough.**
3 Let's move on **to look at sales / the sales figures.**
4 This chart **shows the turnover for 2007.**
5 Let's take a look **at our profits for last year.**
6 That brings me **to the end of my presentation.**

5
1 Graham Pole reports to John Simmons.
2 Graham has missed work on 22 days.
3 John Simmons suggests that Graham should come to discuss any problems with him.
4 Graham should see John Simmons to explain his situation.

6 From: Sarah Kandarthi
Subject: Suggestions for **the** staff party
Just a ~~quickly~~ **quick** reminder that the staff party will be ~~at~~ **on** 5 December. We have not ~~done~~ **made** a final decision on where it will take place, so please ~~to~~ send me your suggestions. If anyone is not able ~~attending~~ **to attend**, please ~~make~~ **let** me know before ~~the~~ next Friday.

7
1 As a result   2 you hear from me
3 For further information   4 Further to   5 because of
6 If you would like   7 I'd like to point out

2.3
Reading: Checking for errors

1
1 For most people, it is ~~more~~ better to have an interesting job than a high salary. (*Comparative form 'better' does not require 'more'.*)
2 The company encourages ~~a~~ people to go on training courses. (*'a' cannot be used with a plural noun.*)
3 It is a job with a lot of variety and ~~which~~ with flexible working hours. (*'which' is used to introduce a relative clause.*)
4 When you join ~~to~~ the company, you become part of a family. (*'join' does not require a preposition.*)
5 But it is not only the company's responsibility. Each employee ~~that~~ has to motivate himself. (*'that' is used to introduce a clause.*)

2 1 more   2 correct   3 which   4 out   5 does
6 correct   7 because   8 a

Writing: Internal communications

3 **Suggested answer:**
Following the changes in the tax law announced last week, the rate of social security tax will increase from 10% to 11% from July. This new rate will apply to all employees. For further information please contact me in the HR department between 9 am and 5 pm.

MODULE 3
3.1
Starting a business

1

2 1 F   2 D   3 B   4 C   5 A

3 1 growth   2 profit   3 enthusiastic   4 tested
5 sense   6 hard   7 fail   8 risks   9 capital   10 run

4
1 Present simple
2 *going to*
3 Future perfect
4 *will* (promise)
5 *will* (prediction)
6 Present continuous

5
1 **By the end of the year we** will have sold over 1 million units.
2 **This time tomorrow I** will be lying on a beach in Bermuda. I can't wait!
3 I'm meeting her **in the pub at 6 o'clock**.
4 The seminar takes place **at 11 am, followed by lunch at 1 pm.**
5 **I think that she** will probably get the job.
6 **I've decided that I** am going to set up my own consultancy business.

6
1 'm having
2 'll be driving
3 I'm going to tell
4 leaves, will get
5 will win, will try
6 will have finished
7 I'll help
8 I'm going to play, I'll be relaxing

3.2
Leaving and taking messages

1
1 the fourteenth of May two thousand and nine
2 two to five pee em
3 Oh-double seven-eight, three-two-two, one-oh-one-oh OR one-zero-one-zero
4 Jay-jee-one-three-ex
5 Oh-apostrophe-are-ee-ay-double ell-why
6 Double you double you double you dot yell dot com
7 Karen at gmail dot eff are

2 1 hold 2 returning 3 read 4 back 5 get 6 reason

3 A 6 B 5 C 0 D 1 E 3 F 2 G 4

4 1 to 2 out 3 regard 4 by 5 back 6 grateful
7 call 8 on 9 read 10 for

5
Message for: Mico Jurevic
From: Jose Moya
Subject: Mr Moya picked up your diary by mistake yesterday.
Action needed: Call Mr Moya back in the office today or on his mobile.
Contact details: Mobile number 06966 39941

6 **A**
Message for: Ms Gerhard
Message from: **Aran** at **Bangkok House Restauran**t
Subject: He has **prepared menu** and **price** for set dinner.
Action: Please call him **on 0208 733 4545**.

B
Message for: Mr Sato
Message from: **John Davies**
Subject: **Confidential**
Action: Please **call him** as soon as possible.

C
Message from: Terry Jones
Subject: Please note that the **offer** on **office chairs** ends **this week**.
Action: Let **him know** soon if we are interested.

D
Message for: Sarah Jenas
Message from: **Maria Sanchez**
Subject: She apologised for **missing** the **appointment on** Friday. Would like to **change to** Thursday afternoon.
Action: Please call to **confirm**.

7

/eɪ/	/iː/	/aɪ/	/əʊ/	/ɑː/	/uː/	/e/
A	E	I	O	R	Q	Z
H	G	Y			U	
J	T				W	

8 1 Jagger 2 Stipe 3 Cobain

3.3
Listening: Short messages

2 **A**
Changes to conference
Date: (**1**) **3 May**
Venue: (**2**) **National Institute**
3–4pm session: Speaker cancelled
New speaker: (**3**) **Steve Johnson**
Title: (**4**) **Mobile Future**

B

Customer Services – Messages

Caller's name: Jackie Brown

Company: **(5) Global Media** Limited

Item Ordered: **(6) Leather sofa**

Problem: Incorrect invoice. We **(7) overcharged** the customer.

Action: Credit **(8) £300** to her account.

C

Date: 4 July

Course Title: **(9) Buying signals**

Participants: **(10) Sales managers**

Venue: Galaxy Hotel

To reserve a place: Send back **(11) registration form** to Lisa Melrose in HR.

D

HR department – Messages

Caller's name: Buddy Richards

Subject: Job interview

Problem: He has an interview on **(12) 10 July** but he is unable to attend because he is **(13) on holiday**. He is very **(14) interested in** the job. Is it possible for us to give him a **(15) telephone interview**?

MODULE 4

4.1

Advertising

1 1 word of mouth 2 loyalty card 3 billboard 4 spam
5 mailshot 6 sample 7 banner 8 TV commercial

2 1 to 2 about 3 for 4 to 5 to 6 to 7 at 8 at

3 1 E 2 A 3 D 4 C

4 1 suppose 2 not sure 3 On the other hand
4 relatively 5 Remember

5 1 mustn't 2 don't have to 3 mustn't 4 don't have to
5 must 6 should

6 1 can't have 2 must have 3 must 4 can't have
5 can't 6 must

7 1 AIDS
2 No (*changes will have to be made*)
3 Yes (*we had already improved it*)
4 They chose not to make the advert 'more pleasant to look at'.

8 1 They should have (ought to have) used an advertising agency.
2 They should have (ought to have) used a different type of advertising.
3 They should (ought to) advertise in the local paper.
4 They should (ought to) introduce a loyalty card.
5 He should have (ought to have) installed an anti-virus programme.

4.2

Delegating

1 1 Throw away your ego
2 Let go in stages
3 Get help from specialists
4 Delegate, don't dump

2 1 priority 2 brief 3 free 4 ensure 5 updates
6 through 7 deadline 8 charge

3 1 Please give priority to the Johnson case.
2 Let me know your answer by Tuesday.
3 You've done a great job on this!
4 One thing that's worrying me is the cost.
5 Can I borrow your computer for a moment?
6 I want you to go to Geneva.
7 When is the deadline for registration?
8 The main findings of the report were positive.

5 1 A 2 F 3 B 4 G 5 C 6 D

6 1 B 2 D 3 A 4 C 5 G 6 F

7 **Suggested answer:**

To: The executive board

Re: Results of recent advertising campaigns

Introduction and aims

This report sets out to examine the results of recent advertising campaigns on sales figures, and to suggest how we can improve our advertising strategy.

Findings: Effect of advertising on sales

In late February we mailed out a special offers catalogue to all our customers. This had positive results and sales in March increased by 35%. In June we carried out a short TV advertising campaign, which was expensive and achieved a very poor response. As you can see from the chart, sales continued to fall following this campaign. In September we launched a series of newspaper adverts which were more successful, although they were also quite expensive. Finally, in November we mailed out our new catalogue. Sales continued to increase slightly following this mailout.

Conclusions

The most successful advertising was the mailout of the special offers catalogue. The other campaigns achieved disappointing results.

Recommendations

We would recommend mailing out a special offers catalogue again. We would not recommend TV and newspaper advertising due to the high costs and poor results. We would also suggest investigating new possibilities, such as internet advertising.

4.3

Reading: Vocabulary and collocation

1   1 C   2 D   3 A   4 C   5 C

2   1 A   2 C   3 D   4 B   5 B   6 D   7 D   8 C   9 A
    10 B   11 B   12 D

MODULE 5

5.1

The workplace

1   1 What kind of art do companies tend to buy?
    2 How does a company agree on what art to buy?
    3 Why do so many companies choose to buy art?
    4 Who should I consult if I want to buy a piece of art?
    5 Does it matter where the art is displayed?
    6 Can you commission a work of art to emphasise your brand?

2   1 aims   2 end   3 commissioned   4 manager
    5 scope   6 much   7 spend   8 specialist   9 cope
    10 oversee   11 requirements   12 on   13 within
    14 checking

3   1 worldwide   2 requirements   3 referrals
    4 satisfaction   5 expertise   6 combination
    7 outcome   8 appointment

4   1 In words ending in -tion or -sion we usually stress the syllable before this ending.
    2 combi**na**tion   di**vi**sion   so**lu**tion   instal**la**tion
    4 de**vel**opment   a**gree**ment   enter**tain**ment
       re**quire**ment   ap**poin**tment   in**vest**ment
    5 When the suffix -ment is added to a verb to make a noun, the stress remains on the same syllable.

5

Direct speech	Reported speech
I **am** too old	was
I **don't know**	**didn't know**
I **haven't seen** him	**hadn't seen**
You **have to** apply	**had to**
I **can** manage	**could**
It**'s raining** here	**was raining**
I **live** in Paris	**lived**
I **was waiting** for an hour	**had been waiting**
I **won't** tell anyone	**wouldn't tell**
I **can't** understand	**couldn't understand**

6   1 Works of art and artistic events.
    2 They must be for public display.
    3 It will give a boost to the arts in Britain.

7   1 A spokesperson for Harris Plumbing said that it wouldn't really affect them, as they did not sponsor any art projects anyway.
    2 A spokesperson for Riverside Centre said that they were not against it, but they wished they would do the same for sports sponsorship.
    3 A spokesperson for Max's Café said that it was right for the government to reduce taxes on companies, but they had to decide where they could spend their money.
    4 A spokesperson for Jones Gallery said that it was about time. They said that this government had a bad record on promoting the arts.
    5 A spokesperson for The Bus Company said that they thought it was a really good idea. It would help to bring art closer to the people.
    6 A spokesperson for Ashton Community Centre said that they hoped this would give employees a chance to show their artistic talents.
    7 A spokesperson for Opera Now said that it was not clear whether this also applied to musical performances, but they hoped so.
    8 A spokesperson for Telecom asked if it was really true.

8   'We apologise for the inconvenience to passengers following the closure of the London to Glasgow line. This is due to an accident involving two freight trains. Fortunately, no-one has been injured. The line will reopen on Tuesday morning after we have made repairs. In the meantime, passengers are asked to use other means of transport.'

5.2
Participating in a meeting

1 1 Chairman 2 minutes 3 attend 4 agenda
5 informal 6 holding 7 reach 8 point
9 along 10 on

2 1 reached an 2 It seems to me 3 I agree
4 I suggest that we / I'd like to suggest that we
5 I disagree with you there 6 come in

3 1 He uses them to warn people if they say something rude.
2 He schedules the meeting early to give people time to relax before the meeting actually starts.
3 It helps people to concentrate.
4 People can give their opinion more openly.
5 He cancels a meeting and asks people to use the time to look for ideas.

4 1 Correct
2 there are no ~~the~~ rules about
3 some ~~of~~ discussion
4 when we ~~do~~ meet
5 Correct
6 was ~~more~~ easier
7 by ~~are~~ negotiating a deal
8 the most difficult ~~which~~ to
9 whether ~~if~~ it was necessary
10 Correct
11 some ~~the~~ said
12 did not ~~have~~ justify
13 must ~~to~~ fly
14 Correct

5 **Suggested answer:**
Subject: Art commission
This report describes the decisions taken on commissioning an artwork for the reception area of the new company offices. The main points agreed are as follows:
- A sculpture will be the best type of artwork for the space. The work is expected to cost around £10,000, but the maximum budget is £20,000.
- We will employ an art consultant for half a day to get advice on how to manage the project (Diego Sanchez will find the right consultant).
- Michiko Makio will make a list of possible artists and present it at the next meeting.
- The artist chosen will make the final decision on the exact character of the sculpture, but will be given some ideas to work from. These suggestions will be presented at the next meeting.

5.3
Speaking: Short presentations

1 1 F 2 T 3 T 4 F

2 **Good points:**
Includes introduction, main body and conclusion.
Separates points using *first, second, third*.
Gives specific example for delivery time.

Bad points:
Doesn't give specific information about first two points, price and quality.

3 1 **In** my view …
2 The second~~ly~~ is the quality
3 the third is the ~~period of~~ delivery **time**
4 the time it **takes** from …
5 the delivery ~~into~~ the factory
6 In some industries, this ~~must be~~ **is** a …
7 I think **it** is very difficult
8 who will ~~can~~ meet all of these conditions
9 the price will ~~be also~~ **also be** high

4 1 First of **all** …
2 The second point to **consider** is that …
3 It is also true **that** many companies …
4 Something **else** that is important is …
5 **For** example, if you need to …
6 **In** conclusion, I think …

MODULE 6
6.1
Recruitment

1 1 C 2 A 3 C 4 A 5 B 6 A 7 D 8 D 9 B
10 C 11 A 12 C

2 1 G 2 E 3 C 4 A 5 H 6 I 7 D 8 B

3 1 dismissed (*You are made redundant when your job is no longer needed. You are usually dismissed when a company is not happy with your work.*)
2 retire (*You retire from a company when you stop working, usually at around 60. You resign from a company to work somewhere else.*)
3 recruit (*You recruit someone when you get them to join the company. You hire someone when you pay them to do a job.*)
4 leave (*You usually leave a company to take another job or do something else, and you receive no extra pay. When you take voluntary redundancy you receive redundancy pay to compensate you for losing your job.*)

4 1 fine 2 stayed 3 look 4 fork 5 tyre

5 1 car park 2 laboratory 3 reception 4 lift
5 staff room/staff noticeboard

6 1 All members are invited to attend a union meeting on Friday 12 July.
2 Anything suspicious should be reported to security immediately.
3 Suggestions can be posted in this box.
4 This building was opened by Queen Elizabeth in 1988.
5 A registration form must be obtained from the Administration Office.

7 1 Holbroke has been sacked by capital investors.
2 400 jobs will be created in the North West.
3 The CEO has resigned after record losses were announced at Teleast.
4 Temporary workers were given only 1 day's notice.
5 A report shows that 300 new doctors are needed.
6 The England football manager has resigned.

8 1 It's better to be respected than to be liked.
2 I dislike being told what to do.
3 It's nice to be considered for a promotion.
4 It don't like to be kept waiting.
5 I don't mind my decisions being questioned.

6.2
Emailing

1 1 F 2 E 3 G 4 A 5 C

2 1 deleted 2 resend 3 forgot 4 know 5 work
6 check 7 received 8 access 9 key 10 click
11 sending 12 copy

3 1 E 2 A 3 D 4 I 5 H 6 C 7 G 8 J 9 F

4 **Suggested answer:**
Dear Liane
Thank you for sending me your presentation. I have looked through it and generally it looks good. Unfortunately, it also contains a few factual mistakes. Perhaps we could meet some time to go through it and discuss these. Let me know a time that suits you.

5 1 remind 2 please 3 appreciate 4 regard 5 reason
6 grateful 7 suggestions 8 note

6.3
Reading: Linking ideas

1 **Suggested answers:**
1 One is to advertise the job in the newspaper.
2 Do you enjoy your job?
3 'I think the design has serious weaknesses.
4 The second was a great improvement.
5 77% were very unhappy.
6 Nowadays, it is unusual to stay in the same job for more than ten years.

2 1 D 2 F 3 G 4 C 5 B

MODULE 7
7.1
Sales

1 1 sales pitch 2 door-to-door selling 3 target-driven
4 tangible results 5 sales techniques

2

Positive	Negative
rewarding, dynamic, challenging, well-paid, tangible, sociable	dishonest, unglamorous, unpopular, repetitive

3 1 rewarding 2 frustrating 3 repetitive 4 variety
5 interesting 6 boredom 7 responsibility
8 well-paid

4 de**b**t autum**n** enviro**n**ment **wh**ole busi**n**ess
mortgage **k**nowledge **g**uard **h**our **wr**ong lis**t**en
building dou**b**t clim**b**

5

Adjective (or adverb)	Comparative form	Superlative form
high	higher	the highest
low	lower	the lowest
good	better	the best
well (adverb)	better	the best
bad	worse	the worst
flexible	more flexible	the most flexible
rich	richer	the richest
far	further	the furthest
pretty	prettier	the prettiest
boring	more boring	the most boring
little	less	the least
much	more	the most

6　1 The　2 than　3 more　4 as　5 even　6 better
7 most　8 worse

7　1 ~~than~~ **as** me
2 the ~~reliablest~~ **most reliable**
3 the ~~better~~ **best** price
4 my ~~nearer~~ **nearest**
5 a ~~more close~~ **closer** look
6 so ~~more~~ **many** people
7 ~~highest~~ **higher** than
8 just as ~~cheaper~~ **cheap**
9 similar prices ~~with~~ **to**
10 ~~many~~ **much** higher

7.2
Selling

1

F¹	A²	I	L		K³	N⁴	O	W	S⁵
	B			R⁶		O			T
	L			E			I⁷		U
B⁸	E	N⁹	E	F	I	T	S		F
U		E	L				S		F
I		E	E		B¹⁰	U	Y		
L		D	C				E		
D			S	T¹¹	R	U	S	T	

2　1 in, mind　2 come, updated　3 prove, on　4 about, put
5 much, give　6 wondering, with

3　1 understand / respond to / establish / meet
2 close / make　3 compare / sell　4 make / receive
5 explain / emphasise / stress

4　1 B　2 E　3 D　4 A　5 H　6 C　7 G

5　1 They are central and convenient for clients.
2 The offices are too small and poorly equipped, and more business is coming from outside the city.
3 More office space, a more modern building and more car parking.
4 He wants to know the fees.

6　**Suggested answer:**
Dear Mr Smith,
Thank you for **your letter concerning new offices**.
We would be delighted **to help you find more convenient premises for your company**.
At the moment we have two suitable **properties for rent**.
One is **the first floor (1400 m²) of a new office block in the Milton Industrial Park**. Its key features are:
- **good access to main roads**
- **flexible working space**
- **modern fittings (lights, computer cables etc.)**

- **parking for 12 cars**

The other is an attractive **office building on the outskirts of the city (1000 m²)**. Its key advantages are that:
- **it has good public transport links**
- **it is located near a public park**
- **a low rent**

Full details of our fees can be **found on our website**.
Please do not hesitate **to contact me for further details**.
I look forward **to hearing from you**.

7.3
Reading: Extracting key information

1　B

2　A A make of chocolate is now being marketed which can help people feel less stressed.
B This product is one of a range now being marketed on the basis that it will help change your mood rather than giving physical benefits.
C Omega-3 is another product which benefits mental well-being.
D Food experts are advising caution and warning that all the things we eat are important.

3　1 D (*everything you eat is important*)
2 A (*It's every marketer's dream to take a product which people like …*)
3 B (*With this new range, the focus is much more on food that will change your mood.*)
4 A (*can reduce anxiety*)
5 D (*people feel that consuming one or two products, they can reap all the benefits*)
6 C (*boosts mental development*)
7 B (*sales of healthy or lifestyle foods are worth over £1 billion*)

MODULE 8
8.1
Training

1　1 C　2 C　3 D　4 A　5 B　6 D　7 A　8 C　9 B
10 D

2

Advantage	Disadvantage
a plus	the downside
one good thing	one drawback
a benefit	one problem
a positive point	one thing against

3　1 ↘↗　2 ↘　3 ↗　4 ↘　5 ↗　6 ↘↗　7 ↘　8 ↘↗
9 ↗　10 ↘

4

+ Gerund (-ing)	+ Infintive (to do)	Both possible
recommend	afford	remember
be interested in	want	stop
involve	would like	like
		start
		prefer

5 1 to speak, to call   2 seeing, calling
3 switching, restarting   4 using   5 to risk   6 attending
7 to come

6 Students' own answers.

7 online, by correspondence, in a group, one to one

8.2
Showing you're listening

I 1 A   2 B   3 B

2 1 +   2 +   3 +   4 –   5 –   6 +   7 +   8 –   9 –

3 + phrases often ask questions; they focus on what the other person is thinking or saying.
– phrases often include the word *I* or *me* and focus on the speaker's feelings, opinions, or experiences.

4 1 do   2 with   3 putting   4 as   5 ~~of~~   6 would
7 I know   8 recruit   9 ask them questions   10 That
11 more   12 doing

5 1 E   2 F   3 C   4 B   5 A

6 1 In addition to being a very effective training course, it can be done in only two days.
2 Because of bad weather, the session was cancelled.
3 Despite only six people enrolling on the course, it went ahead anyway.
4 Following a discussion on the issue, we took a vote.

7 1 As a result   2 Unfortunately   3 despite   4 However
5 Moreover   6 In addition to   7 due to   8 Nevertheless

8.3
Listening: Short monologues

I 1 H   2 E   3 A   4 C   5 F

2 6 G   7 C   8 H   9 A   10 F

MODULE 9
9.1
Branding

I 1 brand identity
2 advertising slogan
3 big impact
4 customer perception
5 attractive packaging
6 marketing tool

2 1 bad
2 local
3 ultimate

3 1 Levi's®
2 BMW
3 HSBC

4 0 A (*a responsibility to be sensitive to other cultures*)
1 D (*it no longer wants to be sold an American lifestyle*)
2 C (*they change their products so that they suit local tastes*)
3 A (*Americans have a poor record of researching foreign markets*)
4 C (*they try to build trust with local consumers*)
5 B (*other policies made the US less popular internationally*)
6 D (*more international marketing case studies are being used*)

5 1 which   2 whose   3 when   4 why   5 who
6 where   7 which   8 which

6 1 Necessary
2 Omitted: It's the first new product we have launched in six years.
3 Necessary
4 Necessary
5 Necessary
6 Omitted: The company we used last year has gone out of business.
7 Necessary
8 Omitted: He's a man I respect very much.

7 Suggested answers:
1 New York is the kind of place *where anything can happen.*
2 Your 20's are a period in your life *when you find your direction.*
3 My parents are the reason *why I became a doctor.*
4 It's the kind of book *which you can't put down.*
5 The iPod is the kind of product *which changes everyone's way of life.*
6 He's the kind of manager *who people respect.*

9.2
Getting through

1 1 D 2 F 3 G 4 E 5 A 6 C

2 **Suggested answers:**
1 I'll look it up.
2 I'll read that back to you.
3 I'm tied up at the moment.
4 We've run out of time, I'm afraid.
5 I'll try to bring it forward to Thursday.
6 I'll call back later.
7 I'll put you through.
8 I'll pass the message on to her.

3 1 connect   2 in   3 take   4 put
5 take   6 moment   7 hold   8 calling
9 back   10 convenient   11 suits   12 pass

4 Dear Rebecca
I am **still** waiting **for** an answer to the email I sent you last week. My colleague Erica **needs** to know your answer before she **goes** to Germany. Please let **me** know by We**dnes**day at the latest.
Thanks
Jane

Hello John
I **tried** to telephone you yesterday, but I think you were out at ~~the~~ lunch with a client. We are having a meeting **tomorrow** at 10 o'clock with a brand consultant to discuss ~~about~~ our new marketing campaign. He is a very in**teres**ting guy who **has** worked with some top companies, so please try to come.
Felix

Dear Mr Duncan
Regarding ~~to~~ your order for a Bosch washing machine, I am afraid that this item **is** not in stock. However, I can offer you **an**other option, which is a German-made machine **too**. I **have attached** a full description of the product to this email and I hope it will meet your re**quirem**ents.
Yours sincerely,
Onkar (Sales)

Dear Maria
I got your message ~~in~~ this morning about the interviews which will take place **next week**. In ~~the~~ answer to your question, I think it **would** be better if they were group interviews. This will give us the **oppor**tunity to see how the different candidates **react** with each other.
Thanks
Jane

9.3
Writing: Reports

1 C The style is a little too conversational; *Thanks, What's more, it'd be good to know, give me a call, a good time to meet* The student didn't cover all the points. The following were not mentioned:
• that the price of cars can vary between locations.
• drop off times.
• that for Newcastle they would need to use a partner firm, Geordie Car Rental.

2 **Suggested answer:**
Dear Mr Duffy
Thank you very much for choosing our company. We **would be very pleased** to have the chance to work with you. **Moreover**, if you **would consider extending** the trial period to 12 months, we could offer you another 8% reduction in the price.
Here are the answers to your other points:
– Our normal collection hours are 7am – 8pm. There **is** a small fee for collection at other times. **Cars may be dropped off at any time**.
– We can cover all the locations mentioned, but it **would** be good to know how many cars you expect to hire from each place. **(In Newcastle we would be working with a partner firm, who are very reliable.)**
– We can also **provide** chauffeur driven cars.
– **The prices of our cars vary a little from one location to another, but this is something we can discuss.**
All in all, I think you can be confident that we **will** handle this business professionally and **at a competitive** price.
Please **contact me to arrange a convenient** time to meet.
Yours sincerely
Steve **Johns**

MODULE 10
10.1
Management

1 1 Develop   2 Recognise, fill
3 Plan, implement   4 Renew

2 1 fail   2 weaknesses   3 success
4 aware   5 rapidly   6 learn

3 1 rapidly   2 strategy   3 recognise   4 awareness
5 success   6 weak   7 set   8 implementation

4
1 can
2 away
3 so
4 Correct
5 than
6 about
7 Correct
8 been
9 to
10 Correct

5
1 Correct
2 Incorrect: will never achieve
3 Incorrect: heat
4 Correct
5 Incorrect: hadn't met
6 Incorrect: have
7 Incorrect: were
8 Correct
9 Incorrect: keeps
10 Incorrect: failed

6 1 C 2 F 3 H 4 G 5 B 6 D 7 A

7 **Suggested answers:**
1 She would not have met other performers, if she *hadn't found a job / worked in a gym*.
2 If she hadn't signed to the One Stone Music record label, her career *would probably not have taken off*.
3 If her former husband hadn't run away with his secretary, her life *would not have changed / would have been very different*.
4 She wouldn't have started writing songs if she *hadn't needed to take her mind off other things*.

10.2
Solving problems

I

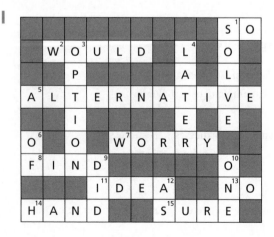

2
1 could / might   2 find   3 person's   4 are
5 were   6 a good idea   7 of   8 few
9 would   10 by   11 to write
12 do   13 so   14 well

3
1 ahead   2 in   3 within
4 over   5 out   6 behind

4 1 B 2 D 3 A 4 C

5
1 Following / Further to
2 In order to
3 Therefore / So

6
1 Because of the high demand for the training course next week, we have decided to move it to a larger venue. The course will now take place at the Marriot Hotel on 4 March.
2 Unfortunately, we have experienced a few problems with the new software. This is due to a programming fault. We are trying to correct it and with luck it will be working again by tomorrow afternoon at the latest.
3 Further to our meeting last week, I have been working on a proposal for our new Chinese partner. However, it will be ready in time for our next meeting. I am attaching it to this email. Could you look at it and tell me how it can be improved?
4 I am still waiting for a response to my request of 12 September concerning purchases of office stationery. I need this information in order to prepare the budgets for next year.
Please send the information as soon as possible. I am running out of time.

10.3
Listening: An interview

I
1 B a big mystery.
2 A include all the things that you have to do.
3 A leave until another day.
4 A use the time to do some personal jobs.
5 B feel tired.
6 B agree to any deadlines.
7 C get home earlier at the end of the day.
8 A wastes the company's time.

2 1 A 2 B 3 C 4 C 5 C 6 A 7 B 8 C

MODULE 11

11.1
Ethical economics

1 1 GDP   2 break-even   3 overheads
4 freight   5 mark-up   6 a commodity
7 export costs   8 market price

2 export insurance staffing maintenance additional

3 1 paid   2 exported   3 transported
4 bought   5 packaged   6 sold

4 1 average   2 tiny   3 small   4 increasing
5 excessive   6 minimum   7 least

5 1 **a** taxi
2 **some** information
3 **the** biggest
4 **The** train
5 **an** enormous increase
6 at **the** work.
7 in **the** Red Lion
8 **a** very bad
9 **the** last five years
10 **some** paper

6 1 I work at (**0**) night and sleep in **the** day.
2 We are based in (**0**) Germany but we operate all over **the** world.
3 In **the** last ten years, we have taken on (**0**) forty new employees.
4 **The** United Nations was founded in 1945 after **the** Second World War.
5 I need to be at (**0**) home in time for (**0**) supper.
6 Will you go to (**0**) university next year?
7 My son is studying at **the** University of California.

7 vulnerable comfortable medicine secretary ordinary
difference interested business valuable withdrawal

8 1 few
2 a
3 on
4 to
5 ~~about~~
6 the past ten years
7 must ~~to~~
8 necessarily
9 to operate
10 make
11 Meeting, seeing

11.2
Discussing trends

1 1 decrease   2 fall   3 soar
4 peak   5 remain stable

2 1 fall   2 increase   3 level out   4 remain

3 1 B   2 B   3 C   4 B   5 C   6 D   7 B   8 C   9 C
10 A

4 1 F   2 A   3 D   4 B   5 H   6 E   7 G

5 **Introducing a proposal**
We would be delighted to work with you
Before I give more details I would like to point out that …
Comparing pros and cons
The advantage of using a hotel would be …
One other thing we should consider is …
Balancing and concluding
In order to keep the overall cost down I would recommend that …
Please don't hesitate to contact me if you would like to discuss any of these points

6 **Suggested answer:**
Dear Mr Cook
Thank you for your letter regarding an evening event for your staff and customers. We would be delighted to work with you. Before I give more details, I would like to point out that we have over ten years experience in organising successful events for large companies.
The main elements of our proposal are as follows:
- The venue we suggest is the Churchill Hotel Banquet Hall. The advantage of using a hotel would be that any guests who need to stay over for the night can stay in the hotel.
- The well-known comedian, Jo Bland, will do a half-hour session at the end of the dinner. After that, a live band will supply the music for dancing.

One other thing we should consider is whether you or one of our staff will want to give a speech and if so what equipment is needed.
As to the cost, I expect the figure to be around £40 per head. In order to keep the overall cost down, I would recommend that guests pay for their drinks at the bar.
Please don't hesitate to contact me if you would like to discuss any of these points. I look forward to hearing from you.
Yours sincerely

11.3
Reading: Longer texts

1 1 B   2 C   3 D   4 A   5 A   6 C

MODULE 12

12.1
Business law

1
sue someone
take **legal** action against someone
take out **litigation** against someone
start legal **proceedings** against someone
prosecute someone for

2
1 court
2 copyright
3 prosecute (sue)
4 defence
5 trademark
6 rights
7 case
8 sue (prosecute)
9 compensation
10 litigation

3
1 C   2 F   3 B   4 E   5 G   6 A

4
1 You're French, aren't you?
2 Do you think they are going to sue?
3 Do you know what this is about ?
4 I was wondering if you could help me?
5 Do you know when I have to register?
6 Can you tell me who is in charge?
7 I'd like to know why she left.
8 You're open to new offers, aren't you?
9 Can you explain how it works?
10 I'd like to know how long you've worked here.

5
1 I'd like to know what you think.
2 Could you tell me how much it costs?
3 Do you think it is legal?
4 I was wondering how long it would take.
5 Can you tell me exactly what they complained about?
6 I wonder if they own the rights to the name?
7 Do you remember which firm you used?

6
1 We met at the Berlin conference, didn't we?
2 Li is your first name, isn't it?
3 The meeting has been postponed, hasn't it?
4 You take sugar in your coffee, don't you?
5 I'm not late, am I?
6 They own the rights to the name, don't they?
7 He works for ABC, doesn't he?

7
/iː/
legal, recent, secret, previous, detail, retail, medium, female
/e/
level, metal, separate, precious, creditor, pressure, decade

12.2
Handling questions

1
1 follow
2 answer
3 come back
4 mean
5 get back
6 mind
7 repeat
8 Thank
9 catch
10 is

2
1 Sorry, I didn't catch that. OR Can you repeat the question?
2 Let me get back to you on that.
3 That's a good question.
4 I'll come back to that point in a moment.
5 Sorry, I don't follow you. OR Sorry, can you explain what you mean exactly?

3
1 A   2 C   3 B   4 D

4
1 made
2 a
3 before / by
4 ~~of~~
5 has been
6 using
7 nothing
8 ~~more~~
9 these
10 as
11 to expand
12 to
13 from

5
Press release C: It is written in the first person, (*We are pleased...*); it doesn't contain information of general or public interest. In other words, it's more like an advertisement than a press release.

6 **Suggested answer:**
The contract to build a new tramline linking the centre of Liverpool to the Birkenhead area has been won by Sestro. The total value of the contract is £16.5 million, but part of this sum will be put towards the building of a community youth centre and skateboard park. A spokesman from Liverpool City Council said that he was very happy that the project would not only benefit travellers in and out of Liverpool city centre but also young people in the area. Work is due to begin in January next year.

7 <u>fu</u>ture oppor<u>tu</u>nity pro<u>du</u>ce <u>m</u>usic val<u>ue</u> <u>due</u>
un<u>u</u>sual

12.3
Speaking: Discussions

1 Employee A's answers are too long and formal.
Employee B's answers are too short and sound rude.

2 1 E 2 I 3 G 4 J 5 A 6 B 7 H 8 F 9 C

3 1 discount
2 the other
3 effective
4 like / such as
5 save
6 commute / come
7 interested
8 do